## DATE DUE

D1064295

## Praise for *Race and Liberty in America*

"*Race and Liberty in America* is the race and civil rights anthology we have been waiting for. In our politicized age we often think of civil rights as a movement of racial pride and identity. But Martin Luther King's movement succeeded precisely because it used the principles of classical liberalism to shatter the idea that race or identity could be a source of entitlement. . . . This book is a timely and necessary corrective."
—Shelby Steele, author, *The Content of Our Character: A New Vision of Race in America*

"Readers will find a wealth of information in Bean's outstanding book *Race and Liberty in America,* a collection of primary source materials covering the great historical debates over race and ethnicity in America. Students, educators, civic leaders, and general readers can all greatly benefit from the book."
—Carol M. Swain, Professor of Political Science and Law, Vanderbilt University; author, *Black Faces, Black Interests*

"If you are interested in the real history of the civil rights movement in America—the radical ideas that set it in motion no matter where they came from— get ready for an intellectual thrill ride. There is no time for political posturing here. *Race and Liberty in America* is full of revelations and stunning in its honesty."
—Juan Williams, Senior Correspondent, National Public Radio; author, *Eyes on the Prize: America's Civil Rights Years, 1954–1965* and *Thurgood Marshall: American Revolutionary*

"A wonderful collection of fascinating documents. . . . *Race and Liberty in America* deserves a wide audience and will enrich the reader's understanding of the nation's most difficult and troubling domestic issue."
—Stephan Thernstrom, Winthrop Research Professor of History, Harvard University; coauthor, *America in Black and White*

"*Race and Liberty in America* is indeed essential reading. All too often classical liberals are attacked for their indifference or insensitivity on matters of race. This superb collection of material dispels that illusion."
—Richard A. Epstein, James Parker Hall Distinguished Service Professor of Law, University of Chicago

super-lawyer Moorfield Storey, frontier novelist Rose Wilder Lane, and black Republican congressman Oscar De Priest. The selections also contain surprising new information about such better-known individuals as Frederick Douglass, Warren G. Harding, Milton Friedman, and Zora Neale Hurston."
—David T. Beito, Professor of History, University of Alabama; author, *Black Maverick: T. R. M. Howard's Fight for Civil Rights and Economic Power*

"After reading *Race and Liberty in America,* my reaction was WOW!! But, in case a one-word reaction is insufficient, I hasten to add that this fantastic book is destined to become America's new textbook about 'race,' civil rights, and what it means to be a classical liberal on the subject of race. Americans are deeply divided about whether to enable their government to pursue 'diversity' or to embrace 'colorblind' public policies. This debate is not well served by the polarizing influence of political labels that divide 'conservatives' and 'liberals.'"
—Ward Connerly, Chairman, American Civil Rights Institute; author, *Creating Equal*

"We are one human race, in need of a savior, and as my uncle Dr. Martin Luther King said, 'we must learn to live together as brothers or perish as fools.' Life, liberty and justice are matters of the heart and go beyond politics and legislation. The essential book *Race and Liberty in America* is a major step in the process."
—Alveda C. King, Founder and Chairman, King for America; daughter of civil rights leader Rev. A. D. Williams King, brother of Martin Luther King Jr.

"Historian Jonathan Bean has provided a signal service by bringing to light the rich tradition of classical liberal thinking about civil rights. The world of ideas has been waiting for a book such as *Race and Liberty in America* for far too long, but Bean's collection of primary sources and thematic commentary has made it worth the wait. The book deserves a prominent place on the bookshelves of all open-minded scholars and should be required reading in classrooms across the nation. This is a transformative book by a courageous scholar."
—Scott Douglas Gerber, Ella & Ernest Fisher Chair in Law, Ohio Northern University; author, *First Principles: The Jurisprudence of Clarence Thomas*

"Short of studying statistics and census reports, the new book *Race and Liberty in America,* edited by Jonathan Bean, offers a 'classical liberal' description of the past,

present, and future impact of race and immigration in America's future. It's a challenging book of ideas offering a balanced discussion on these two issues."
—Lee H. Walker, President, New Coalition for Economic and Social Change

"*Race and Liberty in America* is an original and much-needed anthology, indispensable for any serious discussion of race relations in American history. The first-rate introductions and selections provide a fabulous resource for both teachers and students. Genuinely inspired."
—Paul Moreno, William and Berniece Grewcock Chair in Constitutional History, Hillsdale College

# Race and Liberty in America

# Race and Liberty in America

*The Essential Reader*


Edited by Jonathan Bean

THE UNIVERSITY PRESS OF KENTUCKY

Published in Association with The Independent Institute

Published by The University Press of Kentucky

Scholarly publisher for the Commonwealth,
serving Bellarmine University, Berea College, Centre
College of Kentucky, Eastern Kentucky University,
The Filson Historical Society, Georgetown College,
Kentucky Historical Society, Kentucky State University,
Morehead State University, Murray State University,
Northern Kentucky University, Transylvania University,
University of Kentucky, University of Louisville,
and Western Kentucky University.
All rights reserved.

*Editorial and Sales Offices:* The University Press of Kentucky
663 South Limestone Street, Lexington, Kentucky 40508-4008
www.kentuckypress.com

13 12 11 10 09     5 4 3 2 1

Library of Congress Cataloging-in-Publication Data

Race and liberty in America : the essential reader / edited by Jonathan Bean.
    p.    cm.
    Includes bibliographical references and index.
    ISBN 978-0-8131-2545-9 (hardcover : alk. paper)
    1. Minorities—Civil rights—United States—History—Sources.
2. Civil rights—United States—History—Sources. 3. Civil rights
movements—United States—History—Sources. 4. United States—
Race relations—History—Sources.´I. Bean, Jonathan J.
  E184.A1R248   2009
  305.800973—dc22
                          2009010817

This book is printed on acid-free recycled paper meeting
the requirements of the American National Standard
for Permanence in Paper for Printed Library Materials.

Manufactured in the United States of America.

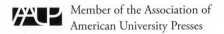 Member of the Association of
American University Presses

*To Joanna and Emily*
*Beloved daughters and members of the one race that God made*

# Contents

# Documents

# Acknowledgments

THIS BOOK RESULTED from the collective support of many individuals. My family deserves the greatest acknowledgment for tolerating the endless clicking of the keyboard. David Theroux, founder and president of the Independent Institute (www.independent.org), first saw the work's importance to the cause of liberty, and has been enormously supportive. His Independent Institute has produced some of the most provocative works on liberty in recent years. The Social Philosophy and Policy Center generously gave me the time to research and write without distraction, with the assistance of Jonathan Miles and John Milliken. Thank you, Fred, Jeff, and Ellen. Robert Weems, David Beito, Paul Moreno, Alex Tabarrok, Ken Masugi, and several anonymous referees read drafts of the manuscript and offered excellent advice on improving it. My research assistant, Colleen Lindsay, was diligent in ferreting out obscure sources. Gerhard Peters maintains a splendid online archive from which I drew several documents, The American Presidency Project (http://americanpresidency.org or http://www.presidency.ucsb.edu/). I recommend it to anyone studying U.S. history. Branch B. Rickey III and Justice George Nicholson helped me learn more about the role of religion in Branch Rickey's life. Steven Greenhut and others at Freedom Newspapers retrieved hard-to-get articles. Similar thanks go to Matthew Schaefer of the Herbert Hoover Library for giving me access to a series of documents related to desegregation of the Commerce Department. Irwin Gellman cheered me on with his encouraging phone calls. We have never met in person, but I owe him a firm handshake of gratitude. Led by Steve Wrinn, the staff members at University Press of Kentucky are a joy to work with: professional, enthusiastic, and constructive. I am grateful to copyeditor Robin DuBlanc for her good judgment and extraordinary eye for detail. To the countless critics whom I engaged along the way, thank you for helping me think through my own arguments. There is more of you here than you imagine.

# Introduction

## Civil Rights and Classical Liberalism

**THIS IS THE FIRST COLLECTION** of writings on race and immigration to document the role of the classical liberal tradition. For many generations, this tradition dominated the civil rights movement, and it continues to exert a profound influence on current events. Classical liberals fought slavery, lynching, segregation, imperialism, and racial distinctions in the law. As immigration advocates, they defended the "natural right" of migration to America. *Race and Liberty* recaptures this lively tradition through the writings of men and women missing from other civil rights anthologies. Academic booklists reflect the politically correct view that left-wing liberals or radicals completely dominated the struggle for racial freedom.[1] Works offering a different point of view are guilty of "backlash," "whitewashing race," or "color-blind racism"—the trendy notion that those who favor nondiscrimination are "objectively racist."[2] Not surprisingly, classical liberals are the invisible men and women of the long civil rights movement.

*Race and Liberty* will interest readers tired of the Left versus Right debates on television or the Left on Left offerings in the classroom. Instructors may use this collection to stimulate discussion of a civil rights tradition deeply rooted in the American experience. While students may agree or disagree with the classical liberal perspective, they will not "shut down" in silence, looking for the "correct" answers they have encountered in other discussion readers. Students live in a highly charged campus climate that presumes racism is everywhere and must be overcome by "affirmative discrimination," diversity studies, multiculturalism, harassment codes, and sensitivity training by "race experts." *Race and Liberty* frees them to consider another way of looking at the world.

1

Above all, this is a story about people and the difference they made in the face of seemingly insurmountable odds. Classical liberalism is a philosophy of *individualism;* its history is peopled by a mix of iconoclasts, contrarians, lone dissenters, courageous rebels, and powerful political leaders. They include Moorfield Storey, first president of the National Association for the Advancement of Colored People (NAACP); Kelly Miller, dean of Howard University and one of the most widely read black writers of the 1920s; Robert Taft, who unseated the Senate's most vicious racist; novelist Zora Neale Hurston; and Branch Rickey, the "missionary" businessman who broke the color bar in baseball by signing Jackie Robinson to the Brooklyn Dodgers. These individuals represent a classical liberal tradition that is neither "progressive" nor "conservative," neither left nor right.

Classical liberals espoused values shared by many other Americans: "unalienable Rights" from God, individual freedom from government control, the Constitution as a guarantor of freedom, color-blind law, and capitalism. These values distinguish classical liberalism from left-wing liberalism, with its emphasis on group rights, government power, and hostility to free market capitalism. Left-wing liberalism trended toward the secular, while classical liberals typically argued for a Creator as the source of our "unalienable Rights." In short, most classical liberals believed in individual freedom, Christianity, the Constitution, colorblindness, and capitalism.

## Classical Liberals on Race

These five core beliefs greatly influenced the classical liberal tradition of racial freedom. Together, they form a coherent worldview different from the left-wing liberal tradition. The classical liberal tradition dominated the struggle for racial freedom well into the twentieth century, and it persists in today's liveliest debates over race and immigration. The core beliefs outlined below framed the classical liberal response to slavery, Jim Crow, lynching, voting rights, racial preferences, and immigration restriction. Here, a few examples illustrate the influence of each factor; the anthology develops the themes in much greater detail.

## Individual Freedom

On issues of racial freedom and immigration, classical liberals advocated freedom from government control. This included the right of businesses to freely contract with labor—whether those workers were African Americans or immigrants seeking entry to the United States. This position pitted classical liberals against progressives on the left, who wanted the government to make "reasonable" exceptions for labor unions and immigration restriction. On the right, nativist conservatives joined with progressives in opposing "open borders," while classical liberals staunchly defended immigration: whether Chinese or Czech, immigrants had a natural right to migrate.

Individual freedom from State control extended far beyond the right to work, however. Antebellum newspaper editor William Leggett denounced proslavery forces that used gag rules or violence to censor free speech. During the Reconstruction era, Congress guaranteed constitutional protection of the individual right to bear arms, a right defeated Confederates tried to limit to white citizens. Classical liberals also defended the constitutional right to life by introducing antilynching legislation. Finally, classical liberals from Louis Marshall (1910s) to Ward Connerly (2000s) sought to rid race from government classification. Removing this power to classify by groups would prevent—or at least hinder—the government from undermining individual freedom.

## Christianity and Judaism

Religion inspired many classical liberals to advance the Golden Rule as a guide to civil rights. Of course, classical liberals had no monopoly on faith; others followed the Social Gospel of the Left or a southern brand of Christianity that defended slavery by citing passages from the New Testament. Nevertheless, religion played an important role in the history of classical liberalism. Christian evangelism was integral to the antislavery movement. For example, Lewis Tappan was a well-known evangelical Christian who used his church ties to create a network of antislavery men and women. Frederick Douglass, an ordained minister, repeatedly used references to the Creator in rebuking—and inspiring—his fellow Christians.

Senator Joseph Hawley (R-CT) opposed the Chinese Exclusion Act (1882) partly because of his missionary work with the Chinese, both in the United States and abroad. Louis Marshall's devout Judaism impelled him to fight for free immigration and against Jim Crow laws. Kelly Miller viewed religion as a "solvent of the race problem" in 1908. To publicly rebuke the Ku Klux Klan's bigotry, President Calvin Coolidge spoke of religious toleration in a speech to the Holy Name Society. Justice Pierce Butler's Catholicism influenced his sole dissent in the infamous *Buck v. Bell* case (1927), which upheld forced sterilization by the states—a "progressive" eugenic policy of weeding out the "imbeciles" among the so-called inferior races. Branch Rickey explained his recruitment of Jackie Robinson as "a call from God."

### The Constitution

Classical liberal advocates of racial freedom consistently maintained that the Constitution was fundamentally sound on the issue of race: *not* a racist or pro-slavery document. Lysander Spooner, Frederick Douglass, Lewis Tappan, and others argued that, strictly speaking, there was no constitutional sanction of slavery. Moreover, the Constitution provided a means of change within the political system. This position contrasted sharply with fiery abolitionist William Lloyd Garrison's view that the Constitution was a diabolical compact with slavery and should be scrapped, along with the Union it sustained. Later, classical liberals looked to the Constitution as guarantor of individual civil rights. When government denied those rights, classical liberals took to the courts, using arguments based on the founding principles of the Constitution and the Declaration of Independence. Law professor Scott Gerber quotes Justice Clarence Thomas, who extolled "the principles of our founding and how they apply to the controversies of our time."[3] That vision has united classical liberal civil rights advocates since the early nineteenth century.

The Fourteenth and Fifteenth amendments, guaranteeing legal equality and voting rights, led classical liberals to insist that all Americans were equal before the law. By embracing the Constitution and the Declaration of Independence as sacred documents of their civic religion, they aligned patriotism with civil rights. For the government to treat individuals or groups as unequal before the law was, in their mind, "un-American." Thus, President Calvin Coolidge publicly rebuked a white racist who objected to a black Republican running for Congress: after noting the patriotic contributions of blacks to the recent war effort, Coolidge stated, "Our Constitution guarantees equal rights to all our citizens, without discrimination on account of race or color. . . . A colored man is precisely as much entitled to submit his candidacy in a party primary, as is any other citizen."[4]

## Colorblindness

Consistent with this view of the Constitution, classical liberals rejected class, caste, or group distinctions in the law. The government should not interfere with fundamental rights that belong to all Americans, regardless of race, color, or creed. Likewise, they often extended this "hands-off" approach to immigration, arguing that the government should not pick and choose the races it admits to this country. As demonstrated by Andrew Kull in *The Color-Blind Constitution,* this powerful ideal inspired generations of civil rights activists, although the Supreme Court never fully accepted it, and left-wing liberals reject it.[5] The countervailing view is that courts may uphold "reasonable" racial distinctions—a position taken in support of segregation and affirmative action. Classical liberals argued that this "reasonableness" standard substitutes the rule of men and women (politicians, bureaucrats, judges) for the rule of law. Therefore, they favored a ban on racial legislation.

Although many writers have expressed the color-blind ideal, none have done so more eloquently than Supreme Court justices John Marshall Harlan and Antonin Scalia, separated by a century but espousing the same sentiment: "Our Constitution is color-blind, and neither knows nor tolerates classes among citizens," Harlan wrote (*Plessy* dissent, 1896). Scalia pronounced that "under our Constitution there can be no such thing as either a creditor or debtor race. . . . In the eyes of government, we are just one race here. It is American." The Constitution's focus, he argued, was on the individual (*Adarand,* 1995).

## Capitalism

Left-wing liberals, Marxists, and black radicals have long held that capitalism is inherently racist.[6] Historian Manning Marable quotes Malcolm X: "You can't have racism without capitalism. If you find antiracists, usually they're socialists or their political philosophy is that of socialism."[7] Many labor historians argue that capitalist employers used racism to "divide and conquer" the working class, thus preventing development of an interracial labor movement. This theme permeates historians' handling of labor-management relations and their negative view of the courts that upheld freedom of contract between capitalists and workers.[8] To rid capitalist societies of racism, the government must force employers to "be good."

Classical liberals turn this view upside down: capitalism undermines racism by penalizing those who act on their "taste for discrimination"—a thesis articulated by Gary Becker in *The Economics of Discrimination* in 1957 but advanced even earlier by advocates of racial freedom who opposed government backing for labor unions.[9] Firms willing to recruit workers and market goods without regard to color or national origin have a competitive advantage. Streetcar companies fought segregated seating because it added to their cost of doing business. The "desegregating of the dollar" also occurred as large corporations reached out to the "Negro market." This theme appeared in the business press of the twentieth century as well as in the writing of Booker T. Washington and Kelly Miller and the popular works of economists Milton Friedman, Thomas Sowell, and Walter Williams.

Capitalism also provided wealthy individuals with funds to help advance the cause of racial freedom. Examples include merchant Lewis Tappan's funding of antislavery activists and the legal defense in the *Amistad* case (see chapter 1); Julius Rosenwald's bankrolling of fifty-five hundred "Rosenwald" schools for southern blacks; and Booker T. Washington's fund-raising for the NAACP's crusade against lynching and segregation.

Moreover, capitalism provided African Americans and other minorities with options foreclosed by restrictive licensing laws and racist labor unions. Thus, Booker T. Washington's *Up from Slavery* (1901) became a self-help bible for generations of black entrepreneurs, including John Johnson (publisher of *Ebony* and *Jet*); Chicago businessman S. B. Fuller; and A. G. Gaston, who amassed a $150 million fortune in Birmingham, Alabama—one of the most racist environments in America. Washington's classic autobiography also inspired the philanthropy of Rosenwald and other businessmen who believed in self-help.[10]

## Classical Liberalism: Neither Left nor Right

Classical liberalism deserves further study as a distinctive civil rights tradition that is neither left nor right. Why, for example, do we know so much about W. E. B. DuBois but little about superlawyer Moorfield Storey, cofounder and president of the NAACP? In *Buchanan v. Warley* (1917), Storey won the first Supreme Court case ruling segregation unconstitutional—thirty-seven years before *Brown v. Board*. Why do we know so little of Louis Marshall, a giant in Jewish American life who fought all racial classifications (including the grouping of "Jews" for political purposes)? Marshall spearheaded the defense of free immigration to the United States until Congress finally passed the National Origin Quota Act of 1924. In the 1920s, he fought quotas limiting the number of Jews entering college—a harbinger of today's affirmative action debate. Marshall also succeeded Storey as lead lawyer for the NAACP and won *Nixon v. Herndon* (1927), a Supreme Court case striking down the racist "white primary" law of Texas. Progressive contemporaries characterized both Storey and Marshall as "ultraconservative" because of their laissez-faire economics, but laissez-faire also motivated their unswerving devotion to a color- and caste-blind Constitution.

The current canon ignores these classical liberals, or distorts their record, partly because they rejected government meddling in race relations—whether the meddling was done by the Right or the Left. On the right, conservatives advocated the "state right" to discriminate in favor of native-born whites. On the left, the progressive credo might read: *government was sometimes the problem but always the solution.* Thus, the solution to segregation was not the elimination of government interference in race relations but rather its transformation from "negative" to "affirmative" discrimination. Similarly, the solution to the supposed racism of capitalism was governmental control of business. To be fair, many "conservatives" see themselves as classical liberals today, even if conservatism was used to justify illiberal policies in the past. The same rings true of left-wing liberals: some were (and are) classical liberals *on the topic of race* (note the inclusion of several right- and left-leaning writers in this volume).

The standard academic dismissal is to lump classical liberals with unsavory conservatives rather than address classical liberal thought as a distinctive tradition separate from right-wing conservatism and left-wing liberalism (although there is overlap with those traditions). Many writers depict today's classical liberals (Ward Connerly, Clarence Thomas, Roger Clegg, and Shelby Steele) as examples of conservative "backlash" rather than as exemplars of a coherent tradition that dates back two centuries. Angela Dillard, author of *Guess Who's Coming to Dinner Now? Multicultural Conservatism in America,* expresses the received wisdom: "The conservative movement, overall, is predominantly white and Christian and has, in both the past and present, used racism, ethnocentrism, homophobia, and anti-Semitism . . . to achieve its goals."[11] Writers like Dillard label classical liberals "conservatives" and then sweep them together with racists, homophobes, and anti-Semites! Not surprisingly, many classical liberals have forgotten their own history. No wonder both Democratic and Republican administrations have kowtowed to the nativist Right's stance on immigration restriction and the Left's agenda on affirmative action; they have no historical compass to guide them elsewhere. When it comes to classical liberalism and civil rights, misinformation prevails in academic and political circles.

## Republicans and Race

One of the initial objections to this project was that the figures chosen were predominantly Republican from the 1850s onward, and since the Republican Party was the "centralizing" party of the nineteenth century, it was not classical liberal. My response is twofold. First, this project focuses on racial freedom, not on other policies that were possibly antithetical to classical liberalism. Second, the "centralization" argument misses the point: while the Republican Party was more "statist" at the national level with regard to the tariff and other issues (for example, Prohibition), it was less statist with regard to race. This antistatism embraced both African Americans and immigrants (hence Republican opposition to the Chinese Exclusion Act). Furthermore, "centralization" is a sweeping term that has misled many writers who view the rise of the Republican Party during Reconstruction as centralizing power in the federal government, to the detriment of states' rights and individual liberty. In fact, most Republicans desired a speedy reestablishment of federalism; however, southern outrages delayed reunion. National constitutional amendments restored a balance between federal and state governments while guaranteeing rights of life and property to all individuals regardless of race. The process was to be self-executing once African Americans secured the vote (1870) and President U.S. Grant suppressed the Ku Klux Klan (1871–1872).

Nor should we forget that local and state governments were extraordinarily active, often oppressively so, in the nineteenth century. Several historians have shown how localities and states wove a web of regulations touching many aspects of life.[12] To focus on racial freedom: which was more statist, southern regulations of race (black codes, segregation, disfranchisement), or passage of constitutional amendments that set a legal framework for all Americans, thus striking down some of these oppressive regulations?

Unfortunately, historians who deplore the expansion of federal power during the Civil War and Reconstruction too often ignore oppressive southern regulations of daily life that violated individual freedom. These political controls ranged from the serious to the absurd: for example, the Birmingham, Alabama, ordinance barring whites and blacks from playing dominoes or checkers together in public places! Or the Maryland ban on interracial tennis (a policy skewered by H. L. Mencken's acidic pen). More seriously, those critical of federal power overlook the absence of law and order that allowed for rampant lynching, often condoned by local authorities. John Sibley Butler compares the state of racial freedom in the Jim Crow South to life under a communist regime:

> In addition to the basic rights being abridged, there was an element of fear based on the weapons power of the police. As would be the case in the Soviet Union, they were not allowed to travel comfortably in all parts of a city, and they could be picked up and detained without due process. Even more analogous to a communist society, the government told blacks where to drink water, where to sit on the bus, which schools they could attend, which bathrooms they could visit, and which communities they could live in. All of these rules were enforced by law. There was total governmental interference in the lives of Afro-Americans.[13]

No wonder many civil rights advocates, from Frederick Douglass to Ward Connerly, felt strongly that the government was the problem, rather than the solution to racial oppression. Neither left nor right, these men and women were radical critics of the status quo and conservative defenders of traditions that included religion, the Constitution, capitalism, and other classical liberal values.

In sum, the classical liberal tradition has a long history and is not simply recent "backlash." Nor is it solely located within the Republican Party: since the late 1960s, the GOP establishment, together with the Democratic Party, has condoned racial preferences and rolled a racial pork barrel over the rights of individuals. Nevertheless, despite partisan backsliding, classical liberals kept to the principles of their tradition. Indeed, persistent patterns emerge that tie together figures separated by a century or more of time.

## Looking Backward . . . and Forward

I hope this brief introduction to the anthology has whetted your appetite to learn more about such forgotten events as President Warren Harding's racial freedom address at Birmingham, Alabama (1921); Calvin Coolidge's speech before Howard University when the KKK was at high tide (1924); and Hamilton Fish's wartime membership in the black "Harlem Hellfighters" unit and his subsequent civil rights activism in Congress. Other memorable individuals include Moorfield Storey; R. C. Hoiles, the editor who denounced the internment of Japanese Americans; and Rose Wilder Lane, a regular columnist for leading black newspapers. The best tribute to these forgotten voices of racial freedom is learning more, and perhaps being inspired by their example. At the very least, we may become better informed citizens regarding the American dilemma of race.

## A Note on the Text

Historians divide the past into periods to help readers understand the themes marking one era from those preceding and following. The documents in each chapter fall into logical periods, but there is overlap. Certain issues dominated one period but culminated in an event in the next era. In such a case, I have kept the flow of the chapter's discussion together even if a document extends into the next chapter's time period.

My commentary is presented in slightly bolder text to distinguish it from the actual documents.

## Notes

1. Clayborne Carson, *Eyes on the Prize: America's Civil Rights Years: A Reader and Guide* (New York: Penguin, 1987); Clayborne Carson, *The Eyes on the Prize Civil Rights Reader: Documents, Speeches, and Firsthand Accounts from the Black Freedom Struggle, 1954–1990* (New York: Penguin, 1991); Peter B. Levy, *Let Freedom Ring: A Documentary History of the Modern Civil Rights Movement* (New York: Praeger, 1992); Jonathan Birnbaum and Clarence Taylor, *Civil Rights since 1787: A Reader on the Black Struggle* (New York: New York University Press, 2000); Manning Marable, *How Capitalism Underdeveloped Black America: Problems in Race, Political Economy, and Society,* rev. ed. (Cambridge, MA: South End, 2000); Raymond N. D'Angelo, *The American Civil Rights Movement: Readings and Interpretations* (Guilford, CT: Dushkin, 2001); Manning Marable, Nishani Frazier, and John Campbell McMillian, *Freedom on My Mind: The Columbia Documentary History of the African American Experience* (New York: Columbia University Press, 2003); Ronald H. Bayor, *The Columbia Documentary History of Race and Ethnicity in America* (New York: Columbia University Press, 2004).

2. Michael K. Brown, *Whitewashing Race: The Myth of a Color-Blind Society* (Berkeley: University of California Press, 2003); Eduardo Bonilla-Silva, *Racism without Racists: Color-Blind Racism and the Persistence of Racial Inequality in the United States,* 2nd ed. (Lanham, MD: Rowman & Littlefield, 2006).

3. Scott Gerber, "Justice Thomas and Mr. Jefferson," *Legal Times,* May 5, 2003, http://www.law.com (accessed June 8, 2006).

4. "Cal Coolidge Tells Kluxer When to Stop," *Chicago Defender,* August 16, 1924, 1.

5. Andrew Kull, *The Color-Blind Constitution* (Cambridge, MA: Harvard University Press, 1992).

6. Marable, *How Capitalism Underdeveloped Black America.*

7. Manning Marable, "By Any Means Necessary: The Life and Legacy of Malcolm X," *Black Collegian Online,* February 21, 1992, http://www.black-collegian .com/african/lifelegacy200.shtml (accessed July 20, 2008).

8. Paul D. Moreno, *Black Americans and Organized Labor: A New History* (Baton Rouge: Louisiana State University Press, 2006).

9. Gary Stanley Becker, *The Economics of Discrimination* (Chicago: University of Chicago Press, 1957).

10. Booker T. Washington, *Up from Slavery: An Autobiography* (Garden City, NY: Doubleday, 1901); John H. Johnson and Lerone Bennett, *Succeeding against the Odds* (New York: Warner, 1989); Mary Fuller Casey, *S. B. Fuller: Pioneer in Black Economic Development* (Jamestown, NC: Bridgemaster, 2003); A. G. Gaston, *Green Power: The Successful Way of A. G. Gaston* (Birmingham: Southern University Press, 1968); Peter Max Ascoli, *Julius Rosenwald: The Man Who Built Sears, Roebuck and Advanced the Cause of Black Education in the American South* (Bloomington: Indiana University Press, 2006).

11. Angela D. Dillard, *Guess Who's Coming to Dinner Now? Multicultural Conservatism in America* (New York: New York University Press, 2001), 12–13.

12. Jonathan R. T. Hughes, *The Governmental Habit Redux: Economic Controls from Colonial Times to the Present* (Princeton, NJ: Princeton University Press, 1991); Ballard C. Campbell, *The Growth of American Government: Governance from the Cleveland Era to the Present* (Bloomington: Indiana University Press, 1995); William J. Novak, *The People's Welfare: Law and Regulation in Nineteenth-Century America* (Chapel Hill: University of North Carolina Press, 1996).

13. John S. Butler, *Entrepreneurship and Self-Help among Black Americans: A Reconsideration of Race and Economics* (Albany: State University of New York Press, 1991), 73.

# 1

## Antislavery
### *1776–1853*

IN THE ERA OF ANTISLAVERY, classical liberal voices for racial freedom drew upon the Constitution, Christianity, and belief in the right to self-ownership. The Declaration of Independence was also a touchstone of abolitionism quoted and discussed by James Forten, David Walker, Lysander Spooner, Frederick Douglass, and nearly every other antislavery writer in the tumultuous period leading up to the Civil War. Strong, often violent, opposition to antislavery activists led them to develop a coherent tradition that dominated the civil rights movement well into the twentieth century and still persists today. Although the author of the Declaration, Thomas Jefferson, was a slaveholder, that fact did not undermine the meaning and power of the natural rights theory set forth in that famous document, which mentions God four times as the source of those "unalienable Rights." Throughout this period, classical liberal Christians found themselves fighting the proslavery interpretations of Christianity advanced by southerners. In response, classical liberals invoked the concept that "all men are . . . endowed by their Creator with certain unalienable Rights, [and] that among these are Life, Liberty and the pursuit of Happiness."

ℭℬ

### *Declaration of Independence (1776)*

#### *Thomas Jefferson*

When in the Course of human events, it becomes necessary for one people to dissolve the political bands which have connected them with another, and to assume among the powers of the earth, the separate and equal station to which the Laws of Nature and of Nature's God entitle them, a decent respect to the opinions of mankind requires that they should declare the causes which impel them to the separation.

We hold these truths to be self-evident, that all men are created equal, that they are endowed by their Creator with certain unalienable Rights, that among these are Life, Liberty and the pursuit of Happiness.

That to secure these rights, Governments are instituted among Men, deriving their just powers from the consent of the governed, That whenever any Form of Government becomes destructive of these ends, it is the Right of the People to alter or to abolish it, and to institute new Government, laying its foundation on such principles and organizing its powers in such form, as to them shall seem most likely to effect their Safety and Happiness. Prudence, indeed, will dictate that Governments long established should not be changed for light and transient causes; and accordingly all experience hath shewn, that mankind are more disposed to suffer, while evils are sufferable, than to right themselves by abolishing the forms to which they are accustomed. But when a long train of abuses and usurpations, pursuing invariably the same Object evinces a design to reduce them under absolute Despotism, it is their right, it is their duty, to throw off such Government, and to provide new Guards for their future security.

## Independence Day Belongs to All Americans (1813)

### James Forten

A free black who fought in the Revolutionary War, James Forten (1766–1842) became a wealthy sailmaker in Philadelphia. In this 1813 petition to the Pennsylvania state legislature he protests a bill that would have deprived free blacks of rights. (The bill failed, but other "free" states passed similar laws.) Schooled by an abolitionist, Forten believed that the Constitution and the Declaration of Independence applied to all men, even if their promise was not yet fulfilled. In his life, we see the forces of Christianity, classical liberalism, and capitalism combine in an individual characterized as a "conservative radical" by one biographer. His career inspired a later generation of abolitionists, including

William Lloyd Garrison and Frederick Douglass. An advocate of colorblindness and Christian uplift, Forten practiced what he preached by employing both blacks and whites in his business, with harmonious results. "'Here,' said he, 'you see what ought to be done in the country at large.'"[1]

ↄ

### Letter I.

We hold this truth to be self-evident, that God created all men equal, and [it] is one of the most prominent features in the Declaration of Independence, and in that glorious fabrick of collected wisdom, our noble Constitution. This idea embraces the Indian and the European, the Savage and the Saint, the Peruvian and the Laplander, the white Man and the African, and whatever measures are adopted subversive of this inestimable privilege, are in direct violation of the letter and spirit of our Constitution. . . .

These thoughts were suggested by the promulgation of a late bill, before the Senate of Pennsylvania, to prevent the emigration of people of colour into this state. It was not passed into a law at this session and must in consequence lay over until the next. . . . Many of us are men of property, for the security of which, we have hitherto looked to the laws of our blessed state, but should this become a law, our property is jeopardized, since the same power which can expose to sale an unfortunate fellow creature, can wrest from him those estates, which years of honest industry have accumulated. Where shall the poor African look for protection, should the people of Pennsylvania consent to oppress him? . . . Many of our fathers, many of ourselves, have fought and bled for the Independence of our country. Do not then expose us to sale. Let not the spirit of the father behold the son robbed of that Liberty which he died to establish, but let the motto of our legislators be: "The Law knows no distinction. . . ."

### Letter II.

Let us put a case, in which the law in question operates peculiarly hard and unjust.— I have a brother, perhaps, who resides in a distant part of the Union, and . . . comes to visit me. Unless that brother be registered in twenty four hours after, and be able to produce a certificate to that effect, he is liable, according to the second and third sections of the bill, to a fine of twenty dollars, to arrest, imprisonment and sale. . . . The same power which protects the white man, should protect A MAN OF COLOUR.

### Letter III.

Who is this Register [Registrar]? A man, and exercising an office, where ten dollars is the fee for each delinquent, will probably be a cruel man and find delinquents where they really do not exist. The poor black is left to the merciless gripe of an avaricious Register, without an appeal, in the event, from his tyranny or oppression! . . . What have the people of colour been guilty of, that they more than others, should be compelled to register their houses, lands, servants and *Children*. Yes, ye rulers of the black man's destiny, reflect upon this; our *Children* must be registered, and bear about them a certificate, or be subject to imprisonment and fine. You, who are perusing this effusion of feeling, are you a parent? Have you children around whom your affections are bound, by those delightful bonds which none but a parent can know? Are they the delight of your prosperity, and the solace of your afflictions? If all this be true, to you we submit our cause. The parent's feeling cannot err. . . .

### Letter IV.

Are not men of colour sufficiently degraded? Why then increase their degradation. It is a well known fact, that black people, upon certain days of publick jubilee, dare not be seen after twelve o'clock in the day, upon the field to enjoy the times; for no sooner do the fumes of that potent devil, Liquor, mount into the brain, than the poor black is assailed like the destroying Hyena or the avaricious Wolf. I allude particularly to the FOURTH OF JULY!—Is it not wonderful, that the day set apart for the festival of Liberty, should be abused by the advocates of Freedom, in endeavouring to sully what they profess to adore. If men, though they know that the law protects all, will dare, in defiance of law, to execute their hatred upon the defenceless black, will they not by the passage of this bill, believe him still more a mark for their venom and spleen.—Will they not believe him completely deserted by authority. . . .

**Letter V.**

The fifth section of this bill, is also peculiarly hard, inasmuch as it prevents freemen from living where they please.—Pennsylvania has always been a refuge from slavery, and to this state the Southern black, when freed, has flown for safety. Why does he this! When masters in many of the Southern states, which they frequently do, free a particular black, unless the Black leaves the state in so many hours, any person resident of the said state, can have him arrested and again sold to Slavery:—The hunted black is obliged to flee, or remain and be again a Slave. I have known persons of this description sold three times after being first emancipated.

It is in vain that we are forming societies of different kinds to ameliorate the condition of our unfortunate brethren, to correct their morals and to render them not only honest but useful members to society. All our efforts, by this bill, are despised, and we are doomed to feel the lash of oppression:—As well may we be outlawed, as well may the glorious privileges of the Gospel, be denied us, and all endeavours used to cut us off from happiness hereafter as well as here! . . .

I have done. My feelings are acute, and I have ventured to express them without intending either accusation or insult to any one. An appeal to the heart is my intention, and if I have failed, it is my great misfortune, not to have had a power of eloquence sufficient to convince. But I trust the eloquence of nature will succeed, and that the law-givers of this happy Commonwealth will yet remain the Blacks' friend, and the advocates of Freemen, is the sincere wish of A MAN OF COLOUR.

Source: James Forten, *Letters from a Man of Colour on a Late Bill Before the Senate of Pennsylvania* (n. p., [1813]), 1–3, 5–6, 8, 10–11.

## Is Christianity So Little Esteemed? (1823)

*William Wilberforce*

While slavery directly threatened black Americans, many others were passionate about ending slavery because it violated the teachings of Jesus Christ. It is part of the American dilemma that Americans inherited both slavery and Christianity from the British. Indeed, the Declaration of Independence (1776) stated that "all men . . . are endowed by their Creator with certain unalienable Rights." Students of American history have paid especial attention to the "unalienable Rights" of "Life, Liberty and the pursuit of Happiness," but have downplayed the emphasis on the Creator endowing human beings with these rights. Yet the religious aspect of the Declaration fueled classical liberal antiracism for the next two centuries.

The fervor of Christian abolitionism came primarily from the New Testament, a body of literature providing the universal principles of natural law to attack slavery. Faith crossed borders and oceans, with Christians in both Britain and America using natural and divine law to argue first for the end of the slave trade (1807) and then to abolish slavery entirely in the British Empire (1833). In Britain, an unlikely Member of Parliament, William Wilberforce (1759–1833), courageously took up the cause of human emancipation, despite strong parliamentary opposition when he began his campaign in the late eighteenth century. The son of a wealthy merchant, young Wilberforce led a life of hedonism until he entered Parliament at age twenty-one. Five years later, he had a conversion experience leading him to devote his life to freeing those in bondage and emancipating the legally free from vice. Wilberforce published *A Letter on the Abolition of the Slave Trade* (1807) on the eve of Parliament's vote to end the trade in human beings. In 1823, "God's politician" began a ten-year campaign to end slavery entirely, releasing his *Appeal to the Religion, Justice and Humanity of the Inhabitants of the British Empire in Behalf of the Negro Slaves in the West Indies,* in which he claimed that total and unqualified emancipation was a moral and ethical duty before God. He died just as Parliament was in the process of abolishing slavery. His friend John Newton, once one of the cruelest of slave traders, later in life went through a similar "born-again" experience and wrote the famous hymn "Amazing Grace"—later the title of the movie about Wilberforce's awe-inspiring campaign against slavery. A historically black college in America is named after him (Wilberforce University).

Under Wilberforce's leadership, the antislavery movement in Britain developed tactics adopted by American abolitionists: speakers on lecture circuits, mass petitions to Congress, distribution of abolitionist tracts, and the use of "respectable" women as advocates. As seen below, American abolitionists faced greater danger, including the "gagging" of petitions to Congress, the seizure of abolitionist mail in the South, and death threats. Despite the differences, in both Britain and the United States, Christianity impelled individuals to organize in opposition to man's ownership of man. Religion, together with invocations of natural law (divinely ordered), weaves through many of the documents in this anthology.

※

*Woe unto him that buildeth his house by unrighteousness, and his chambers by wrong; that useth his neighbour's service without wages, and giveth him not for his work. Jeremiah*

*Do justice, and love mercy. Micah*

The West Indians, in the warmth of argument, have gone still farther, and have . . . distinctly told us, again and again . . . that these poor degraded beings, the Negro slaves, are as well or even better off than our British peasantry,—a proposition so monstrous, that nothing can possibly exhibit in a stronger light the extreme force of the prejudices which must exist in the minds of its assertors. The Briton to compare the state of a West Indian slave with that of an English freeman, and to give the former the preference! It is to imply an utter insensibility of the native feelings and moral dignity of man, no less than of the rights of Englishmen!! I will not condescend to argue this question, as I might, on the ground of comparative feeding and clothing, and lodging, and medical attendance. Are these the only claims? Are these the chief privileges of a rational and immortal being? Is the consciousness of personal independence nothing? Are self-possession and self-government nothing? Is it of no account that our persons are inviolate by any private authority, and that the whip is placed only in the hands of the public executioner; is it of no value that we have the power of pursuing the occupation and the habits of life which we prefer; that we have condition, or at least the hope, of improving our condition, and of rising, as we have seen others rise, from poverty and obscurity to comfort? . . . Are husband and wife, parent and child, terms of no meaning? Are willing services, or grateful returns for voluntary kindnesses, nothing? But, above all, is Christianity so little esteemed among us, that we are to account as of no value the hope, "full of immortality," the light of heavenly truth, and all the consolations and supports by which religion cheers the hearts and elevates the principles, and dignifies the conduct of multitudes of our labouring classes in this free and enlightened country? Is it nothing to be taught that all human distinctions will soon be at an end; that all the labours and sorrows of poverty and hardship will soon exist no more and to know, on the express authority of Scripture, that the lower classes, instead of being an inferior order in the creation, are even the preferable objects of the love of the Almighty?

But such wretched sophisms as insult the understandings of mankind, are sometimes best answered by an appeal to their feelings. Let me therefore ask, is there, in the whole of the three kingdoms, a parent or a husband so sordid and insensible that any sum, which the richest West Indian proprietor could offer him, would be deemed a compensation for his suffering his wife or his daughter to be subjected to the brutal outrage of the cart-whip—to the savage lust of the driver—to the indecent, and degrading, and merciless punishment of a West Indian whipping? If there were one so dead . . . he might consent to sell the liberty of his own children, and to barter away even the blessings conferred on himself by that religion which declared to him that his master, no less than himself, has a Master in heaven—a common Creator, who is no respecter of persons, and in whose presence he may weekly stand on the same spiritual level with his superiors in rank, to be reminded of their common origin, common responsibility, and common day of final and irreversible account.

Source: William Wilberforce, *Appeal to the Religion, Justice and Humanity of the Inhabitants of the British Empire in Behalf of the Negro Slaves in the West Indies* (London: J. Hatchard, 1823), 45–48.

## Let God's People Go! (1829)

### David Walker

In 1829, "a dangerous incendiary pamphlet was found circulating among the blacks at Savannah, Georgia. Later the same pamphlet was discovered in the possession of Negroes in the Upper South."[2] Soon thereafter, Nat Turner led a slave insurrection—the righteous violence predicted by David Walker (1796?–1830) in his *Appeal to the Colored Citizens of the World* (1829). Southern states passed laws prohibiting the education of slaves and the circulation of abolitionist material. Henry Highland Garnet stated that "this little book produced more commotion among slaveholders than any volume of its size"; "it was merely a smooth stone which this David took up, yet it terrified a host of Goliaths. When the fame of this book reached the South, the poor, cowardly, pusillanimous tyrants, grew pale behind their cotton bags, and armed themselves to the teeth."[3]

The regional crackdown on free speech and freedom of the press led many northerners, including William Leggett and Lysander Spooner (below), to defend the right of slaves to overthrow their "masters." Others argued for *northern* secession from the Union to create a haven for runaway slaves. Thus Walker planted the seeds of a regional divide that ended in civil war. Walker's *Appeal* demonstrates the revolutionary potential of the classical liberal tradition, with its unconditional emphasis upon self-ownership and Christian justice.

Walker was a free black who fled the South for Boston, where he operated a successful clothing business. Inspired by Richard Allen, founder of the African Methodist Episcopal Church, Walker denounced white Americans in the harshest terms as hypocrites to their Christian faith and the Declaration of Independence. Walker's jeremiad called upon God to side with the slaves in a violent struggle against their oppressors. Urging white Americans to repent, he offered a glimmer of biracial harmony ("nothing is impossible with God"), yet doubted that whites would soften their hardened hearts. Christianity was the primary defense used by southern slaveholders to uphold slavery. Walker condemned those Christians who selected scriptural passages (Colossians 3:22, Ephesians 6:5) to defend slavery. This debate among Christians went on until war destroyed the institution of slavery.

Walker's *Appeal* galvanized free blacks in the North and paved the way for the radical abolitionism of the 1830s. Yet Walker never lived to see these changes: in 1830 he died suddenly. He had a bounty on his head; many supporters believed that he was poisoned.

❧

We, (colored people of these United States), are the most degraded, wretched, and abject set of beings that ever lived since the world began, and I pray God, that none like us ever may live again until time shall be no more. They tell us of the Israelites in Egypt, the Helots in Sparta, and of the Roman Slaves, which last, were made up from almost every nation under heaven, whose sufferings under those ancient and heathen nations were, in comparison with ours, under this enlightened and christian nation, no more than a cypher—or in other words, those heathen nations of antiquity, had but little more among them than the name and form of slavery, while wretchedness and endless miseries were reserved, apparently in a phial, to be poured out upon our fathers, ourselves and our children by *christian* Americans!

These positions, I shall endeavour, by the help of the Lord, to demonstrate in the course of this *appeal,* to the satisfaction of the most incredulous mind—and may God Almighty who is the father of our Lord Jesus Christ, open your hearts to understand and believe the truth.

. . . The fact is, the labor of slaves comes so cheap to the avaricious usurpers, and is (as they think) of such great utility to the country where it exists, that those who are actuated by sordid avarice only, overlook the evils, which will as sure as the Lord lives, follow after the good. In fact, they are so happy to keep in ignorance and degradation, and to receive the homage and the labor of the slaves, they forget that God rules in the armies of heaven and among the inhabitants of the earth, having his ears continually open to the cries, tears and groans of his oppressed people; and being a just and holy Being will at one day appear fully in behalf of the oppressed, and arrest the progress of the avaricious oppressors; for although the destruction of the oppressors God may not effect by the oppressed, yet the Lord our God will bring other destructions upon them—for not unfrequently will he cause them to rise up one against another, to be split and divided, and to oppress each other, and sometimes to open hostilities with sword in hand.

. . . All persons who are acquainted with history, and particularly the Bible, who are not blinded by the God of this world, and are not actuated solely by avarice—who are able to lay aside prejudice long enough to view candidly and impartially, things as they were, are, and probably will be, who are willing to admit that God made man to serve him *alone,* and that man should have no other Lord or Lords but himself—that God Almighty is the *sole proprietor* or *master* of the WHOLE human family, and will not on any consideration admit of a colleague, being unwilling to divide his glory with another.—And who can dispense with prejudice long enough to admit that we are men, notwithstanding our *improminent noses* and *woolly heads,* and believe that we feel for our fathers, mothers, wives and children as well as they do for theirs.

. . . Are we MEN!!—I ask you, O my brethren! are we MEN? Did our creator make us to be slaves to dust and ashes like ourselves? Are they not dying worms as well as we? Have they not to make their appearance before the tribunal of heaven, to answer for the deeds done in the body, as well as we? Have we any other master but Jesus Christ alone? Is he not their master as well as ours?—What right then, have we to obey and call any other master, but Himself? How we could be so *submissive* to a gang of men, whom we cannot tell whether they are as *good* as ourselves or not, I never could conceive. However, this is shut up with the Lord and we cannot precisely tell—but I declare, we judge men by their works. . . .

The Pagans, Jews and Mahometans try to make proselytes to their religions, and whatever human beings adopt their religions, they extend to them their protection. But Christian Americans not only hinder their fellow creatures, the Africans, but thousands of them will *absolutely beat a coloured person nearly to death, if they catch him on his knees, supplicating the throne of grace.* I have known tyrants or usurpers of human liberty in different parts of this country take their fellow creatures, the colored people, and beat them until they would scarcely leave life in them; what for? Why they say,

"The black devils had the audacity to be found *making prayers and supplications to the God who made them!!! . . .*"

. . . What the American preachers can think of us, I aver this day before my God, I have never been able to define. They have newspapers and monthly periodicals, which they receive in continual succession, but on the pages of which, you will scarcely ever find a paragraph respecting slavery, which is ten thousand times more injurious to this country than all the other evils put together; and which will be the final overthrow of its government, unless something is very speedily done; for their cup is nearly full.—Perhaps they will laugh at, or make light of this; but I tell you Americans! that unless you speedily alter your course, *you* and your *Country are gone!!!!!! . . .*

. . . Treat us like men, and there is no danger but we will all live in peace and happiness together. For we are not like you, hard hearted, unmerciful, and unforgiving. What a happy country this will be, if the whites will listen. What nation under heaven, will be able to do any thing with us, unless God gives us up into his hand? But Americans, I declare to you, while you keep us and our children in bondage, and treat us like brutes, to make us support you and your families, we cannot be your friends. You do not look for it, do you? Treat us then like men, and we will be your friends. And there is not a doubt in my mind, but that the whole of the past will be sunk into oblivion, and we yet, under God, will become a united and happy people. The whites may say it is impossible, but remember that nothing is impossible with God. . . .

See your declaration, Americans!! Do you understand your own language? Hear your language, proclaimed to the world, July 4, 1776—

"We hold these truths to be self evident—that ALL MEN ARE CREATED EQUAL! that they *are endowed by their Creator with certain unalienable rights; that among these are life, liberty, and the pursuit of happiness!!*"

Compare your own language above, extracted from your Declaration of Independence, with your cruelties and murders inflicted by your cruel and unmerciful fathers on ourselves on our fathers and on us, men who have never given your fathers or you the least provocation!!!

Hear your language further!

"But when a long train of abuses and usurpations, pursuing invariably the same object, evinces a design to reduce them under absolute despotism, it is their *right,* it is their *duty,* to throw off such government, and to provide new guards for their future security."

Now, Americans! I ask you candidly, was your sufferings under Great Britain one hundredth part as cruel and tyrannical as you have rendered ours under you? Some of you, no doubt, believe that we will never throw off your murderous government, and "provide new guards for our future security." If Satan has made you believe it, will he not deceive you? . . .

The Americans may be as vigilant as they please, but they cannot be vigilant enough for the Lord, neither can they hide themselves, where he will not find and bring them out.

Source: David Walker and Henry Highland Garnet, *Walker's Appeal, with a Brief Sketch of His Life* (1829; repr., New York: J. H. Tobitt, 1848), 11, 13, 15, 27, 48, 51, 80–81, 85–87.

# Slavery: No Evil? (1835)

## William Leggett

William Leggett (1802–1839) was publisher of the *New York Evening Post*. He broke away from the Democratic Party because of its position on slavery and other issues and created the Loco-Foco (Equal Rights) Party. His equal rights doctrine held that government must treat all citizens equally and may not discriminate in favor of any person or interest. This classical liberal doctrine effectively reduced the role of the state to a minimum and was consistent with Leggett's espousal of laissez-faire. In the mid-1830s, he criticized southerners and northern Democrats for squelching antislavery speech. In this editorial, he denounces slavery as a great evil. This document demonstrates how issues of race became entangled with the right to free speech, another classical liberal value shared widely among those not as passionately interested in the abolition of slavery.

&

Slavery no evil! Has it come to this, that the foulest stigma on our national escutcheon, which no true-hearted freeman could ever contemplate without sorrow in his heart and a blush upon his cheek, has got to be viewed by the people of the south as no stain on the American character? Have their ears become so accustomed to the clank of the poor bondman's fetters that it no longer grates upon them as a discordant sound? Have his groans ceased to speak the language of misery? Has his servile condition lost any of its degradation? Can the husband be torn from his wife, and the child from its parent, and sold like cattle at the shambles [meat market], and yet free, intelligent men, whose own rights are founded on the declaration of the unalienable freedom and equality of all mankind, stand up in the face of heaven and their fellow men, and assert without a blush that there is no evil in servitude? We could not have believed that the madness of the south had reached so dreadful a climax.

Not only are we told that slavery is no evil, but that it is criminal towards the south, and a violation of the spirit of the federal compact, to indulge even a hope that the chains of the captive may some day or other, no matter how remote the time, be broken. Ultimate abolitionists are not less enemies of the south, we are told, than those who seek to accomplish immediate enfranchisement. Nay, the threat is held up to us, that unless we speedily pass laws to prohibit all expression of opinion on the dreadful topic of slavery, the southern states will meet in Convention, separate themselves from the north, and establish a separate empire for themselves. The next claim we shall hear from the arrogant south will be a call upon us to pass edicts forbidding men to think on the subject of slavery, on the ground that even meditation on that topic is interdicted by the spirit of the federal compact.

What a mysterious thing this federal compact must be, which enjoins so much by its spirit that is wholly omitted in its language—nay not only omitted, but which is directly contrary to some of its express provisions! And they who framed that compact, how sadly ignorant they must have been of the import of the instrument they were giving to the world! They did not hesitate to speak of slavery, not only as an evil, but as the direst curse inflicted upon our country. They did not refrain from indulging a hope that the stain might one day or other be wiped out, and the poor bondman restored to the condition of equal freedom for which God and nature designed him. But the sentiments which Jefferson, and Madison, and Patrick Henry freely expressed are treasonable now, according to the new reading of the federal compact. . . .

It is due to ourselves, and it is no less due to the south, that the north should speak out plainly on the questions which the demands of the former present for our decision. On this subject boldness and truth are required. Temporizing, like oil upon the waters, may smooth the billows for a moment, but cannot disperse the storm. Reasonable men and lovers of truth will not be offended with those who speak with boldness what reason and truth conspire to dictate.

Source: William Leggett, editorial, *New York Evening Post*, September 9, 1835, reprinted in *A Collection of the Political Writings of William Leggett*, ed. Theodore Sedgwick (New York: Taylor & Dodd, 1840), 2:64–68.

## Is Jesus Christ in Favor of American Slavery? (1839)

### Beriah Green and the American Anti-Slavery Society

In this tract distributed by the American Anti-Slavery Society (AAS)—a group founded by William Lloyd Garrison and Lewis Tappan (see below), among others—Beriah Green (1795–1874) voiced the religious critique of the evangelicals in opposition to those Christians who defended slavery. Green was a trained theologian and president of the Oneida Institute, a New York college that accepted black and white students. In answering the perennial question of WWJD ("What Would Jesus Do?"), Green and his fellow evangelicals argued that he would abolish slavery.

One year later (1840), Tappan, Green, and Gerrit Smith (1797–1874) broke with the AAS over Garrison's support of women's rights, and his belief that abolitionists should not be tainted by politics. The anti-Garrison faction, led by the evangelicals, ran candidates for public office. They formed the Liberty Party and ran Smith as their presidential candidate (he lost). Although elected to Congress, Smith became disillusioned with politics and left after only two years in office (1853–1854). Smith later retired to spend his time and wealth on church and charity. This political wing of the antislavery movement later aligned with the Republican Party (see chapter 2).

☙

Is Jesus Christ in favor of American slavery? In 1776 THOMAS JEFFERSON, supported by a noble band of patriots and surrounded by the American people, opened his lips in the authoritative declaration: "We hold these truths to be SELF-EVIDENT, *that all men are created equal; that they are endowed by their Creator with certain unalienable rights; that among these are life, LIBERTY and the pursuit of happiness."* And from the inmost heart of the multitudes around, and in a strong and clear voice, broke forth the unanimous and decisive answer: Amen—such truths we do indeed hold to be self-evident. And animated and sustained by a declaration, so inspiring and sublime, they rushed to arms, and as the result of agonizing efforts and dreadful sufferings, achieved under God the independence of their country. The great truth, whence they derived light and strength to assert and defend their rights, they made the foundation of their republic. And in the midst of *this republic,* must we prove, that He, who was the Truth, did not contradict "the truths" which He Himself, as their Creator, had made self-evident to mankind? . . .

Is Jesus Christ in favor of American slavery? It is already widely felt and openly acknowledged at the South, that they can not support slavery without sustaining the opposition of universal christendom. And Thomas Jefferson declared, that "he trembled for his country when he reflected, that God is just; that his justice can not sleep forever; that considering numbers, nature, and natural means only, a revolution of the wheel of fortune, an exchange of situation, is among possible events; that it may become practicable by supernatural influences! The Almighty has no attribute which can take sides with us in such a contest." And must we prove, that Jesus Christ is not in favor of what universal christendom is impelled to abhor, denounce, and oppose;—is not in favor of what every attribute of Almighty God is armed against?

Source: Beriah Green, *The Chattel Principle: The Abhorrence of Jesus Christ and the Apostles; or, No Refuge for American Slavery in the New Testament* (New York: American Anti-Slavery Society, 1839), 3–5. The footnotes in the original have been omitted.

### Liberation of the Amistad Captives (1841)

Lewis Tappan (1788–1873) was an evangelical Christian, businessman, and abolitionist. Tappan used his network of antislavery men, including Abraham Lincoln, to create a credit reporting system that covered North America (later merged into Dun & Bradstreet). Extremely moralistic, Tappan burst into brothels to rescue prostitutes from their sinful ways, and protested the drunken revels that took place on Independence Day in New York City. He paid a stiff price for his abolitionism when a mob sacked and burned his house.

Undeterred, Tappan proved crucial in organizing and funding the successful legal defense of the *Amistad* captives—an incident made famous by Steven Spielberg's epic film *Amistad* (1997). In 1807, Congress banned the importation of slaves from abroad, thus making overseas slave trading a crime. But in 1839, the Spanish ship *Tecora* set sail from Africa to Cuba with captive slaves. After reaching Havana, Cuba, the Spanish owners took the captives aboard the *Amistad* for shipment to their plantations on the other side of Cuba. The slaves mutinied and took over the ship, ending up in U.S. waters, where they were met by the U.S. Navy. The Spanish demanded their "property" while the Spanish government asked the U.S. government to extradite the captives to Cuba, where they could stand trial for murdering several members of the ship's crew. President

Martin van Buren wanted to extradite the captives, but the courts decided that this was a federal matter and the case worked its way to the U.S. Supreme Court. During this two-year period, Lewis Tappan and other abolitionists formed the "Amistad Committee" to raise a legal defense fund, teach the Africans English and Christianity, and use the case to further their abolitionist cause.

In the following documents, Tappan and his committee announce the U.S. Supreme Court's release of the kidnapped Africans after years in captivity. In a separate letter, the freed Africans thank former president John Quincy Adams for his legal defense by presenting him with a Bible. Touched by their gesture, Adams responds by wishing them well on their return to Africa.

ɕʓ

*Lewis Tappan et al.*

The Committee have the high satisfaction of announcing that the Supreme Court of the United States have definitively decided that our long-imprisoned captives who were taken in the Amistad, ARE FREE, on this soil, without condition or restraint. The opinion of the court was pronounced on Tuesday, March 9, by Judge Story. In view of this great deliverance, in which the lives and liberties of thirty-six fellow-men are secured, as well as many fundamental principles of law, justice, and human rights established, the committee respectfully request that public thanks be given on the occasion, to Almighty God in all the churches throughout the land.

S. S. JOCELYN

JOSHUA LEAVITT

LEWIS TAPPAN

*Cinque, Kinna, and Kale*

To the Honorable John Quincy Adams:

Most Respected Sir,—The Mendi people give you thanks for all your kindness to them. They will never forget your defence of their rights before the great court at Washington. They feel that they owe to you, in a large measure, their deliverance from the Spaniards, and from slavery or death. They will pray for you as long as you live, Mr. Adams. May God bless and reward you. We are about to go home to

Africa. We go to Sierra Leone first, and then we reach Mendi very quick. When we get to Mendi we will tell the people of your great kindness. Good missionary will go with us. We shall take the bible with us. It has been a precious book in prison, and we love to read it now we are free! Mr. Adams, we want to make you a present of a beautiful bible! Will you please to accept it, and when you look at it, or read it, remember your poor and grateful clients? We read in this holy book, "If it had not been the Lord who was on our side, when men rose up against us, then they had swallowed us up quick, when their wrath was kindled against us. Blessed be the Lord, who hath not given us a prey to their teeth. Our soul is escaped as a bird out of the snare of the fowler; the snare is broken and we are escaped. Our help is in the name of the Lord, who made Heaven and Earth.

"For the Mendi people,

CINQUE,

KINNA,

KALE

Boston, Nov. 6, 1841.

### John Quincy Adams

To the Mendian Africans, Cinque, Kinna, Kale and thirty-two others, about to return to their native land:

BOSTON, 19th November, 1841

My Friends,—I have received the elegant Bible, which you have presented to me, through your true and faithful friend, Mr. Lewis Tappan. I accept it, and shall keep it as a kind remembrancer [*sic*] from you, to the end of my life. It was from that book that I learnt to espouse your cause when you were in trouble, and to give thanks to God for your deliverance.

I am glad to learn that you have the prospect of returning safe and free to your native country; and I hope and pray that you may pass the remainder of your lives in peace and comfort there. Remember with kindness those worthy persons who befriended you in your captivity here, and who now furnish you with the means of returning home, and tell your countrymen of the blessings of the book which you have given to me. May the Almighty Power who has preserved and sustained you hitherto, still go with you, and turn to your good, and to that of your country, all that you have suffered, and all that may hereafter befall you.

From your friend,

JOHN QUINCY ADAMS

BOSTON, Nov. 19, 1841

Sources: Lewis Tappan et al., "To The Friends of the African Captives," *Emancipator*, March 25, 1841, 191; "Departure of the Mendi Africans," *Boston Courier*, December 2, 1841, 1.

### *Man Cannot Own Property in Man* or *Woman* (1841)

#### *William Ellery Channing*

Self-ownership was fundamental to the classic liberal critique of slavery. By definition, slaves did not own their own bodies, control their own labor, or possess the freedom to live as they wished. White Americans recognized self-ownership as the underlying value of "life, liberty, and property" yet excluded slaves from these inalienable rights simply because of race. The challenge for antislavery activists was to persuade white Americans that the Declaration of Independence applied to *all* men and women.

Self-ownership provided a compelling argument for the abolition of slavery. It also helped defend against the southern allegation that northern workers were "wage slaves." Thus, the antislavery movement contributed to the redefinition of "free labor," from economic independence to the free exchange of labor for wages. Wage slavery was an "abuse of language," said abolitionist William Lloyd Garrison. Frederick Douglass, who knew real slavery firsthand, exulted at a paying job: "I was now my own master." Or, as another abolitionist said of a worker, "Does he not own himself?"[4]

In *Slavery* (1841), Unitarian minister William Ellery Channing (1780–1842) rejected southern efforts to squelch (or "gag") discussion of slavery: "Slavery ought to be discussed," he wrote. "We ought to think, feel, speak, and write about it."[5] Channing had a keen intellect and a passion for religious and social controversy. His influence extended to reform-minded churches throughout the North. His target audience was the growing body of reformers motivated by "Christian philanthropy" to do good. Coupling the natural instinct and right of self-ownership with the Golden Rule of Christianity, Channing called upon

Americans to recognize the common humanity of all people, regardless of their superficial "outward distinctions." It was wrong for Christians "to cast him [the slave] out from God's spiritual family into the brutal herd."[6] This excerpt ends by arguing that "God's laws" nullified any human laws that allowed man to own property in man.

Women activists shared the classical liberal philosophy of Channing and other abolitionists. Indeed, the two movements—abolitionism and women's rights—drew upon the same principles for much of the nineteenth century. Angelina Grimké (1805–1879) was the daughter of a wealthy South Carolinian slave owner. She hated slavery from an early age and left for the North, where she worked with her sister, Sarah Grimké, on the antislavery lecture circuit. The mere fact that these women spoke out in public upset many people in the North and South, including many abolitionists.

Nevertheless, Grimké was one of the most vocal and influential women in the abolitionist movement. Grimké combined feminism and abolitionism into a passionate plea for human rights, regardless of race or sex. In an 1837 letter, Grimké wrote, "The investigation of the rights of the slave has led me to a better understanding of my own. . . . Human beings have rights, because they are moral beings: the rights of all men grow out of their moral nature. . . . Now if rights are founded in the nature of our moral being, then the mere circumstance of sex does not give to man higher rights and responsibilities than to woman. . . . I recognize no rights but human rights—I know nothing of men's rights and women's rights; for in Christ Jesus, there is neither male nor female."[7]

℮ↄ

The slave-holder claims the slave as his Property. The very idea of a slave is, that he belongs to another, that he is bound to live and labor for another, to be another's instrument, and to make another's will his habitual law, however adverse to his own. . . . Such is slavery, a claim to man as property. . . .

1. It is plain, that, if one man may be held as property, then every other man may be so held. If there be nothing in human nature, in our common nature, which excludes and forbids the conversion of him who possesses it into an article of property; if the right of the free to liberty is founded, not on their essential attributes as rational and moral beings, but on certain adventitious, accidental

circumstances, into which they have been thrown; then every human being, by a change of circumstances, may justly be held and treated by another as property. If one man may be rightfully reduced to slavery, then there is not a human being on whom the same chain may not be imposed. . . . Does not an unhesitating, unerring conviction spring up in my breast, that no other man can acquire such a right in myself? Do we not repel, indignantly and with horror, the thought of being reduced to the condition of tools and chattels to a fellow creature? Is there any moral truth more deeply rooted in us, than that such a degradation would be an infinite wrong? And, if this impression be a delusion, on what single moral conviction can we rely? This deep assurance, that we cannot be rightfully made another's property, does not rest on the hue of our skins, or the place of our birth, or our strength, or wealth. These things do not enter our thoughts. The consciousness of indestructible rights is a part of our moral being. . . .

4. That a human being cannot be justly held and used as property, is apparent from the very nature of property. Property is an exclusive right. It shuts out all claim but that of the possessor. What one man owns, cannot belong to another. What, then, is the consequence of holding a human being as property? Plainly this. He can have no right to himself. His limbs are, in truth, not morally his own. He has not a right to his own strength. It belongs to another. His will, intellect, and muscles, all the powers of body and mind which are exercised in labor, he is bound to regard as another's. . . . To deny the right of a human being to himself, to his own limbs and faculties, to his energy of body and mind, is an absurdity too gross to be confuted by any thing but a simple statement. Yet this absurdity is involved in the idea of his belonging to another. . . .

6. Another argument against the right of property in man, may be drawn from a very obvious principle of moral science. It is a plain truth, universally received, that every right supposes or involves a corresponding obligation. . . . Is the slave under a moral obligation to confine himself, his wife, and children, to a spot where their union in a moment may be forcibly dissolved? Ought he not, if he can, to place himself and his family under the guardianship of equal laws? Should we blame him for leaving his yoke? Do we not feel, that, in the same condition, a sense of duty would quicken our flying steps? Where, then, is the obligation which would necessarily be imposed, if the right existed which the master claims? The absence of obligation proves the want of the right. The claim is groundless. It is a cruel wrong.

7. I come now to what is to my own mind the great argument against seizing and using a man as property. He cannot be property in the sight of God and justice, because he is a Rational, Moral, Immortal Being; because created in God's image, and therefore in the highest sense his child. . . . We have thus seen, that a human being cannot rightfully be held and used as property. No legislation, not that of all countries or worlds, could make him so. Let this be laid down, as a first, fundamental truth. Let us hold it fast, as a most sacred, precious truth. Let us hold it fast against all customs, all laws, all rank, wealth, and power. Let it be armed with the whole authority of the civilized and Christian world.

I have taken it for granted that no reader would be so wanting in moral discrimination and moral feeling, as to urge, that men may rightfully be seized and held as property, because various governments have so ordained. What! Is human legislation the measure of right? Are God's laws to be repealed by man's? Can government do no wrong? To what a mournful extent is the history of human governments a record of wrongs! How much does the progress of civilization consist in the substitution of just and humane, for barbarous and oppressive laws! The individual, indeed, is never authorized to oppose physical force to unrighteous ordinances of government, as long as the community choose to sustain them. But criminal legislation ought to be freely and earnestly exposed. Injustice is never so terrible, and never so corrupting, as when armed with the sanctions of law. The authority of government, instead of being a reason for silence under wrongs, is a reason for protesting against wrong.

Source: William Ellery Channing, *The Works of William E. Channing*, 11th ed.
(1841; repr., Boston: George G. Channing, 1849), 2:17–30.

## The Unconstitutionality of Slavery (1845)

### Lysander Spooner

**Lysander Spooner (1808–1887) was one of the intellectual giants of nineteenth-century liberalism. Spooner was an anarcho-libertarian writer, an abolitionist, and a businessman who challenged the U.S. Post Office monopoly of the mail by establishing the Fed Ex of his day: the American Letter Mail Com-**

pany. The government forced Spooner out of business, but by showing that mail could be delivered cheaply, his company spurred Congress to cut postal rates.

Spooner's greatest contributions came in the field of constitutional theory; he is reemerging in the twenty-first century as an influence on libertarian legal theory.[8] Spooner's arguments ranged from a strict construction of the Constitution (presented here) to later arguments for no Constitution at all (or none binding on any but those who signed the agreement). In the following document, Spooner argues against the Garrisonian position that the Constitution was a diabolical proslavery compact. Spooner's early writings had a profound influence on those who wished to work within the political system. Influenced by Spooner, Frederick Douglass argued eloquently that the Constitution was an antislavery document (see "Fourth of July 1852 Oration" below).

ఇర్

### Chapter 1—What is Law?

In answering this question, I shall attempt to show that law is an intelligible principle of right, necessarily resulting from the nature of man; and not an arbitrary rule, that can be established by mere will, numbers or power. . . .

There is no other standard, than natural rights, by which civil law can be measured. Law has always been the name of that rule or principle of justice, which protects those rights. Thus we speak of *natural law.* Natural law, in fact, constitutes the great body of the law that is *professedly* administered by judicial tribunals: and it always necessarily must be—for it is impossible to anticipate a thousandth part of the cases that arise, so as to enact a special law for them. Wherever the cases have not been thus anticipated, the natural law prevails. . . .

. . . Government can have no powers except such as individuals may *rightly* delegate to it: that no law, inconsistent with men's natural rights, can arise out of any contract or compact of government: *that constitutional law, under any form of government, consists only of those principles of the written constitution, that are consistent with natural law, and man's natural rights;* and that any other principles, that may be expressed by the letter of any constitution, are void and not law, and all judicial tribunals are bound to declare them so. . . .

### Chapter 3—The Colonial Charters

When our ancestors came to this country, they brought with them the common law of England, including the writ of *habeas corpus,* (the essential principle of which, as will hereafter be shown, is to deny the right of property in man,) the trial by jury, and the other great principles of liberty, which prevail in England, and which have made it impossible that her soil should be trod by the foot of a slave.

These principles were incorporated into all the charters, granted to the colonies. . . .

Those charters were the fundamental constitutions of the colonies, with some immaterial exceptions, up to the time of the revolution. . . .

No one of all these charters that I have examined—and I have examined nearly all of them—contained the least intimation that slavery had, or could have any legal existence under them. Slavery was therefore as much unconstitutional in the colonies, as it was in England. . . .

### Chapter 4—Colonial Statutes

. . . When slavery was first introduced into the country, there were no laws at all on the subject. Men bought slaves of the slave traders, as they would have bought horses; and held them, and compelled them to labor, as they would have done horses, that is, by brute force. By common consent among the white race, this practice was tolerated without any law. At length slaves had in this way become so numerous, that some regulations became necessary, and the colonial governments began to pass statutes, which *assumed* the existence of slaves, although no laws defining the persons who might be made slaves, had ever been enacted. . . .

### Chapter 5—The Declaration of Independence

. . . If it [the Declaration of Independence] were the law of the country even for a day, it freed every slave in the country—(if there were, as we say there were not, any legal slaves then in the country.) And the burden would then be upon the slaveholder to show that slavery had *since* been *constitutionally* established. And to show this, he must show an express *constitutional* designation of the particular individuals, who have since been made slaves. . . .

If, then, it be a "self-evident truth," that all men have a natural and inalienable right to life, liberty, and the pursuit of happiness, *that truth* constitutes a part of all our laws and all our constitutions, unless it have been unequivocally and authoritatively denied. . . .

### Chapter 6—The State Constitutions of 1789

I have found, in none of the State constitutions, . . . (existing in 1789,) any other evidence or intimation of the existence of slavery. . . .

### Chapter 7—The Articles of Confederation

The Articles of Confederation, (formed in 1778,) contained no recognition of slavery. . . .

### Chapter 8—The Constitution of the United States

It is perfectly clear, in the first place, that the constitution of the United States did not, *of itself, create or establish slavery* as a new institution; or even give any authority to the state governments to establish it as a new institution.—The greatest sticklers for slavery do not claim this. The most they claim is, that it recognized it as an institution already legally existing, under the authority of the State governments; and that it virtually guarantied to the States the right of continuing it in existence. . . .

. . . If *all* "the people of the United States" were made citizens of the United States, by the United States constitution, at its adoption, it was then forever too late for the *State* governments to reduce any of them to slavery. They were thenceforth citizens of a higher government, under a constitution that was "the supreme law of the land," "anything in the constitution or laws of the States to the contrary notwithstanding. . . ."

. . . Why, then, do not men say distinctly, that the constitution *did* sanction slavery, instead of saying that it *intended* to sanction it? We are not accustomed to use the word "*intention*," when speaking of the other grants and sanctions of the constitution. We do not say, for example, that the constitution *intended* to authorize congress "to coin money," but that it *did* authorize them to coin it. Nor do we say that it intended to authorize them "to declare war;" but that it did authorize them to declare it. . . . Why, then, in the case of slavery, do men say merely that the constitution *intended* to sanction it, instead of saying distinctly, as we do in the other cases, that it *did* sanction it? The reason is obvious. If they were to say unequivocally that it *did* sanction it, they would lay themselves under the necessity of pointing to the words that sanction it; and they are aware that the words alone of the constitution do not come up to that point. . . .

The error and fraud of this whole procedure . . . It personifies the constitution as a crafty individual; capable of both open and secret intentions; capable of legally participating in, and giving effect to all the subtleties and double dealings of knavish men; and as actually intending to secure slavery, while openly professing to "secure and establish liberty and justice."

Source: Lysander Spooner, *The Unconstitutionality of Slavery* (Boston: Bela Marsh, 1845), 5–6, 14, 21–23, 33, 37–38, 51, 55–58.

## Fourth of July Oration (1852)

### *Frederick Douglass*

By any measure, Frederick Douglass (1818–1895) was the "Lion" of nineteenth-century civil rights liberalism. Born a slave, Douglass never knew the identity of his white father. His mother died when he was young, and young Frederick passed from plantation to plantation, transferred several times by his various "owners." During his youth Douglass learned to read from a slaveholder's wife and from every printed material he could find in Baltimore, where he lived for a time. Eventually, he escaped aboard a train to Massachusetts and thereafter began a career based on a titanic intellect, a great capacity for writing, and a voice to thunder his spoken prose denouncing slavery as a great wrong. His *Narrative of the Life of Frederick Douglass, an American Slave* (1845) reached a wide audience, and he spent the next half century pouring forth books, articles, and essays and published several newspapers.

In this famous speech, Douglass criticizes Americans for failing to live up to the ideals of the Declaration of Independence and the Constitution. Yet he also abandons the Garrisonian position that the Constitution was corrupt and the Union must be dissolved to cut all support of slavery. In later years, following Spooner, Douglass fully developed a strict construction of the Constitution as an antislavery document. Douglass thus joined those classical liberal antislavery activists who believed change was possible within the political system.

℃

I am not included within the pale of this glorious anniversary! Your high independence only reveals the immeasurable distance between us. The blessings in which you, this day, rejoice, are not enjoyed in common. The rich inheritance of justice, liberty, prosperity and independence, bequeathed by your fathers, is shared by you, not by me. The sunlight that brought life and healing to you, has brought stripes and death to me. This Fourth [of] July is yours, not mine. You may rejoice, I must mourn. . . .

What, to the American slave, is your 4th of July? I answer: a day that reveals to him, more than all other days in the year, the gross injustice and cruelty to which he is the constant victim. To him, your celebration is a sham; your boasted liberty, an unholy license; your national greatness, swelling vanity; your sounds of rejoicing are empty and heartless; your denunciations of tyrants, brass fronted impudence; your shouts of liberty and equality, hollow mockery; your prayers and hymns, your sermons and thanksgivings, with all your religious parade, and solemnity, are, to him, mere bombast, fraud, deception, impiety, and hypocrisy—a thin veil to cover up crimes which would disgrace a nation of savages. There is not a nation on the earth guilty of practices, more shocking and bloody, than are the people of these United States, at this very hour. . . .

By an act of the American Congress [the Fugitive Slave Act], not yet two years old, slavery has been nationalized in its most horrible and revolting form. By that act, Mason & Dixon's line has been obliterated; New York has become as Virginia; and the power to hold, hunt, and sell men, women, and children as slaves remains no longer a mere state institution, but is now an institution of the whole United States. The power is co-extensive with the star-spangled banner and American Christianity. . . .

### Religion

I take this law to be one of the grossest infringements of Christian Liberty, and, if the churches and ministers of our country were not stupidly blind, or most wickedly indifferent, they, too, would so regard it. . . .

. . . You declare, before the world, and are understood by the world to declare, that you "hold these truths to be self evident, that all men are created equal; and are endowed by their Creator with certain inalienable rights; and that, among these are, life, liberty, and the pursuit of happiness;" and yet, you hold securely, in a bondage which, according to your own Thomas Jefferson, "is worse than ages of that which your fathers rose in rebellion to oppose," a seventh part of the inhabitants of your country. . . .

### The Constitution

But it is answered in reply to all this, that precisely what I have now denounced is, in fact, guaranteed and sanctioned by the Constitution of the United States; that the right to hold and to hunt slaves is a part of that Constitution framed by the illustrious Fathers of this Republic. . . .

. . . But I differ from those who charge this baseness on the framers of the Constitution of the United States. It is a slander upon their memory, at least, so I believe. There is not time now to argue the constitutional question at length—nor have I the ability to discuss it as it ought to be discussed. The subject has been handled with masterly power by Lysander Spooner, Esq., by William Goodell, by Samuel E. Sewall, Esq., and last, though not least, by Gerrit Smith, Esq. These gentlemen have, as I think, fully and clearly vindicated the Constitution from any design to support slavery for an hour.

Fellow-citizens! there is no matter in respect to which, the people of the North have allowed themselves to be so ruinously imposed upon, as that of the pro-slavery character of the Constitution. In that instrument I hold there is neither warrant, license, nor sanction of the hateful thing; but, interpreted as it ought to be interpreted, the Constitution is a GLORIOUS LIBERTY DOCUMENT. Read its preamble, consider its purposes. Is slavery among them? Is it at the gateway? or is it in the temple? It is neither. While I do not intend to argue this question on the present occasion, let me ask, if it be not somewhat singular that, if the Constitution were intended to be, by its framers and adopters, a slaveholding instrument, why neither slavery, slaveholding, nor slave can anywhere be found in it. . . .

Allow me to say, in conclusion, notwithstanding the dark picture I have this day presented of the state of the nation, I do not despair of this country. There are forces in operation, which must inevitably work the downfall of slavery. "The arm of the Lord is not shortened," and the doom of slavery is certain. I, therefore, leave off where I began, with hope. While drawing encouragement from the Declaration of Independence, the great principles it contains, and the genius of American Institutions, my spirit is also cheered by the obvious tendencies of the age. Nations do not now stand in the same relation to each other that they did ages ago. No nation can now shut itself up from the surrounding world. . . .

In the fervent aspirations of William Lloyd Garrison, I say, and let every heart join in saying it:

God speed the year of jubilee
The wide world o'er!

Source: Frederick Douglass, *Oration Delivered in Corinthian Hall, Rochester* (Rochester: Lee, Mann, 1852), 15, 20, 25, 27, 34–39.

## Notes

1. Julie Winch, "'A Person of Good Character and Considerable Property': James Forten and the Issue of Race in Philadelphia's Antebellum Business Community," *Business History Review* 75, no. 2 (2001): 274.

2. C. Eaton, "A Dangerous Pamphlet in the Old South," *Journal of Southern History* 2, no. 3 (1936): 323.

3. David Walker and Henry Highland Garnet, *Walker's Appeal, with a Brief Sketch of His Life* (1829; repr., New York: J. H. Tobitt, 1848), vi.

4. Eric Foner, *The Story of American Freedom* (New York: Norton, 1998), 66.

5. William Ellery Channing, *The Works of William E. Channing*, 11th ed. (1841; repr., Boston: George G. Channing, 1849), 2:10.

6. Ibid., 2:14, 28.

7. Angelina Grimké, "Rights and Responsibilities of Women," in *The Libertarian Reader*, ed. David Boaz (New York: Free Press, 1997), 92–93.

8. Randy E. Barnett, *Restoring the Lost Constitution: The Presumption of Liberty* (Princeton, NJ: Princeton University Press, 2004).

## Recommended Reading

*Amazing Grace.* 2007. Directed by Michael Apted. Bristol Bay Productions.

Belmonte, Kevin Charles. *Hero for Humanity: A Biography of William Wilberforce.* Colorado Springs, CO: Navpress, 2002.

Colaiaco, James A. *Frederick Douglass and the Fourth of July.* New York: Palgrave Macmillan, 2006.

Douglass, Frederick. *The Frederick Douglass Papers.* 7 vols. Edited by John W. Blassingame, John R. McKivigan, and Peter P. Hinks. New Haven, CT: Yale University Press, 1979–2003.

Eaton, C. "A Dangerous Pamphlet in the Old South." *Journal of Southern History* 2, no. 3 (1936): 323–34.

Foner, Eric. *The Story of American Freedom.* New York: Norton, 1998.

Hayward, Jack Ernest Shalom. *Out of Slavery: Abolition and After.* London: F. Cass, 1985.

Hinks, Peter P. *To Awaken My Afflicted Brethren: David Walker and the Problem of Antebellum Slave Resistance.* University Park: Pennsylvania State University Press, 1997.

Lean, Garth. *God's Politician: William Wilberforce's Struggle.* Colorado Springs, CO: Helmers & Howard, 1987.

Leggett, William, and Lawrence H. White. *Democratick Editorials: Essays in Jacksonian Political Economy.* Indianapolis: Liberty, 1984.

McElroy, Wendy, and Lewis C. Perry. *Freedom, Feminism and the State.* Oakland, CA: Independent Institute, 1991.

McFeely, William S. *Frederick Douglass.* New York: Norton, 1991.

Metaxas, Eric. *Amazing Grace: William Wilberforce and the Heroic Campaign to End Slavery.* New York: HarperSanFrancisco, 2007.

Myers, Peter C. *Frederick Douglass: Race and the Rebirth of American Liberalism.* Lawrence: University Press of Kansas, 2008.

Quarles, Benjamin. *Frederick Douglass.* Washington, DC: Associated Publishers, 1948.

Spooner, Lysander. *The Lysander Spooner Reader.* San Francisco: Fox & Wilkes, 1992.

Thompson, C. Bradley. *Antislavery Political Writings, 1833–1860: A Reader.* Armonk, NY: M. E. Sharpe, 2004.

Wilberforce, William. *Real Christianity.* Edited by Bob Beltz. Ventura, CA: Regal, 2006.

Winch, Julie. *A Gentleman of Color: The Life of James Forten.* New York: Oxford University Press, 2002.

———. "James Forten, Conservative Radical." In *Black Conservatism: Essays in Intellectual and Political History,* edited by Peter R. Eisenstadt, 3–24. New York: Garland, 1999.

———. "'A Person of Good Character and Considerable Property': James Forten and the Issue of Race in Philadelphia's Antebellum Business Community." *Business History Review* 75, no. 2 (2001): 261–96.

Wyatt-Brown, Bertram. *Lewis Tappan and the Evangelical War against Slavery.* 1969. Reprint, Baton Rouge: Louisiana State University Press, 1997.

# 2

# The Republican Era

## 1854–1876

WITH THE ELECTORAL SUCCESS of the newly formed Republican Party (established in 1854), many classical liberals joined the party because of its opposition to slavery. Republicans, including Abraham Lincoln, declared slavery to be a moral wrong yet confined the political issue to whether slaves ought to exist in the territories of the United States. This expediency, or fear of getting ahead of public opinion, disillusioned classical liberals, who hoped for a firmer stance against slavery. When southern states seceded from the Union (1860–1861), President Lincoln backed his party's passage of a constitutional amendment that would have inserted the right to own slaves within the federal Constitution. At the outset, Lincoln seemed willing to do anything to appease southerners and bring them back into the Union. In a published letter to newspaper editor Horace Greeley (August 19, 1862), Lincoln stated, "My paramount object is to save the Union, and not either to save or to destroy slavery. If I could save the union without freeing any slave, I would do it—if I could save it by freeing all the slaves I would do it—and if I could do it by freeing some and leaving others alone, I would also do that."[1] Lysander Spooner and Frederick Douglass criticized Lincoln for not making emancipation the centerpiece of his administration. Readers will find a trio of documents below contrasting the views of Lincoln, Spooner, and Douglass on slavery and the Civil War.

After the war, with North and South still divided over race, Republicans faced off against southern Democrats for generations to come. Despite its temporizing, the Republican Party was arguably the party of civil rights, as seen in many of the documents below. The Democratic Party was simply "wrong on race," as

Bruce Bartlett argues in a book by that title.[2] Notwithstanding the Republican Party's failings, many civil rights activists agreed with Frederick Douglass that "for colored men the Republican party is the deck—all outside is the sea."[3]

## Slavery, a Relic of Barbarism

Members of the newly formed Republican Party were deeply split over tactics: some favored colonization (sending blacks to Africa or Latin America), others immediate emancipation, and still more restriction of slavery in the western territories. The territorial issue was critical because the North and South had compromised to maintain the Union: beginning with the "Missouri Compromise" (1820), Congress created an even balance of slave and free territories. This balance unraveled in the 1850s. Senator Stephen A. Douglass (D-IL) advanced the doctrine of "popular sovereignty" to remove the issue from congressional debate. Embodying this new doctrine, the Kansas-Nebraska Act (1854) stated that residents of the newly created territories would decide whether to accept slavery. In the Kansas Territory, a proslavery faction fought for a majority against antislavery settlers. Partisans from free and slave states rushed into the territory to join the guerilla warfare (1855–1858). The pitched battles were so violent that the territory became known as "bleeding Kansas." The two sides drafted competing constitutions, but the issue was not resolved until 1861, when Congress accepted a favorable vote for admission as a free state. However, by then, southern states were seceding from the Union to form the Confederate States of America.

The infamous *Dred Scott* decision (1857), rendered by a southern-dominated U.S. Supreme Court, had ended the possibility of compromise. Chief Justice Roger Taney ruled that Congress had no power to limit slavery in the territories or elsewhere. Taney claimed that those who wrote the Constitution never intended African Americans to have any rights because blacks were "beings of an inferior order, and altogether unfit to associate with the white race, either in social or political relations, and so far inferior that they had no rights which the white man was bound to respect."[4] This extreme view ignored the existence of free blacks, the unanimous passage of the Northwest Ordinance (1787) barring slavery north of the parallel 36°30', and other relevant historical facts. Moreover, *Dred Scott* declared the Republican Party to be at odds with the Constitution. "Bleeding Kansas" and *Dred Scott* explain the outrage evident in the Republican Party platforms.

ℰℛ

## Republican Party Platforms (1856, 1860)

*Republican Party*

### 1856

That, with our Republican fathers, we hold it to be a self-evident truth, that all men are endowed with the inalienable right to life, liberty, and the pursuit of happiness. . . . Our Republican fathers, when they had abolished Slavery in all our National Territory, ordained that no person shall be deprived of life, liberty, or property, without due process of law, it becomes our duty to maintain this provision of the Constitution against all attempts to violate it for the purpose of establishing Slavery in the Territories. . . .

That the Constitution confers upon Congress sovereign powers over the Territories of the United States for their government; and that in the exercise of this power, it is both the right and the imperative duty of Congress to prohibit in the Territories those twin relics of barbarism—Polygamy, and Slavery. . . . [Polygamy was a reference to the Mormon community in Utah. Such denunciations of polygamy appeared in subsequent GOP platforms.]

### 1860

That the new dogma [*Dred Scott*] that the Constitution, of its own force, carries slavery into any or all of the territories of the United States, is a dangerous political heresy. . . .

That the normal condition of all the territory of the United States is that of freedom: That, as our Republican fathers, when they had abolished slavery in all our national territory, ordained that "no persons should be deprived of life, liberty or property without due process of law," it becomes our duty, by legislation, whenever such legislation is necessary, to maintain this provision of the Constitution against all attempts to violate it; and we deny the authority of Congress, of a territorial legislature, or of any individuals, to give legal existence to slavery in any territory of the United States.

Sources: *Republican Party Platform, 1856*, American Presidency Project, http:// americanpresidency.org (accessed October 29, 2006); *Republican Party Platform, 1860*, American Presidency Project, http://americanpresidency.org (accessed October 29, 2006).

## Abraham Lincoln and Classical Liberals: Union or Slavery?

The presidential election of Abraham Lincoln in 1860 cheered moderate Republicans and alarmed (or angered) southerners to the point of secession from the Union. Classical liberals faulted Lincoln for placing preservation of the Union over the abolition of slavery. Years earlier, Lincoln had condemned slavery as a moral wrong but focused only on what could be done with the territories, rather than those millions already enslaved. In Lincoln's first Inaugural Address, he supported a constitutional amendment to protect slavery, promised to uphold the fugitive slave laws (i.e., return escaped slaves to their "masters"), and appeased southerners in other ways—all in an effort to persuade southerners to rejoin the Union.

Lincoln's critics included Lysander Spooner, who condemned the Republicans for failing to uphold the Constitution as an antislavery document. If the Republicans truly believed slavery was a moral wrong, they would abolish slavery everywhere in the Union. Frederick Douglass was more hopeful that the Civil War might bring the end of slavery. Yet it took Douglass years to persuade Lincoln to enlist blacks in the Union army, a move precipitated in the end by military considerations rather than the moral necessity of allowing slaves, ex-slaves, and "free" blacks to fight for their freedom (recall *Dred Scott:* even "free" blacks had "no rights which the white man was bound to respect"). Even after Lincoln signed the Emancipation Proclamation, freeing blacks in areas occupied by the Union army, Douglass feared that the "Great Emancipator" would accept reunion with slavery. "Abolition war" was Douglass's true desire. These documents highlight the controversy emerging from the constitutional element of classical liberalism (Lincoln versus Spooner). Abolitionists (Spooner, Douglass) stressed the urgency of the hour while moderates (Lincoln) counseled patience.

ော

## Address of the Free Constitutionalists (1860)

### Lysander Spooner

A few friends of freedom, who believe the Constitution of the United States to be a sufficient warrant for giving liberty to all the people of the United States, make the following appeal against any support being given to the Republican Party at the ensuing election.

Boston, September, 1860.

The real question, that is now convulsing the nation, is not—as the Republican party would have us believe—whether slaves shall be carried from the States into the Territories? but whether anywhere, within the limits of the Union, one man shall be the property of another? . . . If there are to be slaves in the country, a humane man, instead of feeling himself degraded by their presence, would desire to have them in his neighborhood, that he might give them his sympathy, and if possible ameliorate their condition. And the man, who, like the Republican party, consents to the existence of slavery, so long as the slaves are but kept out of his sight, is at heart a tyrant and a brute. And if, at the same time, like the more conspicuous members of that party, he makes loud professions of devotion to liberty and humanity, he thereby just as loudly proclaims himself a hypocrite. And those Republican politicians, who, instead of insisting upon the liberation of the slaves, maintain, under the name of *State Rights,* the inviolability of the slaveholder's right of property in his slaves, in the States, and yet claim to be friends of liberty, because they cry, *"Keep the slaves where they are;" "No removal of them into the Territories;" "Bring them not into our neighborhood,"*—are either smitten with stupidity, as with a disease, or, what is more probable, are nothing else than selfish, cowardly, hypocritical, and unprincipled men, who, for the sake of gaining or retaining power, are simply making a useless noise about nothing, with the purpose of diverting men's minds from the true issue, and of thus postponing the inevitable contest, which every honest and brave man ought to be ready and eager to meet at once. . . .

If the constitution of the United States—"the supreme law of the land"—declares A to be a citizen of the United States (we use the term *citizen* in its technical sense) then, constitutionally speaking, he is a citizen of the United States everywhere throughout the United States,—any thing in the constitution or laws of any State to the contrary notwithstanding; and no State law or constitution can depose him from that *status,* or deprive him of the enjoyment of the least of those rights, which the national constitution guarantees to the citizens of the United States. . . .

The palpable truth is, that the four millions of human beings now held in bondage in this country are, in the view of the constitution of the United States, full citizens of the United States, entitled, without any qualification, abatement, or discrimination whatever, to all the rights, privileges, and protection which that constitution guarantees to the white citizens of the United States, and that their citizenship has been withheld from them only by ignorance, and fraud, and force.

Such being the truth in regard to this portion of the citizens of the United States, it is the constitutional duty of both the general and State governments to protect them in their personal liberty, and in all the other rights which those governments secure to the other citizens of the United States.

It is as much the constitutional duty of the general government, as of the State governments, to protect the citizens of the United States in their personal liberty; for if it cannot secure to them their personal liberty, it can secure to them no other of the rights or privileges which it is bound to secure to them.

To enable the general government to secure to the people their personal liberty, it is supplied with all necessary powers. It is authorized to use the writ of *habeas corpus,* which of itself is sufficient to set at liberty all persons illegally restrained. It is authorized to arm and discipline the people as militia, and thus enable them to do something towards defending their own liberty. It is authorized "to make all laws which shall be necessary and proper for carrying into execution" the powers specifically enumerated. That is to say, it is authorized "to make all laws which shall be necessary and proper for carrying" home to each individual every right and every privilege which the constitution designs to secure to him; and the United States courts are required to take cognizance "of all cases in law and equity arising under this constitution, the laws of the United States, and treaties made, or which shall be made, under their authority." In other words, they are authorized to take cognizance of all cases in which the question to be tried is the right which any individual has under the constitution, laws, or treaties of the United States. The United States are also bound to guarantee to all the citizens of the United States, within the States, the benefits of a republican form of government. There is, then, obviously no lack of powers delegated to the general government, to secure the personal liberty of all its citizens. . . .

Still further: The principal, if not the sole object of our having two governments for the same citizen, would be entirely defeated, if each government had not an equal right to defend him against enslavement by the other. What is the grand object of having two governments over the same citizen? It is, that, if either government prove oppressive, he may fly for protection to the other. This right of flying from the oppression of one government to the protection of the other, makes it more difficult for him to be oppressed, than if he had no alternative but submission to a single government. This certainly is the only important, if not the only possible, advantage of our double system of government. Yet if either of these two governments can enslave their common citizen, and the other has no right to interfere for his protection, the principal, if not the only, benefit of our having two governments, is lost. . . .

There is, therefore, no room or basis under the constitution for the four different factions that now exist in this country, in regard to slavery, either in the States, or in the territories. There is room only for this single question, viz.: Does the Constitution of the United States, "the supreme law of the land," make one man the property of another? . . .

We ask all the people of the United States to take their position distinctly on the one side or the other side of this question, at the ensuing election; and not to waste their energies or influence upon any of the frivolous and groundless issues, which divide the four different factions now contending for possession of the government.

Of all these factions, the Republican is the most thoroughly senseless, baseless, aimless, inconsistent, and insincere. It has no constitutional principles to stand upon, and it lives up to no moral ones. It aims at nothing for freedom, and is sure to accomplish it. The other factions have at least the merits of frankness and consistency. They are openly on the side of slavery, and make no hypocritical grimaces at supporting it. The Republicans, on the other hand, are double-faced, double-tongued, hypocritical, and inconsistent to the last degree. We speak now of their presses and public men. Duplicity and deceit seem to be regarded by them as their only available capital. This results from the fact that the faction consists of two wings, one favorable to liberty, the other to slavery; neither of them alone strong enough for success; and neither of them honest enough to submit to present defeat for their principles. How to keep these two wings together until they shall have succeeded in clutching the spoils and power of office, is the great problem with the managers. The plan adopted is, to make, on the one hand, the most desperate efforts to prove that their consciences and all their moral sentiments are opposed to slavery, and that they will do every thing they *constitutionally* can, against it; and, on the other, to make equally desperate efforts to prove that they have the most sacred reverence for the constitution, and that the constitution gives them no power whatever to interfere with slavery in the States. So they cry to one wing of their party, "Put us in power, and we will do every thing we *constitutionally* can for liberty." To the other wing, they cry, "Put us in power. You can do it with perfect safety to slavery—for *constitutionally* we can do nothing against it, where it is."

It is lucky for these Jesuitical demagogues that there happen to be, bordering upon the United States, certain wilderness regions, over which the United States have hitherto usurped jurisdiction. This gives them an opportunity to make a show of living up to their professions, by appearing to carry on a terrific war against slavery, *outside the United States, where it is not;* while, *within the United States, "where it is,"* they have no *political* quarrel with it whatever, but only make a pretence of having very violent moral sentiments. . . .

We understand the reasons given, in private, by these men, why they do not declare that slavery is unconstitutional, and that the general government has power to abolish it, to be, *That the people are not ready for it! That the Republicans must first get possession of the government!* That is to say, these men must persist in their false asseverations, that the general government has no power to abolish slavery; that they, if placed in possession of that government, never will abolish it; but will, on the contrary, sustain it in the States where it is—they must persist in these asseverations, until they get the general government into their hands; then, as they wish it to be inferred, they will avow the fraud by which they obtained their power; will take it for granted that the people *are* ready to be informed what the constitutional law of the country really is; and will proceed to put it into execution, by giving liberty to all! . . .

But if, as is very likely to be the result, no one of these electoral [presidential] candidates should be chosen, the votes given for them will nevertheless not have been thrown away. The great object is to procure the defeat of the Republicans. If defeated on the sixth of November, the faction itself will be extinct on the seventh. Those of its members who intend to support slavery, will then go over openly into its ranks; while those who intend to support liberty, will come unmistakably to her side. She will then know her friends from her foes. And thenceforth the issue will be distinctly made up, whether this be, or be not, a free country for all? And this one issue will hold its place before the country, until it shall be decided in favor of freedom.

Source: Lysander Spooner, *Address of the Free Constitutionalists to the People of the United States* (Boston: Thayer & Eldridge, 1860), 2–4, 19–20, 23, 40–42, 50–51, 53–54.

## First Inaugural Address (1861)

### Abraham Lincoln

Apprehension seems to exist among the people of the Southern States that by the accession of a Republican Administration their property and their peace and personal security are to be endangered. There has never been any reasonable cause for such apprehension. Indeed, the most ample evidence to the contrary has all the while existed and been open to their inspection. It is found in nearly all the published speeches of him who now addresses you. I do but quote from one of those speeches when I declare that—

> I have no purpose, directly or indirectly, to interfere with the institution of slavery in the States where it exists. I believe I have no lawful right to do so, and I have no inclination to do so. . . .

There is much controversy about the delivering up of fugitives from service or labor. The clause I now read is as plainly written in the Constitution as any other of its provisions:

> No person held to service or labor in one State, under the laws thereof, escaping into another, shall in consequence of any law or regulation therein be discharged from such service or labor, but shall be delivered up on claim of the party to whom such service or labor may be due.

It is scarcely questioned that this provision was intended by those who made it for the reclaiming of what we call fugitive slaves; and the intention of the lawgiver is the law. All members of Congress swear their support to the whole Constitution—to this provision as much as to any other. To the proposition, then, that slaves whose cases come within the terms of this clause "shall be delivered up" their oaths are unanimous. Now, if they would make the effort in good temper, could they not with nearly equal unanimity frame and pass a law by means of which to keep good that unanimous oath? . . .

I hold that in contemplation of universal law and of the Constitution the Union of these States is perpetual. Perpetuity is implied, if not expressed, in the fundamental law of all national governments. It is safe to assert that no government proper ever had a provision in its organic law for its own termination. Continue to execute all the express provisions of our National Constitution, and the Union will endure forever, it being impossible to destroy it except by some action not provided for in the instrument itself. . . .

It follows from these views that no State upon its own mere motion can lawfully get out of the Union; that "resolves" and "ordinances" to that effect are legally void, and that acts of violence within any State or States against the authority of the United States are insurrectionary or revolutionary, according to circumstances. . . .

In [defending the Union] there needs to be no bloodshed or violence, and there shall be none unless it be forced upon the national authority. The power confided to me will be used to hold, occupy, and possess the property and places belonging to the Government and to collect the duties and imposts; but beyond what may be necessary for these objects, there will be no invasion, no using of force against or among the people anywhere. Where hostility to the United States in any interior locality shall be so great and universal as to prevent competent resident citizens from holding the Federal offices, there will be no attempt to force obnoxious strangers among the people for that object. While the strict legal right may exist in the Government to enforce the exercise of these offices, the attempt to do so would be so irritating and so nearly impracticable withal that I deem it better to forego for the time the uses of such offices. . . .

One section of our country believes slavery is "right" and ought to be extended, while the other believes it is "wrong" and ought not to be extended. This is the only substantial dispute. The fugitive-slave clause of the Constitution and the law for the suppression of the foreign slave trade are each as well enforced, perhaps, as any law can ever be in a community where the moral sense of the people imperfectly supports the law itself. The great body of the people abide by the dry legal obligation in both cases, and a few break over in each. This, I think, can not be perfectly cured, and it would be worse in both cases "after" the separation of the sections than before. The foreign slave trade, now imperfectly suppressed, would be ultimately revived without restriction in one section, while fugitive slaves, now only partially surrendered, would not be surrendered at all by the other. . . .

. . . I understand a proposed amendment to the Constitution—which amendment, however, I have not seen—has passed Congress, to the effect that the Federal Government shall never interfere with the domestic institutions of the States, including that of persons held to service. To avoid misconstruction of what I have said, I depart from my purpose not to speak of particular amendments so far as to say that, holding such a provision to now be implied constitutional law, I have no objection to its being made express and irrevocable. . . .

In your hands, my dissatisfied fellow-countrymen, and not in mine, is the momentous issue of civil war. The Government will not assail you. You can have no conflict without being yourselves the aggressors. You have no oath registered in heaven to destroy the Government, while I shall have the most solemn one to "preserve, protect, and defend it."

I am loath to close. We are not enemies, but friends. We must not be enemies. Though passion may have strained it must not break our bonds of affection. The mystic chords of memory, stretching from every battlefield and patriot grave to every living heart and hearthstone all over this broad land, will yet swell the chorus of the Union, when again touched, as surely they will be, by the better angels of our nature.

Source: Abraham Lincoln, *Inaugural Address,* March 4, 1861, http:// americanpresidency.org (accessed July 5, 2008).

## The Mission of the War (1863)

### *Frederick Douglass*

An abolition war! Well, let us thank the Democracy [Democratic Party] for teaching us this word. The charge, in a comprehensive sense, is true, and it is not a pity that it is true, but it would be a vast pity if it were not true. Would that it were more true than it is.

When our Government and people shall bravely avow this to be an abolition war, then country will be safe; then our work will be fairly mapped out; then the uplifted arm of the nation will swing unfettered, and the spirit, pride and power of the rebellion will be broken.

Had slavery been broken down in the border states at the very beginning of this war, as it ought to have been, there would now be no rebellion in the southern states. Instead of having to watch Kentucky and Maryland, our armies would have marched in overpowering numbers upon the rebels and overwhelmed them. I now hold that a sacred regard for truth, as well as a sound policy makes it our duty to own and avow before Heaven and Earth that this war is, and of right ought to be, an abolition war. This is its central principle and comprehensive character, and includes everything else which the struggle involves.

It is a war for the Union, a war for the Constitution, and a war for Republican institutions, I admit; but it is logically such a war, only in the sense that the greater includes the lesser. Slavery has proved itself a strong element of our national life. In every rebel state it has proved itself stronger than the Union, the Constitution, and Republican institutions.

This strong element must be bound and cast out of our national life before Union, Constitution, and Republican institutions can become possible. An aboli-

Frederick Douglass (1818–1895). (Library of Congress, Prints & Photographs Division, LC-USZ62–15887.)

tion war therefore includes Union, Constitution, and Republican institutions, and all else that goes to make up the greatness and glory of our common country.

The position of the Democratic Party in relation to the war ought to surprise no one. It is consistent with the history of the party for thirty years past. Slavery, and only slavery, has been its recognized master during all that time. It early won for itself the title of being the natural ally of the South, and of slavery. It has always been for peace or against peace, for war or against war, precisely as dictated by slavery.

Ask why it was for the Florida war, and its answer is "slavery." Ask why it was for the Mexican war and it answers "slavery." Ask why it was for the annexation of Texas, and the answer is "slavery." Ask why it was opposed to the habeas corpus when the negro was the applicant, and the answer is "slavery." Ask why it is now in favor of the habeas corpus when traitors and rebels are the applicants for its benefit, and the answer is "slavery!"

Ask why it was for mobbing down freedom of speech a few years ago, when that freedom was claimed by abolitionists, and "slavery" is the answer. Ask

why it now furiously asserts freedom of speech when sympathizers with traitors claim that freedom, and again "slavery" is the answer. Ask why it denied
the right of a state to protect itself and its citizens from possible abuses of the
fugitive slave bill, and you have the same old answer. Ask why it now asserts
the sovereignty of the states separately, as against the states united, and again
"slavery" is the answer. Ask why it was opposed to giving persons claimed as
fugitive slaves jury trial before returning them to slavery? Ask why it is now
in favor of giving jury trial to traitors before sending them to the forts for safe
keeping? Ask why it was for war with England at the beginning of our civil
war? Ask why it has attempted to hinder and embarrass the loyal Government
at every step of its progress, and you have but one answer, and that answer is
again and again, "slavery!" . . .

Our danger lies in the absence of all moral feeling in the utterances of our
rulers. In his letter to Mr. Greeley, the president has told the country that, if he
could save the union with slavery he would do that; if he could save it without the
abolition of slavery, he would do that. In his last message he shows the same indifference as to slavery, by saying that he hoped that the rebellion could be put down
without the abolition of slavery. When the late Stephen A. Douglas uttered the
sentiment that he did not care whether slavery were voted up or voted down in the
territories, we thought him lost to all genuine feeling on the subject of slavery, and
no man more than Mr. Lincoln denounced that sentiment. But today, after nearly
three years of slaveholding rebellion, we find Mr. Lincoln uttering something like
the same sentiment. Douglas wanted his popular sovereignty, and cared nothing
for the fortunes of the slave. Mr. Lincoln wanted the Union and would accept
that with or without slavery. Had a warm heart and high moral feeling controlled
his utterance, he would have welcomed with joy unspeakable and full of glory,
the opportunity afforded by the rebellion to free his country from the matchless
crime and infamy of slavery. But policy, policy, everlasting policy, has robbed our
statesmanship of broad soul moving utterance. . . .

President Lincoln introduced his Administration to the country as one which
would faithfully catch, hold, and return runaway slaves to their masters. He
avowed his determination to protect and defend the slave holders right to plunder
the black laborer of his hard earnings. Europe was early assured by Mr. Seward

that no slave should gain his freedom by this war. Both the President and the Secretary of State have made some progress since then. . . .

The hour is one of hope as well as danger. We should take counsel of both.

But whatever may come to pass, one thing is clear: the principle involved in this contest; the necessities of both sections of the country; the obvious requirements of the age, and every suggestion of enlightened policy, demand the utter extirpation of slavery from every foot of American soil, and the complete enfranchisement of the entire colored population of the country.

Source: Frederick Douglass, "The Mission of the War," speech delivered in the Concert Hall, Philadelphia, 1863, *Frederick Douglass Papers*, Manuscript Division, Library of Congress, Washington, DC, http://memory.loc.gov/ammem/doughtml/dougFolder5.html (accessed July 1, 2008).

## Restoring Liberty and Order: Reconstruction

After the defeat of the Confederacy, a "grasp of war" theory held the Republican Congress together as it amended the constitutional federal system. While Congress held the defeated Confederacy in the "grasp of war," it set conditions for readmittance of states while guaranteeing individual rights of self-ownership, equality before the law, the right to vote, and the right to bear arms irrespective of race. Despite the changes, Republicans returned to a federal system respecting the separate spheres of national and state governments.

In the transition, southern Democrats chafed at Republican rule and tried their best to reimpose conditions of servitude by passing laws known as "black codes." These codes deprived African Americans of certain rights: the right to bear arms, to travel freely, and to labor freely without the slavelike conditions placed upon them by the codes. Congress restored these freedoms by passing the Civil Rights Act of 1866. That context helps to explain the meaning of Richard Henry Dana Jr.'s outrage (below) and the northern reaction to southern black codes.

Even after repeal of the black codes, African Americans continued to labor under the unjust application of the law. Local courts refused to protect the property rights of blacks, including the right of contract. In some counties, whites could violate contracts with impunity, although this was not the case everywhere. For more on the insecurity of property rights, see Frederick Douglass's speech ("Slavery by Another Name") in chapter 3.

ℰ✌ℑ

## Grasp of War Speech (1865)

*Richard Henry Dana Jr.*

Richard Henry Dana Jr. (1815–1882) was the son of a Cambridge, Massachusetts, poet and journalist. After traveling the world, the younger Dana graduated from Harvard College and became a successful lawyer, sharing his father's gift for writing. The realism of Dana's *Two Years before the Mast* (1840) influenced an entire generation of sea novels, including Herman Melville's *Moby Dick* (1851).

Beginning in the 1840s, Dana was active in the "free soil" movement to rid slavery from the territories. Defending fugitive slaves, he became famous as a champion of civil rights in the courtroom. On one occasion, a proslavery thug nearly killed Dana by beating him with an iron bar. During the Civil War, Dana became a Republican and President Abraham Lincoln appointed him U.S. district attorney for Massachusetts. After the war, Dana coined the term "grasp of war" to describe how congressional Republicans might rally to put down unacceptable southern violations of civil rights. Those states were in the "grasp of war" until they respected the civil rights of the freedmen. With this legal theory in hand, the Republican Congress required the southern states to dismantle the black codes and ratify several constitutional amendments before readmitting them to the Union (see entries below).

ℰ✌ℑ

What is a WAR? War is not an attempt to kill, but it is coercion for a purpose. When a nation goes into war, she does it to secure an end, and the war does not cease until the end is secured. . . . Why, suppose a man has attacked your life, my friend, in the highway, at night, armed, and after a death-struggle, you get him down—what then? When he says he has done fighting, are you obliged to release him? Can you not hold him until you have got some security against his weapons? [Applause.] Can you not hold him until you have searched him, and taken his weapons from him? Are you obliged to let him up to begin a new fight for your life? The same principle governs war between nations. When one nation has conquered another, in a war, the victorious nation does not retreat from the country and give up possession of it, because the fighting has ceased. No; it holds the conquered enemy in the grasp of war until it has secured whatever it has a right to require. . . .

What are their laws? Why, their laws, many of them, do not allow a free negro to live in their states. When we emancipated the slaves, did we mean they should be banished—is that it? [Voices—"No."] Is that keeping public faith with them? And yet their laws declare so, and may declare it again.

That is not all! By their laws a black man cannot testify in court; by their laws he cannot hold land; by their laws he cannot vote. Now, we have got to choose between two results. With these four millions of negroes, either you must have four millions of disfranchised, disarmed, untaught, landless, thriftless, non-producing, non-consuming, degraded men, or else you must have four millions of land-holding, industrious, arms-bearing, and voting population. [Loud applause.] Choose between these two! . . .

We have a right to require, my friends, that the freedmen of the South shall have the right to hold land. [Applause.] Have we not? We have a right to require that they shall be allowed to testify in the state courts. [Applause.] Have we not? We have a right to demand that they shall bear arms as soldiers in the militia. [Applause.] Have we not? We have a right to demand that there shall be an impartial ballot. [Great applause.] . . .

. . . Let the states make their own constitutions, but the constitutions must be satisfactory to the Republic [applause], and—ending as I began—by a power which I think is beyond question, the Republic holds them in the grasp of war until they have made such constitutions. [Loud applause.]

Source: Richard Henry Dana, "Grasp of War Speech," in *Speeches in Stirring Times and Letters to a Son* (Boston: Houghton, Mifflin, 1910), 243–59.

## *Freedom Amendments (1865–1870)*

### Thirteenth Amendment to the U.S. Constitution (1865)

1. Neither Slavery nor involuntary servitude, except as punishment for crime whereof the party shall have been duly convicted, shall exist within the United States, or any place subject to their jurisdiction.

2. Congress shall have power to enforce this article by appropriate legislation.

### Fourteenth Amendment to the U.S. Constitution (1868)

1. All persons born or naturalized in the United States, and subject to the jurisdiction thereof, are citizens of the United States and of the State wherein they reside. No State shall make or enforce any law which shall abridge the privileges or immunities of citizens of the United States; nor shall any State deprive any person of life, liberty, or property, without due process of law; nor deny to any person within its jurisdiction the equal protection of the laws. . . .

2. Representatives shall be apportioned among the several States according to their respective numbers, counting the whole number of persons in each State, excluding Indians not taxed. But when the right to vote at any election for the choice of Electors for President and Vice-President of the United States, Representatives in Congress, the executive and judicial officers of a State, or the members of the legislature thereof, is denied to any of the male inhabitants of such State, being twenty-one years of age, and citizens of the United States, or in any way abridged, except for participation in rebellion, or other crime, the basis of representation therein shall be reduced in the proportion which the number of such male citizens shall bear to the whole number of male citizens twenty-one years of age in such State.

3. No person shall be a Senator or Representative in Congress, or Elector of President and Vice-President, or hold any office, civil or military, under the United States, or under any State, who, having previously taken an oath, as a member of Congress, or as an officer of the United States, or as a member of any State Legislature, or as an executive or judicial officer of any State, to support the Constitution of the United States, shall have engaged in insurrection or rebellion against the same, or given aid or comfort to the enemies thereof. But Congress may by a vote of two-thirds of each House, remove such disability.

4. The validity of the public debt of the United States, authorized by law, including debts incurred for payment of pensions and bounties for services in suppressing insurrection or rebellion, shall not be questioned. But neither the United States nor any State shall assume or pay any debt or obligation incurred in aid of insurrection or rebellion against the United States, or any claim for the loss or emancipation of any slave; but all such debts, obligations and claims shall be held illegal and void.

5. The Congress shall have the power to enforce, by appropriate legislation, the provisions of this article.

### Fifteenth Amendment to the U.S. Constitution (1870)

1. The right of citizens of the United States to vote shall not be denied or abridged by the United States or by any State on account of race, color, or previous condition of servitude.

2. The Congress shall have the power to enforce this article by appropriate legislation.

## Racial Freedom and the Individual Right to Bear Arms

The Mississippi constitution of 1832 and the "black code" of 1866 show that representative southern state's imposition of restrictions to the right to bear arms. Congress then required the southern states to pass constitutions consistent with the rights guaranteed in the federal Constitution, including the right to bear arms. The change can be seen in Mississippi's revised constitution of 1868. In practice, however, white Democrats seized weapons from blacks and whites who voted for the Republican Party. They then terrorized the Republican opposition through murder, physical assault, and voter intimidation (see the documents below in the Ku Klux Klan section).

Judging from the record, both northerners and southerners viewed gun ownership as an individual right not limited to state militia—the interpretation of the U.S. Supreme Court in *District of Columbia v. Heller* (2008). Indeed, the postwar problem was one of disloyal and loyal militias rivaling for power, while southern states tried to revoke the right to bear arms from blacks only. Henceforth, in the violent atmosphere of the South, the right to bear arms became a civil rights issue for African Americans, echoing down to advocates of self-defense such as Robert F. Williams, author of *Negroes with Guns* (1962).[5]

ℰℛ

## Mississippi Constitution (1832)

### Article I—Declaration of Rights

Sect. 23. Every citizen has a right to bear arms in defence of himself and of the state.

Source: Mississippi Constitution, 1832, http://www.stateconstitutions.umd.edu/index.aspx (accessed July 14, 2008).

## Mississippi Black Code (1866)

### Article IV—Penal Code

Section 1. *Be it enacted by the legislature of the state of Mississippi,* that no freedman, free Negro, or mulatto not in the military service of the United States government, and not licensed so to do by the board of police of his or her county, shall keep or carry firearms of any kind, or any ammunition, dirk, or Bowie knife; and, on conviction *thereof in the county* court, shall be punished by fine, not exceeding $10, and pay the costs of such proceedings, and all such arms or ammunition shall be forfeited to the informer; and it shall be the duty of every civil and military officer to arrest any freedman, free Negro, or mulatto found with any such arms or ammunition, and cause him or her to be committed for trial in default of bail. . . .

Section 3. *Be it further enacted,* that if any white person shall sell, lend, or give to any freedman, free Negro, or mulatto any firearms, dirk, or Bowie knife, or ammunition, or any spirituous or intoxicating liquors, such person or persons so offending, upon conviction thereof in the county court of his or her county, shall be fined not exceeding $50, and may be imprisoned, at the discretion of the court, not exceeding thirty days. . . .

Section 4. *Be it further enacted,* that all the penal and criminal laws now in force in this state defining offenses and prescribing the mode of punishment for crimes and misdemeanors committed by slaves, free Negroes, or mulattoes be and the same are hereby reenacted and declared to be in full force and effect against freedmen, free Negroes, and mulattoes, except so far as the mode and manner of trial and punishment have been changed or altered by law.

Source: *Laws of the State of Mississippi, Passed at a Regular Session of the Mississippi Legislature, Held in Jackson, October, November and December, 1865, Jackson, 1866,* 82–93, 165–67, http://www.sagehistory.net/reconstruction/docs/MissBlCode.htm (accessed June 24, 2006).

### *Editorials on the Civil Rights Act of 1866 (1866)*

*Harper's Weekly*

While Presidents Abraham Lincoln and Andrew Johnson favored "easy" terms for the South, events in the former Confederacy galvanized congressional Republicans, outraged by southern laws that revived the draconian restrictions of the old slave codes. The black codes enraged northern public opinion and led Congress to pass the Civil Rights Act of 1866, which effectively overturned the codes and defined the status of freedmen as persons deserving "fundamental rights," not de facto slaves.

ᘒ

**March 31, 1866**

This bill—which is truly a Magna Charta—overthrows all hostile legislation of the States against equality of civil rights. The Black Codes, which seek to retain as many of the disabilities of slavery as possible, disappear before this just and beneficent decree. It announces distinctly to those who would still cling to feudalism in America that feudalism is henceforth impossible. It tends to speedy pacification by showing to those who still doubted the national purpose that all the consequences of emancipation have been well weighed and fully accepted by the country. It destroys false hopes. It clears away misunderstandings. It proclaims that when the United States abolished slavery they meant what they said, and knew what they did.

### April 14, 1866

The policy of such a measure is plain from the fact that the civil rights of millions of the native population of the United States are destroyed in certain parts of the country on the ground of color; that this invasion springs from the spirit and habit of slavery, and that, if not corrected by the supreme authority, the inevitable result will be a confirmation of that spirit, and a consequent perpetual menace of the public peace by deepening the conviction of the outraged class of the population that the chance of legal redress is hopeless. The good policy is evident from the further fact that the country earnestly desires repose, but that repose is and ought to be impossible while millions of loyal and tried friends of the Government are exposed, as in the absence of such a bill they are exposed, to the vengeance of those who are still, and naturally, alienated from the Government. Nothing can tend so surely to confirm the peace of the Union as the kindly but firmly expressed intention of the Government to protect and enforce the equal civil rights of every citizen; understanding by civil rights, according to Chancellor Kent, "the right of personal security, the right of personal liberty, and the right to acquire and enjoy property." This is substantially the explanation given by President Johnson of the right conferred by the Emancipation [Thirteenth] Amendment. "Liberty," he said to the colored soldiers and to Judge Wairdlaw, "means freedom to work and enjoy the products of your own labor." The Civil Rights Bill merely secures that freedom; for no man enjoys the fruit of his labor if he can not own property, and sue and testify and convey. . . .

The President's objection to the bill as special legislation is a manifest misapprehension. The bill is universal in its application. If the rights of any citizen of whatever birth or color are invaded any where in the country the bill provides the remedy, without any exclusion or exception whatever. But the veto lays great weight upon the fact that "worthy, intelligent, and patriotic foreigners" must reside here five years before they can become citizens, and expresses the opinion that the bill discriminates against them in favor of those to whom the avenues of freedom and intelligence are just opened. But the President hardly puts the case fairly. Let us ask it in another way. . . . If it be right to take a foreigner totally ignorant of our language and government and the whole spirit of our system and give him a vote at the end of five years, can it be wrong to take a man like Robert Small[s], who instinctively knows and loves and struggles for the Government, and at the end of three years of emancipation give him, not so much as a vote, but the name and rights of a citizen? . . ."[6]

. . . What is the President's plan? Is it to leave them to the Black Codes? Is it to call them free, thereby exasperating the late masters, and then suffer those masters unchecked to forbid them to own property, to bear arms, to testify, and to enjoy any of the rights of freedom? Is it to trust to time, and to hope that when the present generation, to whom we gave our word, is exterminated, some kind of justice may be done their posterity by those who come after us? The present danger to the Union is not in the direction feared by the President. It is not from the United States doing a simple Constitutional act of justice; it is from the States perpetuating the old injustice from which our troubles sprang. State rights interpreted by slavery brought us bitter alienation and bloody war. State rights interpreted by liberty can alone give us Constitutional unity and enduring peace.

Sources: "The Civil Rights Bill," *Harper's Weekly*, March 31, 1866, 194, and April 14, 1866, 226.

## Mississippi Constitution (1868)

Article I.—Bill of Rights
Sec. 15. All persons shall have a right to keep and bear arms for their defence.

Source: *The 1868 Constitution of the State of Mississippi*, http://www.stateconstitutions .umd.edu/index.aspx (accessed July 14, 2008).

# Ku Klux Klan Act of 1871

Rights guaranteed on paper meant little to African Americans and others victimized by the lawlessness of the Ku Klux Klan (KKK). The following documents preface the Ku Klux Klan Act (below) with brief testimony by those who were dispossessed, attacked, or witnessed the lynching of others, simply for voting "the [R]epublican ticket." President U. S. Grant responded by asking Congress for this anticonspiracy act, and then sent federal troops and marshals to put down the KKK. The military intervention was an effort to protect the life, liberty, and property of individuals facing Democratic-KKK conspiracies to rid the region of the Republican Party.

The following documents offer testimony to the violence in the South. The first document is an account by Jack Johnson, a black tenant farmer in South Carolina when the Ku Klux Klan and associated ruffians terrorized Republicans, black and white. His testimony before Congress occurred after he fled the region. White Democrats, together with the Ku Klux Klan, intimidated voters; nevertheless, the black-majority county carried the Republican ticket to office, thus sparking violent reprisals.

The second entry is a plea from a Republican woman to President Grant, begging him for protection. Congress passed the Ku Klux Klan Act, excerpted in the third document. The KKK Act authorized the president to take military action against state-private conspiracies, and also made state authorities personally liable for damages to individuals.

ତ୬

## *KKK Victim Testifies Before Congress (1871)*

*Jack Johnson*

JACK JOHNSON (colored) sworn and examined.

By the CHAIRMAN:

Q. How old are you?

A. Forty-five on the 25th of next August.

Q. What did you do there [in Laurens County, South Carolina]?

A. I was farming pretty much all the time until emancipation, and then I still farmed on, but cut rock and built chimneys.

Q. You were a stone-mason, then?

A. Yes, sir.

Q. Were you called on there by the Ku-Klux at any time?

A. Yes, sir; I was called on by one man on the way from the riot at Laurens from the fuss. . . . He says to me, "What ticket did you vote?" I told him I voted the republican ticket. "God Damn you," says he, "have you got a tie-rope here?" Says I, "Mr. Reizer, I don't think I have done anything to call for that." He says, "No, God damn you, you haven't done anything; you go against our party; you go against us who have been a friend to you all your days. I suppose you hallooed the other day, Hurrah for Governor Scott. Didn't you vote for Governor Scott?" I told him I did, and I thought I was right in doing so. He says, "Why did you think so?" I told him I thought that was the right way, and it was right for me to go that way. He says, "Suppose you want to be burned right here?" I says, "No, I am not prepared to die," and I stooped down to pick up some cotton on the ground, and he struck me on the head and knocked me down on the face.

Q. What with?

A. With a club about a yard long, and I turned and got hold by his coat and tried to struggle up, and he jerked out his pistol and said, "God damn you, if that is what you're after, I'll kill you right now." I told him I didn't want him to kill me. He beat me on the head. I don't know what passed, but he beat on me to his satisfaction, and I went to raise again, and he says, "God damn you, I've a great mind to shoot you through and through." I says, "Mr. Reizer, you are beating me for nothing. O Lord, I hope you'll not kill me." He says, "Do you think the Lord has any feeling for you or anybody else that voted the ticket you have?" I told him yes, I thought he ought to have. When I said that he struck me right across the top of my forehead, and I caught his hand, and he says, "God damn you, I left eight of your republican party biting up dirt at Laurens, and you'll be biting dirt before morning. . . . He went on then toward the house to have his horse fed. I struggled along to the fence and got on the fence and got over and went through to my wife's house, and she said they had been there hunting me. I told her to please give me a little piece of bread and meat and I would try to get away from there. . . .

Q. How is it there in regard to the other colored people? Do they feel at liberty to vote as they please, or has this system of intimidation been carried on to any extent?

A. Well, they are down up there now, for all the republican men that have been the leaders, speaking and going about through there, has left there—has come out and left them. My wife come from there about four weeks ago. . . .

Q. Did you do anything else than vote?

A. No sir, only to vote; only this, I took a great propriety in counseling the people which way to vote—the colored people. I had been riding about a good deal. I was the only colored man that had a mule anywheres nigh house, and I would go 'way off to speeches, and come back and tell the news how the speeches were; that was all I did, and for that they were very down on me.

Source: U.S. Congress, *Testimony Taken by the Joint Select Committee to Inquire into the Condition of Affairs in the Late Insurrectionary States, South Carolina* (Washington, DC: GPO, 1871–1872), 2:1165–68.

### Republicans Report Terror to President U. S. Grant (1871)

On April 19, Mrs. S. E. Lane . . . wrote to USG. . . . "I write to ask your help, your protection for us, a few families located in Chesterfield District S.C. . . . True & hearty Republicans, & as individuals & families, kind & friendly to all around us—but Sir, we are in terror from Ku-Klux threats & outrages—there is neither law or justice in our midst,—our nearest neighbor—a prominent Repub'can now lies dead—murdered, by a disguised Ruffian Band, which attacked his House at midnight a few nights since—his wife also was murdered—she was buried yesterday, & a daughter is lying dangerously ill from a shot-wound.—my Husband's life is threatened—a northern man who has bought a Plantation here—a friend's also,—a northern man—Revd Dr Fox, formerly of N. Y,—only because they are Republicans—we are in constant fear & terror—our nights are sleepless, we are filled with anxiety & dismay. Ought this to be?—it seems almost impossible to believe that we are in our own Land. . . ." On the same day, Henry J. Fox, Oro, S.C, wrote to John P. Newman. "We have tried all means of obtaining releif [*sic*] and have failed—we try now, a womans expediant. The writer of the enclosed letter a Mrs Lane, the wife of a presbyterian clergyman has not overstated our terror. She does not know as I do, all the grounds of alarm. I have to sleep out in the woods. We beg you to read the letter to the president. Help us if you can. I have just come from the scene of blood and death. We are marked as the next. . . . Our mails are

Thomas Nast cartoon illustrating the Democratic slogan of 1868: "This is a white man's government." The cartoon is subtitled: "We regard the Reconstruction Acts (so called) of Congress as usurpations, and unconstitutional, revolutionary, and void—*Democratic Platform*." (Library of Congress, Prints & Photographs Division, LC-USZ62–121735. The cartoon originally appeared in *Harper's Weekly,* September 5, 1868.)

tampered with, & it would set our minds at rest, if we can know this reaches you. One line is enough."

Source: Ulysses S. Grant, *The Papers of Ulysses S. Grant*, vol. 21, ed. John Y. Simon (Carbondale: Southern Illinois University Press, 1998), 263n. © 1998 by the Ulysses S. Grant Association, reprinted by permission of the publisher Southern Illinois University Press.

## The Ku Klux Klan Act (1871)

### U.S. Congress

*An Act to enforce the Provisions of the Fourteenth Amendment to the Constitution of the United States, and for other Purposes.*

SEC. 2. That if two or more persons within any State or Territory of the United States . . . shall conspire together, or go in disguise upon the public highway or upon the premises of another for the purpose, either directly or indirectly, of depriving any person or any class of persons of the equal protection of the laws, or of equal privileges or immunities under the laws, or for the purpose of preventing or hindering the constituted authorities of any State from giving or securing to all persons within such State the equal protection of the laws, or shall conspire together for the purpose in any manner impeding, hindering, obstructing or defeating the due course of justice in any State or Territory, with intent to deny to any citizen of the United States the due and equal protection of the laws, or to injury any person in his person or his property for lawfully enforcing the right of any person or class of persons to the equal protection of the laws, or by force, intimidation, or threat to prevent any citizen of the United States lawfully entitled to vote from giving his support or advocacy in a lawful manner towards or in favor of the election of any lawfully qualified person as an elector of President or Vice-President of the United States, or as a member of the Congress of the United States, or to injure any such citizen in his person or property on account of such support or advocacy, each and every person so offending shall be deemed guilty of a high crime, and upon conviction thereof in any district or circuit court of the United States or district or supreme court of any Territory of the United States having jurisdiction of similar offences, shall be punished by a fine not less than five hundred nor more than five thousand dollars, or by imprisonment, with or without hard labor, as the court may determine, for a period of not less than six months nor more than six years, as the court may determine, or by both such fine and imprisonment as the court shall determine. . . .

SEC. 3. That in all cases where insurrection, domestic violence, unlawful combinations, or conspiracies in any State shall so obstruct or hinder the execution of the laws thereof, and of the United States . . . , and the constituted authorities of such State shall either be unable to protect, or shall, from any cause, fail in or refuse protection of the people in such rights, such facts shall be deemed a denial by such State of the equal protection of the laws to which they are entitled under the constitution of the United States. . . .

SEC. 4. That whenever in any State or part of a State the unlawful combinations named in the preceding section of this act shall be organized and armed, and so numerous and powerful as to be able, by violence, to either overthrow or set at defiance the constituted authorities of such State, . . . it shall be lawful for the President of the United States, when in his judgment the public safety shall require it, to suspend the privileges of the writ of *habeas corpus,* to the end that such rebellion may be overthrown.

## No Federal Power over Private Discrimination (1883)

### U.S. Supreme Court

Reconstruction legislation restricted *state* actors from infringing the legal rights of citizens. The Civil Rights Act of 1875 went further in prohibiting private racial discrimination in "public accommodations" (inns, restaurants, and other business establishments held open to the public). The Republican-dominated U.S. Supreme Court ruled the act unconstitutional because it exceeded the bounds of the Fourteenth Amendment, which did not authorize Congress to exercise local police power over private matters. This issue of racial discrimination in "public accommodations" reemerged with the Civil Rights Act of 1964.

တၟ

Civil rights, such as are guaranteed by the Constitution against State aggression, cannot be impaired by the wrongful acts of individuals, unsupported by State authority in the shape of laws, customs, or judicial or executive proceedings. The wrongful act of an individual, unsupported by any such authority, is simply a private wrong, or a crime of that individual; an invasion of the rights of the injured party, it is true, whether they affect his person, his property, or his reputation; but if not sanctioned in some way by the State, or not done under State authority, his rights remain in full force, and may presumably be vindicated by resort to the laws of the State for redress. An individual cannot deprive a man of his right to vote, to hold property, to buy and sell, to sue in the courts, or to be a witness or a juror; he may, by force or fraud, interfere with the enjoyment of the right in a particular case; he may commit an assault against the person, or commit murder, or use ruffian violence at the polls, or slander the good name of a fellow citizen; but, unless protected in these wrongful acts by some shield of State law or State authority, he cannot destroy or injure the right.

Source: *Civil Rights Cases*, 109 U.S. 3 (1883).

## Notes

1. Henry Ketcham, *The Life of Abraham Lincoln* (New York: A. L. Burt, 1901), 303.

2. Bruce R. Bartlett, *Wrong on Race: The Democratic Party's Buried Past* (New York: Palgrave Macmillan, 2008).

3. Frederick Douglass, quoted in "The President and the Colored Citizens," *Harper's Weekly*, June 22, 1872, 483.

4. *Dred Scott v. Sandford*, 60 U.S. (19 How.) 393 (1857).

5. Robert Franklin Williams, *Negroes with Guns* (New York: Marzani & Munsell, 1962).

6. Robert Smalls was a runaway slave who became a war hero in the service of the Union navy. Glenda E. Gilmore, "Smalls, Robert," in *African American National Biography*, ed. Henry Louis Gates Jr. and Evelyn Brooks Higginbotham, Oxford African American Studies Center, http://www.oxfordaasc.com/article/opr/t0001/e0528 (accessed July 28, 2008).

# Recommended Reading

Bensel, Richard Franklin. *Yankee Leviathan: The Origins of Central State Authority in America, 1859–1877*. New York: Cambridge University Press, 1990.

Foner, Eric. *Free Soil, Free Labor, Free Men: The Ideology of the Republican Party before the Civil War*. New York: Oxford University Press, 1970.

———. *Reconstruction: America's Unfinished Revolution, 1863–1877*. New York: Harper & Row, 1988.

Halbrook, Stephen P. *Freedmen, the Fourteenth Amendment, and the Right to Bear Arms, 1866–1876*. Westport, CT: Praeger, 1998.

Hummel, Jeffrey Rogers. *Emancipating Slaves, Enslaving Free Men: A History of the American Civil War*. Chicago: Open Court, 1996.

Shapiro, Samuel. *Richard Henry Dana, Jr., 1815–1882*. East Lansing: Michigan State University Press, 1961.

Spooner, Lysander. *The Lysander Spooner Reader*. San Francisco: Fox & Wilkes, 1992.

Trelease, Allen W. *White Terror: The Ku Klux Klan Conspiracy and Southern Reconstruction*. 1971. Reprint, Baton Rouge: Louisiana State University Press, 1999.

Wyatt-Brown, Bertram. "The Civil Rights Act of 1875." *Western Political Quarterly* 18, no. 4 (1965): 763–75.

# 3

## Colorblindness in a Color-Conscious Era

*1877–1920*

AFTER FEDERAL TROOPS LEFT the U.S. South, Reconstruction ended and the nation focused on new concerns (the tariff, currency debates, foreign wars). Yet racial issues did not go away. In the South, the Democratic Party disfranchised blacks through the use of poll taxes, constitutional literacy tests, election fraud, and voter intimidation. Southern states passed laws forcing the separation of races in schools, on streetcars, and elsewhere in society. White mobs repeatedly lynched blacks, thus sending a harrowing message to an entire race: "Stay in your place." Meanwhile, American shores received record numbers of immigrants from southeastern Europe and Asia. "Progressives" and nativist conservatives advocated immigration restriction in a nation known for its open borders, ultimately succeeding with the National Origins Quota Act of 1924.

Classical liberals found themselves on the defensive: battling immigration restriction, fighting white racism in the South, defending nonwhites in overseas territories, and offering individual property rights as a solution to the "Indian problem." By the end of this period, Progressives dubbed classical liberals "conservative" for trying to prohibit state action not only in the economy but in preserving racial freedom and open borders.

# Immigration

## Chinese Exclusion Act: Right of Migration "God-Given"
## (1877, 1882)

Only fifteen senators, all Republican, voted against the Chinese Exclusion Act (1882)—a law that ended the era of free immigration and stigmatized an entire race. This was not the first anti-immigration campaign in America: the 1850s witnessed a massive reaction of native-born Protestants against Irish and German Catholic immigrants until the Civil War subsumed that concern in the blood and gore of battle. After the war, Chinese immigration increased in the West, where the immigrants worked for railroads, mining companies, and other businesses. The campaign to drive the Chinese out was intensely vicious. Native-born workers set fire to the settlements of the Chinese and voted for politicians who pledged to rid the West Coast of the Chinese. The governor of California characterized the Chinese as an inferior race and asked the state legislature for laws discriminating against the immigrants. Businessmen sided with their Chinese employees against the workers who claimed that foreigners took "their" jobs. The Chinese did not suffer silently: they fought deportation in the courts and spoke out publicly. In a published newspaper letter, Norman Asing, a Chinese American citizen, responded to critics, "The declaration of your independence, and all the acts of your government, your people, and your history, are against you."[1]

As the congressional debate heated up, Senator Oliver P. Morton (R-IN) led the pro-immigration forces. After his death in 1877, the Senate published Morton's eloquent report defending the right of all races to immigrate. Opponents of exclusion repeatedly drew upon his report in the debate that culminated in the Chinese Exclusion Act. Senators George Hoar (R-MA), Joseph Hawley (R-CT) and Representative Charles Joyce (R-VT) argued for immigration as a fundamental right of free men and women. Excluding entire races was counter to the principles of the Constitution, Christianity, and capitalism. Proponents of the Chinese Exclusion Act, led by organized labor, countered that the Chinese were "different": they would not assimilate and also undercut "white" wages.

**Opponents judged, correctly, that this act would be remembered as a blot on American history.**

ℭℌ

### *Oliver P. Morton, R-IN (1877)*

The foundation-stone in our political edifice is the declaration that all men are equal; that they are endowed by their Creator with inalienable rights; that among these are life, liberty, and the pursuit of happiness; that to obtain these, governments are instituted among men, deriving their just powers from the consent of the governed. We profess to believe that God has given to all men the same rights, without regard to race or color. . . .

A cardinal principle in our government, proclaimed in the Declaration of Independence, in the Articles of Confederation, and recognized by our Constitution, is, that our country is open to immigrants from all parts of the world; that it was to be the asylum of the oppressed and unfortunate. It is true, that when the government was formed, and for nearly three–quarters of a century, no immigration was contemplated except from nations composed of white people; but the principles upon which we professed to act, and the invitation we extended to the world, cannot and ought not to be limited or controlled by race or color, nor by the character of the civilization of the countries from which immigrants may come. . . . Nor should the operation of these principles be limited on account of the religious faith of nations. Absolute religious toleration was regarded by our fathers as of vital importance. Not only were the different sects of Christians to be tolerated, but the deist, the atheist, the Mohammedan, and the Buddhist were to be free to express and enjoy their opinions. . . .

. . . If the Chinese in California were white people, being in all other respects what they are, I do not believe that the complaints and warfare made against them would have existed to any considerable extent. Their difference in color, dress, manners, and religion have, in my judgment, more to do with this hostility than their alleged vices or any actual injury to the white people of California. . . .

But before entering upon the discussion of any other principles, I may be permitted to observe that, in my judgment, the Chinese cannot be protected in

E PLURIBUS UNUM (EXCEPT THE CHINESE).

"E Pluribus Unum (Except the Chinese)" ran on April 1, 1882, in *Harper's Weekly*. Congress passed the bill to exclude Chinese immigrants five weeks later—the first immigration act to bar an entire race from the United States. (*Harper's Weekly*, April 1, 1882, 207.)

the Pacific States while remaining in their alien condition. . . . Complete protection can be given them only by allowing them to become citizens and acquire the right of suffrage, when their votes would become important in elections, and their persecutions, in great part, converted into kindly solicitation. . . .

The testimony shows that the intellectual capacity of the Chinese is fully equal to that of white people. Their ability to acquire the mechanic arts, and to imitate every process and form of workmanship, ranks very high, and was declared by many of the witnesses [before Congress] to be above that of white people; and their general intellectual power to understand mathematics, and master any subject presented to the human understanding, to be quite equal to that of any other race.

*George Hoar, R-MA (1882)*

I refuse consent to this legislation. I will not consent to a denial by the United States of the right of every man who desires to improve his condition by honest labor—his labor being no man's property but his own—to go anywhere on the face of the earth that he pleases. . . .

We go boasting of our democracy, and our superiority, and our strength. The flag bears the stars of hope to all nations. A hundred thousand Chinese land in California and everything is changed. God has not made of one blood all the nations any longer. The self–evident truth becomes a self–evident lie. . . .

The advocates of this legislation appeal to a twofold motive for its support.

First. They invoke the old race prejudice which has so often played its hateful and bloody part in history.

Second. They say that the Chinese laborer works cheap and lives cheap, and so injures the American laborer with whom he competes. . . .

What argument can be urged against the Chinese which was not heard against the negro within living memory? . . .

Twenty years have not passed by since the children of the African savage were emancipated from slavery. In that brief space they have vindicated their title to the highest privileges and their fitness for the highest duties of citizenship. These despised savages have sat in the House and in the Senate. I have served with them for twelve years in both branches. Can you find an equal number, chosen on any principle of selection, whose conduct has been marked by more uniform good sense and propriety? I have seen most accomplished debaters unhorsed with as much dexterity as courtesy by one of this despised race. . . .

It is scarcely forty years since the Irishman, who has been such a source of wealth and strength to America, began his exodus across the sea. There are men

**THE AMERICANESE WALL, AS CONGRESSMAN BURNETT WOULD BUILD IT.**
UNCLE SAM: You're welcome in—if you can climb it!

*Puck* cartoon satirizing the literacy bill designed to bar immigrants from the "land of the free" (1916). (Library of Congress, Prints & Photographs Division, LC-USZ62–52584.)

in this body, whose heads are not yet gray, who can remember how the arguments now used against the Chinese filled the American mind with alarm when used against the Irishman. . . .

But the Chinese, it is said, will not assimilate with us. It is said the two races have been side by side for thirty years and no step taken toward assimilation. It is admitted that they have learned our industries rapidly and intelligently. That they do not incline to become Christians or republicans may perhaps be accounted for by the treatment they have received. They are excluded by statute from the public schools. They have no honest trial by jury. . . .

Humanity, capable of infinite depths of degradation, is capable also of infinite heights of excellence. The Chinese, like all other races, has given us its examples of both. To rescue humanity from this degradation is, we are taught to believe, the great object of God's moral government on earth. It is not by injustice, exclusion, caste, but by reverence for the individual soul that we can aid in this consummation. It is not by Chinese policies that China is to be civilized. I believe that the immortal truths of the Declaration of Independence came from the same source with the Golden Rule and the Sermon on the Mount. We can trust Him who promulgated these laws to keep the country safe that obeys them. The laws of the universe have their own sanction. They will not fail.

*Joseph Hawley, R-CT (1882)*

A few words in this proposed law may be quoted for a century, not as the opening lines of the Declaration of Independence are quoted, as a comfort, a prophecy, a battle-cry, but on the same page with the edict of Nantes, the innumerable decrees tormenting and banishing and excluding the Jews, the belated hobgoblin idiocies that are now torturing that race in some parts of Europe, the barbarisms that were once heaped upon the barbarous negro, and more appropriately still with the laws of Japan and of this same China, which treated all of us, gentle and lovely bearers of rum, opium, and Testaments, as "outside barbarians." Or it may be that this bill will be quoted with the alien and sedition law, the repeal of the Missouri compromise, and the fugitive-slave law, as an illustration of the truth that fifty million sovereigns can be as despotic as one sovereign.

[Senate vote for Chinese Exclusion: yeas 29, nays 15, abstentions 32.]

### *Charles Joyce, R-VT (1882)*

The great principle of the right of every man to life, liberty, and the pursuit of happiness is the corner-stone of our republican edifice, and this principle carries with it the right to seek that liberty and happiness anywhere on earth he may choose to go. This right of emigration is a part and parcel of his liberty, an inherent, vested, God-given right, indispensable to his happiness, and one which is far above and beyond all human laws and constitutions. . . .

The late Senator Morton, when speaking of this subject, declared: That a man's right to withdraw from his native country and make his home in another, and thus cut himself off from all connection with his native country, is a part of his natural liberty, and without that his liberty is defective. We claim that the right to liberty is a natural, inherent, God-given right, and his liberty is imperfect unless it carries with it the right of expatriation. . . .

No, Mr. Speaker, let them come, and wherever and whenever these two civilizations, or these two classes of labor come together, you will find the crescent will give way to the cross, and freedom will triumph over slavery; and instead of destroying the votaries of this false religion and degrading dogma, Christianity will enroll them among her supporters and use them to extend and strengthen her kingdom.

[House vote for Chinese Exclusion: yeas 167, nays 66, abstentions 59.]

Sources: Oliver P. Morton, *Views of the Late Oliver P. Morton on the Character, Extent, and Effect of Chinese Immigration to the United States*, U.S. Senate doc. no. 20, 45th Cong., 2nd sess., January 17, 1878, 1–2, 4, 10; George Hoar et al., *Congressional Record*, March 1, 9, and 22, 1882, 1517–23, 1738, 2184–85.


## Immigrant Patriotism: A Businessman's Point of View (1912)

### *John Foster Carr*

During the early twentieth century, American business clashed with labor unions, which sought to restrict immigration. The business community supported free immigration and promoted society's acceptance of immigrants. The following article ran in the *American Leader*, the English-language journal of the Association of Foreign Language Newspapers, an assimilationist advocate of open borders. Carr (1869–1939) ran a thriving business publishing foreign-language guides for specific immigrant groups (Italian, Polish, and so on). He cooperated closely with immigrant groups, teaching them not only how to get by in America but offering tips on how to "become" an American: civic lessons, work expectations, dress, gender relations, shopping in the marketplace, and much more. Advocates of free immigration understood that assimilation was the most effective argument for admitting aliens—they would one day become fellow Americans.

მ

The Immigration Commission recommends restriction of immigration as demanded by economic, moral and social considerations. Yet it has effectually disproved the chief charges against the immigrant. . . . If the immigrant almost uniformly shows at better advantage than the native it is because our immigration law demands a higher standard of health and civic virtue than we can maintain among ourselves. It is well enforced. The immigrant is almost uniformly honest and hard-working and possessed of the adventurous spirit and enterprise of our own immigrant ancestors.

But if the old charges are disproved, new ones are set up in their stead. The immigrant is accused of lowering wages and conditions of living. He is accused of being a bird of passage. And the Commission attempts to distinguish between an old immigration and a new. Apart from differences of race and nationality, I do not hesitate to say that there is no human difference whatever between the old immigration and the new, except improved quality. . . .

We need the new mobile immigrant. The business of the country, the work of the nation, demands restriction of legislation, not restriction of immigration. . . .

But is it true that the new immigrant has lowered wages and the standard of living? . . . It will be news to you employers that wages have anywhere been reduced in this country. To you certainly the fact is plain enough that while immigration has had no lowering effect on wages, wages have had a very important effect on immigration. The immigrant comes to the United States not through a vague migratory instinct, but—I repeat it—at the call of the well paid job. . . .

The immigrant must wear American clothes. Italian cloaks and sashes, Syrian trousers, Russian head gear are ridiculously out of fashion. But when he buys American clothes, he must pay high American prices for them. Except in the camps, it is impossible for him to resist wholly the temptation of American food. He insists on having white bread, our grocer's delicacies that are expensively boxed and canned. He eats meat here, when perhaps he never tastes it at home except on rare holy days.

The social standard is immeasurably higher in the United States and it is expensive. Every Italian peasant becomes a gentleman, a Signore, the moment his foot touches Ellis Island; and he would be insulted here if he were called a "contadino." In no part of America can he walk bare-footed on the road. He usually carries an umbrella, a luxury unknown to him at home. . . . It is obviously impossible for manual laborers to work for wages substantially less than the rate usually prevailing here. And after a few weeks in this country they get to know the market values of labor as accurately as a farmer knows the price of hay. . . .

The new, rapid, educative forces of city life are now accomplishing miracles of assimilation. The change in the immigrant is most remarkable when you consider that generally it is a change from the most primitive agricultural life known on this planet to the most rapid-moving urban life of our western civilization. . . .

We need every strong, healthy, moral man or woman who has ambition enough for better living and personal progress to make the long journey from Europe to America. No excess of population crowds the country. Seven-eighths of the area of the nation is unfilled. And we are engaged in tremendous constructive work in building up this Republic to a point of greatness undreamed of in the world's history. There is an unending demand for vast armies of men. There are our railways to be completed, the huge municipal improvements which we have planned, subways and towers and docks, the building of myriads of new and better houses, new roads, the call of our countless industries for labor, skilled and unskilled. For all these things we need the strong arms of many workers.

Source: John Foster Carr, "Keep Open the Gates: Immigration Considered from the Business Man's Point of View," *American Leader* 1, no. 4 (1912): 31–40.

### One Nation, Open to Immigrants (1922, 1924)
*Louis Marshall*

Louis Marshall (1856–1929) was born in Syracuse, New York, to German-Jewish immigrants. Although born into a poor family, Marshall graduated from

Columbia University Law School and formed a prosperous law firm in New York City. Described an "ultraconservative" in the Progressive Era, Louis Marshall was anything but: his classical liberal passions moved him to found the American Jewish Committee, become a lawyer for the National Association for the Advancement of Colored People (NAACP), and defend Leo Frank (a man accused of rape and then lynched). He led the opposition to immigration restriction and fought the government's efforts to classify Jews as a "race." Contemporaries said that American Jews lived under "Marshall Law"—an exaggeration, to be sure, but indicative of the civic influence he wielded. A corporate and constitutional lawyer, Marshall was a lifelong supporter of the Republican Party but resisted efforts to group Jews as a voting bloc. Jews (and others) could maintain their traditions in private life, but he believed that the government—including political parties and interest groups—should not identify people by their race or ethnicity.

Marshall's contributions to civil rights were not limited to immigrant rights. (Chapter 4 examines in greater detail his battle against racism and anti-Semitism.) In court, he won *Nixon v. Herndon* (1927), a U.S. Supreme Court decision nullifying the "white primaries" of the southern Democratic Party. He also persuaded the Supreme Court to overturn the Oregon Compulsory Law: a Ku Klux Klan–initiated law requiring all students—including Catholics—to attend public school (*Pierce v. Society of Sisters,* 1925). Advocates of compulsory public schooling argued that the State had an overriding interest in educating youth, even if parents preferred parochial education for their children. The law reflected nativist fears that Catholic schoolchildren would not assimilate unless forced into public schools. In a unanimous decision, the U.S. Supreme Court ruled that the law violated the Fourteenth Amendment of the Constitution. In a famous line, Associate Justice James Clark McReynolds wrote that children were not "mere creature[s] of the state."

The drive for immigration restriction grew stronger in the 1920s as the Ku Klux Klan urged its millions of members to defend "100% Americanism" (that is, white, Anglo-Saxon, Protestant Americans—no Catholics, no Jews, no blacks, no foreign-born immigrants). In the following testimony before Congress, Marshall defends immigration and attacks the evil of immigration quotas—a battle he had been fighting for more than a decade that he ultimately lost in 1924, when Congress passed the National Origins Quota Act, which effectively shut down immigration from southern and eastern Europe.

$\infty$

### January 1922

In the first place, this is a country of immigrants. Every man, every woman, every child living in this country is either an immigrant or the descendant of immigrants. Some of them will not have to go back very far for the date of their arrival here. . . .

A number of fundamental principles were quite generally recognized and are now crystallized into our immigration legislation. These principles, to which no honest citizen can make the slightest objection, are that nobody shall be admitted as an immigrant or otherwise who is mentally, morally, or physically unfit, nobody likely to be a drag upon the country by becoming a public charge; nobody who would prove a source of danger to the country by his opposition to those moral concepts for which we stand. We will have no polygamists, none of immoral tendencies, none who have been convicted of crime or of acts of moral turpitude. Nor will we harbor those who are the enemies of organized government—no anarchists, no communists—nobody who believes in force directed against government or in agitation for the destruction of constitutional government. None of these categories is to be admitted. Nobody will raise his voice more earnestly than I in opposition to the admission of any of these objectionable classes.

But when we come to those men and women who are of the same character and the same mental and moral and physical characteristics as those who in the past have proven their worth as immigrants, I say that it is not true Americanism and that it is not right or just that we shall bar the doors of opportunity against them. . . .

Some continue to manifest the spirit of war, so that they are still talking in terms of animosity, hatred, contempt, and uncharitableness when they refer to the different families of the human race. The sooner we get over that tendency the better it will be for the country. When one becomes a citizen of the United States he is an American citizen in every sense of the word. Whatever his nationality or origin may have been, it is forgotten. Wherever his cradle may have been rocked is unimportant. He brings to this country such gifts as he possesses. All of them combined have created that remarkable being, the finest the world has ever known, the composite American. I, therefore, feel a sadness in my heart whenever I hear men say: "This man is an Irishman;" "This man is a Scotchman;" "The Dutch have these qualifications;" "The Greeks have those;" "He is a Dago;" "He is this, that, or the other thing." The sooner we stop it the better it will be for the unity of the Nation, and for the welfare of the world.

### January 1924

Mr. Marshall. The one fundamental thought which is contained in this bill, to which I take exception and which, I think, constitutes its real weakness, is that section which I think it will be conceded, is the central idea of the bill. It indicates how many immigrants are to be admitted into this country under the quota principle. . . .

. . . One would say, having recently read the proclamation of the Imperial Wizard of the Ku-Klux Klan that the ideas which underlie its theories of Government in the United States find an echo in this legislation because the people who are to be admitted are white, largely Protestant, and are of so-called Anglo-Saxon stock, while those who are to be excluded are not Protestants and are not Anglo-Saxon, although they are white. . . .

. . . A gentleman, who is a zoologist, Madison Grant, created the Nordic race. But he was not a real scientist, after all, because he promulgated that notion in a book which he called "The Passing of a Great Race," meaning thereby to say that that noble creation of his mind, the Nordic race, was disappearing.

Well, being a Darwinist in theory, I wondered how this scientific man could square the idea of the passing of that great race with the doctrine of the survival of the fittest. And when the other day, Professor Osborn, of the Museum of Natural History, also lamented that there was a steady disappearance in many parts of the world and in many parts of our country of the Nordic stock, I wondered why this fabled race was so frail and fragile. . . .

And now it is proposed to tell these [non-Nordic] people, who fought and bled for this country, who have worked for it in the field and in the work shop, in summer and in winter, "You are an inferior race. You are not the equal of the people who came from northern and western Europe. We consider you as the dregs of humanity. . . ."

Mr. Raker. . . . What is the right principle in your view?

Mr. Marshall. What I said at the outset, namely, no quota provision at all, but a continuation of the policy of excluding only those who are mentally, morally and physically unfit, who are enemies of organized government, and who are apt to become public charges. . . .

Mr. Raker. And there is to be no restraint as to numbers from any locality?

Mr. Marshall. Yes. I object to any restraint by numbers as being absolutely unjust and without any proper basis in economics, morals, right, or justice.

### February 1924

I am not a member of the Allied Patriotic Societies which have been represented here, but I am proud to be a member of the greatest allied patriotic society in the world, and that is to be an American citizen. I am one who regards the citizenship of this country to be one unitary thing. I regard it as a peril to our country to talk about races or language groups. . . .

. . . The best educational medium that is to be found for transforming the foreign-speaking immigrant to full-fledged American citizenship is [the] foreign-language press. There is no question about the young, the children; they become American citizens almost when they begin to breathe the air of our country. They become familiar with our slang, almost before they can speak other words in English. But they are brought up in our public schools, and they read the English language and they speak in the English language, and they go through the elementary schools and high schools, and through the universities, and enter the professions and become real Americans. The elders likewise feel the need of intellectual sustenance. They can not read English, because the fathers and the mothers have to work hard during the daytime, and they, therefore, wishing to read are limited to a medium which they can understand, and they find it in the Italian newspapers, or other foreign newspapers, which I have frequently read, with a view of testing what they have to say. They find it in the Yiddish newspapers, and the Spanish newspapers, and in other languages. I can speak particularly of the Yiddish newspapers. How many times do you find in the daily press in English disquisitions on the Declaration of Independence, or on the Constitution of the United States? Frequently you find such histories serially published in the daily press in these foreign languages. Almost all of them specialize in that respect, believing that they have a duty to perform to this country, of educating the foreign-speaking residents here in the spirit of America in the language which they understand. . . .

And do you think that they will bite the hand that feeds them or that they will become the enemy of the land that has given them these glorious opportunities? I have said thousands of times—perhaps before these committees—that I was taught by my mother, who was an immigrant, to pray daily three times for this blessed country and its institutions. And that same feeling, I tell you, is innate in practically every one of these immigrants who comes here for the establishment of a home. . . .

If we countenance the idea which has found voice among those who foster this antiimmigration legislation, an evil day portends for our Republic. We should be a great united family and we should not look with contempt upon any member of our population. . . . If you place on your statute books a law which, in effect, says to us: You are inferior; you are not a first-class American, but a second-class American; what shall we think of it? Shall we sit by without protesting in the only way in which an American can protest?

Sources: Louis Marshall, *Immigration*, testimony before the House of Representatives, Committee on Immigration and Naturalization, 67th Cong., 2nd sess., January 26, 1922, 311–14, 325; Louis Marshall, *Restriction of Immigration*, testimony before the House of Representatives, Committee on Immigration and Naturalization, 68th Cong., 1st sess., January 3, 1924, 286–93, 302; Louis Marshall, *Selective Immigration Legislation*, testimony before the Senate, Committee on Immigration, 68th Cong., 1st sess., February 20, 1924, 120–24.

# Imperialism: Nonwhites in Occupied Territories

## The Conquest of the United States by Spain (1899)

### *William Graham Sumner*

William Graham Sumner (1840–1910) was a leading advocate of laissez-faire economics and opponent of socialism. As an academic, Professor Sumner

(Yale University) made important contributions to sociology and wrote on topics ranging from economics to foreign policy. He was a superb polemicist who took part in the great debates of his day. Sumner rejected "natural rights" but espoused other classical liberal values. For example, he opposed the Spanish-American War and the U.S. acquisition of colonies (Philippines, Puerto Rico, Guam). In this speech, delivered at the end of the war, Sumner warned Americans not to create an empire. Sumner's address was in keeping with the classical liberal belief in nonaggression and liberty: "leaving people to live out their own lives in their own way." The following excerpts compare the oppression of non-whites, who are to be "civilized," and the plight of blacks, Indians, and Chinese in America.

℘

There is not a civilized nation which does not talk about its civilizing mission just as grandly as we do. . . . We assume that what we like and practice, and what we think better, must come as a welcome blessing to Spanish-Americans and Philippinos. This is grossly and obviously untrue. They hate our ways. They are hostile to our ideas. Our religion, language, institutions and manners offend them. They like their own ways, and if we appear amongst them as rulers, there will be social discord on all the great departments of social interest. The most important thing which we shall inherit from the Spaniards will be the task of suppressing rebellions. . . . Now, the great reason why all these enterprises which begin by saying to somebody else: We know what is good for you, better than you know yourself, and we are going to make you do it—are false and wrong, is that they violate liberty; or, to turn the same statement into other words: the reason why liberty, of which we Americans talk so much, is a good thing, is that it means leaving people to live out their own lives in their own way, while we do the same. If we believe in liberty, as an American principle, why do we not stand by it? . . .

The Americans have been committed from the outset to the doctrine that all men are equal. We have elevated it into an absolute doctrine as a part of the theory of our social and political fabric. It has always been a domestic dogma in spite of its absolute form, and as a domestic dogma it has always stood in glaring contradiction to the facts about Indians and negroes, and to our legislation about Chinamen. In its absolute form it must, of course, apply to Kanakas, Malays, Tagals and

Chinese just as much as to Yankees, Germans and Irish. It is an astonishing event that we have lived to see American arms carry this domestic dogma out where it must be tested in its application to uncivilized and half-civilized peoples. At the first touch of the test we throw the doctrine away and adopt the Spanish doctrine. We are told by all the imperialists that these people are not fit for liberty and self-government; that it is rebellion for them to resist our beneficence; that we must send fleets and armies to kill them if they do it; that we must devise a government for them and administer it ourselves. . . .

I submit that it is a strange incongruity to utter grand platitudes about the blessings of liberty, etc., etc., which we are going to impart to these people, and to begin by refusing to extend the Constitution over them, and still more, by throwing the Constitution into the gutter here at home. If you take away the Constitution, what is American liberty and all the rest? Nothing but a lot of phrases. . . .

. . . Three years ago we were on the verge of a law to keep immigrants out who were not good enough to be in with us. Now we are going to take in 8,000,000 barbarians and semi-barbarians, and we are paying $20,000,000 to get them. For thirty years the negro has been in fashion. He has had political value and has been petted. Now we have made friends with the Southerners. They and we are hugging each other. We are all united. The negro's day is over. He is out of fashion. We cannot treat him one way and the Malays, Tagals and Kanakas another way. A Southern senator two or three days ago thanked an expansionist senator from Connecticut for enunciating doctrines which proved that, for the last thirty years, the Southerners have been right all the time, and his inference was incontrovertible. So the "great principles" change all the time, or, what is far more important, the phrases change. Some go out of fashion; others come in, but the phrase-makers are with us all the time. . . . All the validity that the great principles ever had they have now. Anybody who ever candidly studied them and accepted them for no more than they were really worth can stand by them now as well as ever. The time when a maxim or principle is worth something is when you are tempted to violate it. . . .

. . . Worse still: Americans cannot assure life, liberty and the pursuit of happiness to negroes inside of the United States. When the negro postmaster's house was set on fire in the night in South Carolina, and not only he, but his wife and children, were murdered as they came out, and when, moreover, this incident passed without legal investigation or punishment, it was a bad omen for the extension of liberty, etc., etc., to Malays and Tagals by simply setting over them the American flag.

Source: William G. Sumner, "The Conquest of the United States by Spain," *Yale Law Journal* 8, no. 4 (1899): 172–73, 176, 180, 189–91.

## The Moro Massacre (1906)
### *Moorfield Storey*

Moorfield Storey (1845–1929) was founder of the Anti-Imperialist League and first president of the NAACP. As a staunch anti-imperialist, Storey defended the rights of those overseas as well as the rights of African Americans. Here he protests a massacre of six hundred men, women, and children in the Philippines. Foreshadowing arguments that would be made in the 1960s, Storey (as Sumner had done) links the plight of blacks with that of colored people abroad. Thus, Storey writes, "The spirit which slaughters brown men in Jolo is the spirit which lynches black men in the South."

ၹ

The island of Jolo is one of the smaller Philippine islands. . . . In a crater at the top of a steep mountain were gathered a body of Moros, or, as Gen. Wood in his official report says, the position was "defended by an invisible army of Moros." This place was attacked by our troops, and, to quote the official report, "all the defenders of the Moro stronghold were killed. Six hundred bodies were found on the field. * * * [asterisk ellipsis in the original] The action resulted in the extinction of a band of outlaws. . . ."

No prisoners were taken. No wounded remained alive when the conflict was over and 600 human beings were slain without mercy. Not even women and children in the villages were spared. Every American must regret deeply when any of our brave countrymen are killed or wounded, but that regret must be far greater when they are sent to their deaths for such work as this. . . .

What was their side of the story? No man lives to tell it. They have been exterminated. Is it possible that this is all the greatest and freest nation in the world, as we like to believe ourselves, can do for a people over whom we insist on extending our benevolent sway? . . .

The spirit which slaughters brown men in Jolo is the spirit which lynches black men in the South. When such crimes go unpunished, far more when the men who commit them are praised and rewarded, the youth of the country is taught an evil lesson. Race prejudice is strengthened and the love of justice, the corner-stone of free institutions, is weakened. When a man is lynched the community which tolerates the offence suffers more than the victim. When we honor brutality in our army we brutalize ourselves. Our colleges have failed if they have not taught a better civilization than this, our churches have failed if this is their Christianity.

Source: Moorfield Storey, "The Moro Massacre," *Public*, April 7, 1906, 15–16.

## American Indians:
## Freedom through Property Rights?

After military defeat and confinement to reservations, American Indians were effectively wards of the U.S. government. American voters became concerned with the cost, while humanitarians hoped to mainstream American Indians and set them on the path to citizenship. The Dawes Act (1887) was the most important measure committing the U.S. government to this policy of assimilation. Periodically amended, the Dawes Act remained in effect until 1934. The law divided up tribal lands and gave the property to individual Indians. This "allotment" policy assumed that private property ownership would turn Indians into capitalistic, patriotic American farmers. This and subsequent efforts at assimilation were dismal failures as unscrupulous whites took advantage of Indian poverty by purchasing their land cheaply and Native Americans faced difficulty adjusting to the new order. Corrupt government agents, aided by Congress, declared much of the Indian land to be "surplus," available for sale to non-Indians. Meanwhile, reformers lost interest in "Indian Emancipation." This tragic history illustrates that some classical liberal efforts at promoting racial freedom failed (whether *any* Indian policy could succeed is another matter). The 1885 report by the Indian commissioner captures well the philosophy driving Indian legislation.

☙

## Annual Report of Commissioner of Indian Affairs (1885)

Every Indian may own a homestead! For it will be his homestead if he takes land in severalty and dissolves the tribal relation. Contrast his situation with that of millions of white families in the country, to say nothing of the larger number of homeless people in the Old World, and of the negroes of the Southern States. What a heritage! A homestead [of] his own, with assistance by the Government to build houses and fences and open farms; with a fund preserved and guarded by the Government for years to assist in teaching him and his children the arts of civilization; with the title to the homestead held in trust for a generation, if need be, so as to protect him from the selfish greed and relentless grasp of the white man; with the means not only for material development and progress, but also for the liberal education of his children. . . .

When the farm and the school have become familiar institutions among the Indians, and reasonable time has intervened for the transition from barbarism or a semi-civilized state to one of civilization, then will the Indian be prepared to take upon himself the higher and more responsible duties and privileges which appertain to American citizenship. A wider and better knowledge of the English language among them is essential to their comprehension of the duties and obligations of citizenship. . . .

When this point in their upward progress has been attained they will be a part and parcel of the great brotherhood of American citizens, and the last chapter in the solution of the Indian problem will be written. After that we shall hear no more of the Indian as a separate and distinct race; we shall hear no more of him as a "ward of the nation"; but like the alien and the negro, who by our laws are admitted to the great family of American citizens, each individual must stand upon his own bottom, enjoying equal rights and bearing equal responsibilities. . . .

Speaking of losing his rights as an Indian if he should become a citizen, [one young Indian] says:

Lose my rights as an Indian! What are the rights that an Indian has? Is it the drawing of rations and beef every week? No, the Indians have no rights. Then how is it that I shall lose my Indian rights? Is it not the Government policy to abandon all this? Some of the good people do not want Indians to become citizens of the United States, because they want to treat them as separate nations. The negroes became citizens while they were just as ignorant as can be, even now. Why cannot the Indians be allowed citizenship? Free us from the rights of support and ignorance, and give us the rights of civilized citizenship. We are bound to be citizens, and why not now?

Source: U.S. Department of the Interior, Office of Indian Affairs, *Annual Report of Commissioner of Indian Affairs to the Secretary of the Interior for the Year 1885* (Washington, DC: GPO, 1885), v–vii.

### The Dawes Law: Indian Emancipation Act? (1887)

*U.S. Congress*

Be it enacted . . . That in all cases where any tribe or band of Indians has been, or shall hereafter be, located upon any reservation created for their use . . . , the President of the United States [is authorized] . . . to allot the lands in said reservation in severalty to any Indian located thereon in quantities as follows:

To each head of a family, one-quarter of a section;

To each single person over eighteen years of age, one-eighth of a section;

To each orphan child under eighteen years of age, one-eighth of a section; and

To each other single person under eighteen years [of age]. . . , one-sixteenth of a section. . . .

Sec. 6. . . . And every Indian born within the territorial limits of the United States to whom allotments shall have been made . . . , and every Indian born within the territorial limits of the United States who has voluntarily taken up, within said limits, his residence separate and apart from any tribe of Indians therein, and has adopted the habits of civilized life, is hereby declared to be a citizen of the United States.

Source: *U.S. Statutes at Large*, vol. 24 (1887), 388–90.

## Black and White: Justice Delayed and Denied

### God Almighty Made But One Race (1884)

*Frederick Douglass*

Frederick Douglass's marriage to a white woman stirred controversy among blacks and whites alike. In an interview with the *Washington Post*, Douglass denied that he was a member of any race based upon skin color; rather, he belonged to the only race that God had made: the human race

ↇ

"The opinion has been expressed," said THE POST, "that the colored people, who look to you as a leader, will consider your position in the light of your present action, as equivocal."

"I do not presume to be a leader," answered Mr. Douglass, "but if I have advocated the cause of the colored people it is not because I am a negro, but because I am a man. The same impulse which would move me to jump into the water to save a white child from drowning, causes me to espouse the cause of the downtrodden and oppressed wherever I find them. Mr. Lincoln and Mr. Sumner were leaders of the colored people, far greater than I, an humble citizen, can ever hope to be. They were both white men. . . .

"All this excitement, then, is caused by my marriage with a woman a few shades lighter then myself. If I had married a black woman there would have been nothing said about it. Yet the disparity in our complexions would have been the same. I am not an African, as may be seen from my features and hair, and it is equally easy to discern that I am not a Caucasian. There are many colored ladies of my acquaintance who are as good as I, and who are a great deal better educated, yet, in affairs of this nature, who is to decide the why and the wherefore. . . ."

"I conceive," said he in conclusion, "that there is no division of races. God Almighty made but one race. I adopt the theory that in time the varieties of races will be blended into one. Let us look back when the black and the white people were distinct in this country. In two hundred and fifty years there has grown up a million of intermediate. And this will continue. You may say that Frederick Douglass considers himself a member of the one race which exists. "

Source: Frederick Douglass, "Mr. Douglass Interviewed" *Washington Post*, January 26, 1884, 1.

## The Silent South (1885)

*George Washington Cable*

George Washington Cable (1844–1925) was the son of slaveholders, veteran of the Confederate army, author of acclaimed southern fiction, and a passionate civil rights activist. Such were the fascinating apparent contradictions of a man rated one of the world's great authors in his time (best known for the novel *Grandissimes* and the short stories *Old Creole Days*). Cable was a "southern heretic," one of those "round pegs who did not fit the square holes of what white Southerners were thought to be."[2] At the peak of his literary career, Cable launched a one-man campaign to publicize the plight of southern blacks, urging the "best people," the "enlightened minority" of the South to speak out against the rising tide of racial hatred.

Cable outraged white southerners by publishing a penetrating analysis of race relations, *The Silent South, Together with the Freedman's Case in Equity and the Convict Lease System* (1885). He then went on speaking tours throughout the region. "Compulsory reconstruction" was at an end, Cable argued, and now "voluntary reconstruction is on trial." It was up to the South to get its racially divided house in order. Cable rejected the arguments of those who blamed the Ku Klux Klan, lynching, and Jim Crow on "feelings engendered by the war." Long before the war, southern whites had treated blacks as "aliens" and "brutes." In fact, contrary to neo-Confederate mythology, the "tyrannous sentiments of the old regime" stood in the way of southern progress.

One can imagine the fury sparked by Cable's "heretical ideas on the race issue."[3] Cable even advocated racially integrated schools, which he saw work in practice, not merely theory. No longer welcome in the South, Cable relocated to Northampton, Massachusetts, where he started the Open Letter Club, a correspondence network that aimed to identify members of the "Silent South" who wanted change but had hitherto been "silent." The club was short lived as correspondents reported the dangers they faced if they spoke out against the demagogic race-baiting politicians who ruled the New South. One letter writer from the University of Texas wrote: "If I open my mouth it means decapitation, and the warning axe hangs ready."[4] The Silent South, then, remained silent.

In *The Silent South*, excerpted below, Cable asked, "Must such men [demagogic race baiters], such acts [of violence], such sentiments [of hatred] stand alone to represent us of the South before an enlightened world?" The unfortunate answer was yes.

ᘓᕼᘐ

The late Southern slave has within two decades risen from slavery to freedom, from freedom to citizenship, passed on into political ascendancy, and fallen again from that eminence. The amended Constitution holds him up in his new political rights as well as a mere constitution can. On the other hand, certain enactments of Congress, trying to reach further, have lately been made void by the highest court of the nation. And another thing has happened. The popular mind in the old free States, weary of strife at arm's length, bewildered by its complications, vexed by many a blunder, eager to turn to the cure of other evils, and even tinctured by that race feeling whose grosser excesses it would so gladly see suppressed, has retreated from its uncomfortable dictational attitude and thrown the whole matter over to the States of the South. . . .

First, then, what are these sentiments [hostile to the Negro]? Foremost among them stands the idea that he is of necessity an alien. He was brought to our shores a naked, brutish, unclean, captive, pagan savage, to be and remain a kind of connecting link between man and the beasts of burden. The great changes to result from his contact with a superb race of masters were not taken into account. As a social factor he was intended to be as purely zero as the brute at the other end of his plow-line. The occasional mingling of his blood with that of the white man worked no change in the sentiment; one, two, four, eight, multiplied upon or divided into zero, still gave zero for the result. Generations of American nativity made no difference; his children and children's children were born in sight of our door, yet the old notion held fast. He increased to vast numbers, but it never wavered. He accepted our dress, language, religion, all the fundamentals of our civilization, and became forever expatriated from his own land; still he remained, to us, an alien. . . .

Yet it was found not enough. The slave multiplied. Slavery was a dangerous institution. Few in the South today have any just idea how often the slave plotted for his freedom. Our Southern ancestors were a noble, manly people, springing from some of the most highly intelligent, aspiring, upright, and refined nations of the modern world; from the Huguenot, the French Chevalier, the Old Englander, the New Englander. Their acts were not always right; whose are? But for their peace of mind they had to believe them so. They therefore spoke much of the negro's contentment with that servile condition for which nature had designed him. Yet there was no escaping the knowledge that we dared not trust the slave caste with any power that could be withheld from them. So the perpetual alien was made also a perpetual menial, and the belief became fixed that this, too, was nature's decree, not ours. . . .

It is the fashion to say we paused to let the "feelings engendered by the war" pass away, and that they are passing. But let not these truths lead us into error. The sentiments we have been analyzing, and upon which we saw the old compulsory reconstruction go hard aground—these are not the "feelings engendered by the war." We must disentangle them from the "feelings engendered by the war," and by reconstruction. They are older than either. But for them slavery would have perished of itself, and emancipation and reconstruction been peaceful revolutions. . . .

Thus we reach the ultimate question of fact. Are the freedman's liberties suffering any real abridgment? The answer is easy. The letter of the laws, with a few exceptions, recognizes him as entitled to every right of an American citizen; and to some it may seem unimportant that there is scarcely one public relation of life in the South where he is not arbitrarily and unlawfully compelled to hold toward the white man the attitude of an alien, a menial, and a probable reprobate, by reason of his race and color. One of the marvels of future history will be that it was counted a small matter. . . .

Suppose, for a moment, the tables turned. Suppose the courts of our Southern States, while changing no laws requiring the impaneling of jurymen without distinction as to race, etc., should suddenly begin to draw their thousands of jurymen all black, and well-nigh every one of them counting not only himself, but all his race, better than any white man. Assuming that their average of intelligence and morals should be not below that of jurymen as now drawn, would a white man, for all that, choose to be tried in one of those courts? Would he suspect nothing? Could one persuade him that his chances of even justice were all they should be, or all they would be were the court not evading the law in order to sustain an outrageous distinction against him because of the accidents of his birth? Yet only read white man for black man, and black man for white man, and that I speak as an eye-witness has been the practice for years, and is still so today. . . .

In this and other practices the outrage falls upon the freedman. Does it stop there? Far from it. It is the first premise of American principles that whatever elevates the lower stratum of the people lifts all the rest, and whatever holds it down holds all down. For twenty years, therefore, the nation has been working to elevate the freedman. It counts this one of the great necessities of the hour. It has poured out its wealth publicly and privately for this purpose. It is confidently hoped that it will soon bestow a royal gift of millions for the reduction of the illiteracy so largely shared by the blacks. . . . All this and much more has been or is being done in order that, for the good of himself and everybody else in the land, the colored man may be elevated as quickly as possible from all the debasements of slavery and semi-slavery to the full stature and integrity of citizenship. And it is in the face of all this that the adherent of the old regime stands in the way to every public privilege and place—steamer landing, railway platform, theatre, concert-hall, art display, public library, public school, courthouse, church, everything flourishing the hot brand-ing-iron of ignominious distinctions. He forbids the freedman to go into the water until he is satisfied that he knows how to swim, and for fear he should learn hangs mill-stones about his neck. This is what we are told is a small matter that will settle itself. Yes, like a roosting curse, until the outraged intelligence of the South lifts its indignant protest against this stupid firing into our own ranks.

I say the outraged intelligence of the South; for there are thousands of South-ern-born white men and women, in the minority in all these places in churches, courts, schools, libraries, theatres, concert-halls, and on steamers and railway car-riages, who see the wrong and folly of these things, silently blush for them, and withhold their open protests only because their belief is unfortunately stronger in the futility of their counsel than in the power of a just cause. I do not justify their silence; but I affirm their sincerity and their goodly numbers. Of late years, when condemning these evils from the platform in Southern towns, I have repeatedly found that those who I had earlier been told were the men and women in whom the community placed most confidence and pride—they were the ones who, when I had spoken, came forward with warmest hand-grasps and expressions of thanks, and pointedly and cordially justified my every utterance. And were they the young South? Not by half. The gray-beards of the old times have always been among them, saying in effect, not by any means as converts, but as fellow-discoverers, "Whereas we were blind, now we see. . . ."

What need to say more? The question is answered. Is the freedman a free man? No. . . . The South stands on her honor before the clean equities of the issue. It is no longer whether constitutional amendments, but whether the eternal principles of justice, are violated. And the answer must—it shall—come from the South. . . . But, as I have said over and over to my brethren in the South, I take upon me to say again here, that there is a moral and intellectual intelligence there which is not going to be much longer beguiled out of its moral right of way by questions of political punctilio, but will seek that plane of universal justice and equity which it is every people's duty before God to seek, not along the line of politics—but across it and across it and across it as many times as it may lie across the path, until the whole people of every once slave-holding State can stand up as one man, saying, "Is the freedman a free man?," and the whole world shall answer, "Yes."

Source: George Washington Cable, *The Silent South, Together with the Freedman's Case in Equity and the Convict Lease System* (New York: C. Scribner's Sons, 1885), 2, 6–7, 9, 13–14, 16–21, 25, 36–38.

## Slavery by Another Name (1888)

### Frederick Douglass

Late in life, Frederick Douglass cried out against the disfranchisement of southern blacks. In the following speech, Douglass notes how one-party Democratic rule left southern blacks victims of unjust laws and insecure property rights: "In law, free; in fact, a slave." Douglass demanded a Republican Party platform committed to honest elections in the South. The GOP followed through with a last-ditch effort to pass a Federal Elections Bill (1890). Douglass and the old guard of Republican civil rights activists knew that a solid Democratic South was bad for America and also bad for the GOP (see "Federal Elections Bill" below). On the issue of economic progress, Douglass was far more optimistic five years later (see "Self-Made Men" below). Economic historians also note the gains made by black farmers despite the odds against them.[5] Nevertheless, the need for political freedom to secure economic liberty was too obvious to ignore.

∾

Do you ask a more particular answer to the question of why the negro of the plantation has made so little progress, why his cupboard is empty, why he flutters in rags, why his children run naked and his wife is barefooted and hides herself behind the hut when a stranger is passing? I will tell you. It is because the husband

and father is systematically and almost universally cheated out of his hard earnings. The same person that once extorted his labor under the lash now extorts it by a mean, fraudulent device, which is more effective than the lash. That device is the trucking system, a system which never permits him to see or to save a dollar of his hard earnings. He struggles from year to year, but like a man in a morass, the more he struggles the deeper he sinks. The highest wages paid him are eight dollars a month, and this he receives only in orders on a store, which, in many cases, is owned by his employer. This scrip has a purchasing power on that one store, and that one store only. A blind man can see that the laborer is, by this arrangement, bound hand and foot, and is completely in the power of his employer, who can charge the poor fellow just what he pleases and give them what kind of goods he pleases, he does both. . . .

But this is not the only evil or the greatest involved in this Satanic arrangement. It promotes dishonesty. It promotes theft. The negro sees himself paid but limited wages—far too limited to support himself and family, and that, too, is in worthless scrip; he sees himself grossly defrauded on it, and he is tempted to fight the devil with fire, and gets the worst of it every time. Finding himself systematically robbed, he takes his revenge by stealing a pig, or a chicken, or a bushel of corn—finds himself in the hands of the law, his liberty, such as it is, taken from him, and himself put to work for years in a chain-gang; and he comes out, if he ever lives to get out, a ruined man, broken in body, soul and spirit. . . .

I come now to another feature of Southern policy which bears hard upon and heavily on the negro laborer and land renter. It is found in the landlord and tenant laws of the South. I will read an extract or two from these laws, that you may see how completely and rigidly the rights of the landlords are guarded and how entirely the tenant is in the clutches of the landlord. [Douglass reads from various laws.] . . .

Again, let us see what are the relations subsisting between the negro in the state and national governments. What support, what assistance, aye, what protection, has he received from either of them? Take his relation to the National Government, and we shall find him a deserted, a defrauded, a swindled outcast; in law, free; in fact, a slave; in law, a citizen; in fact, an alien; in law, a voter; in fact, a disfranchised man. In law, his color is no barrier against him; in fact, his color exposes him to be treated as a criminal. Towards him every attribute of a just government is contradicted and withheld. . . .

But there are many other reasons for the condition of the freedmen, and why the old masters of the South should be well satisfied with the present state of things. It not only gives them all the power they want over the negro, but gives them increased power over the North and the Nation. Where before they had only an apportionment of three-fifths power of representation in Congress and the Electoral College, then now have five-fifths. By suppressing the Republican vote and counting the colored citizens in the basis of representation, they now have a decided advantage over the Northern people. . . .

On the other hand, if the default is not in the structure of the Government, but in the treachery and indifference of those who administer it, the American people owe it to themselves, owe it to the world and to the Negro to sweep from place in power those who are thus derelict in the discharge of their duty, and to see that no men shall hereafter take their places in the Government, who will not enforce the Constitutional rights of every class of American citizens.

I am a Republican. I believe in the Republican party. My political hopes for the future of the colored race are centered in the character and composition, and the wisdom and justice, in the courage and fidelity of the Republican party. I am unable to see how an honest and intelligent colored man can be a Democrat, or play fast and loose between the two parties. But, while I am a Republican and believe in the party, I dare to tell that party the truth. In my judgment it can no longer repose on the history of its grand and magnificent achievements. . . .

[The Republican Party] must not stand still or take any step backward. Its mission is to lead, not to follow; to make circumstances, not to be made by them. It is held and firmly bound by every sentiment of justice and honor to make a living fact of the now dead letter of the Constitutional Amendments. It must make the path of the black citizen to the ballot-box as safe and smooth as is the path of the white citizen in the same place. . . .

If it fails to do all this, it will utterly fail to deserve the support of honest men. The supreme moment of the Republican party is at hand. The question "to be or not to be," will be decided in Chicago, and I reverently trust in Providence that it may be decided rightly. If the platform it shall adopt shall be in accordance with the earlier antecedents; if the party shall have the courage in its maturity which it possessed in its infancy; if it shall express the determination to vindicate the honor and integrity of the Republic, by stamping out the fraud, injustice and violence which make the elections in the South a farce, a disgrace and scandal to the Republic, and shall place on that platform a man with a clear head and a heroic heart, the country will triumphantly elect him. . . .

I am, however, not here to name men [after mentioning Justice John Marshall Harlan favorably as a possible presidential candidate. See Harlan entry below]. My mission now, as all along, during nearly fifty years, is to plead the cause of the dumb millions of my countrymen, and to hasten the day when the principles of liberty and humanity expressed in the Declaration of Independence and the Constitution of the United States shall be the law and practice of every section and for all the people of this great country, without regard to race, color, sex or religion.

Source: Frederick Douglass, "Article Delivered on the 26th Anniversary of the Abolition of Slavery in the District of Columbia," 1888, Frederick Douglass Papers, Manuscript Division, Library of Congress, Washington, DC, http:// memory.loc.gov/ammem/doughtml/dougFolder5.html (accessed July 1, 2008).

## The Federal Elections Bill (1890, 1891)

### George Hoar

After Reconstruction, Republicans accused Democrats of stealing elections through vote fraud in the North and the disfranchisement of African Americans in the South. Frederick Douglass had agitated for fair elections (see above), and the Republican Party platform of 1888 pledged support for a federal election bill to restore voting rights: "We hold the free and honest popular ballot and the just and equal representation of all the people to be the foundation of our Republican government and demand effective legislation to secure the integrity and purity of elections, which are the fountains of all public authority. We charge that the present Administration and the Democratic majority in Congress owe their existence to the suppression of the ballot by a criminal nullification of the Constitution and laws of the United States."[6]

Republican disenchantment with election fraud resulted in the failed Federal Election Bill of 1890, one of the most hotly contested voting rights bills in U.S. history. The House passed the bill, but it died upon Democratic filibuster in the Senate. According to historian Thomas Upchurch, "the Federal Elections Bill debate captivated the American public like few other congressional debates had done."[7] The grand irony is that House sponsor Henry Cabot Lodge proposed literacy tests as a fair way to weed out "unfit" voters, thus inspiring Mississippi and other southern states to adopt such measures and then enforce them unevenly against blacks and whites. The failure of the bill also meant that southern racists felt free of outside intervention as the Republican Party lost interest in the race issue. Lynchings bloodied southern soil, and the states adopted segregation statutes. As Senator Ben Tillman (D-SC) put it, "We took the government away. We stuffed ballot boxes. We shot them. We are not ashamed of it."[8] Tillman and others even had the support of the *New York Times* for repealing the Fifteenth Amendment. The *Times* charged that "the Republican Party committed a great public crime when it gave the right of suffrage to the blacks." Repealing the amendment would be "the just remedy, a proper reparation for a great wrong."[9]

By gambling for racial freedom—and losing—the civil rights activists left an unexpected legacy. Subsequent civil rights history would have been different had this law passed. The following documents offer contemporary reflections on the bill's defeat by Senate sponsor George Hoar (R-MA), an abolitionist, longtime civil rights advocate, and, like many classical liberals, anti-imperialist.

ᘓ

### Senate Speech (1890)

This bill undertakes to defend the Constitution of the United States against an attempt to overthrow it by depriving the majority of the people of their right honestly and freely to elect Representatives in the other House of Congress, and by substituting for such election processes of fraud, intimidation, and bribery. . . .

It is said that this measure imputes dishonor to one part of the country. I shall show presently that it takes for granted no condition of fact there which its own authorities and leaders have not again and again declared to exist. But it strikes at evil in all parts of the country alike. . . .

Mr. President, this is not a question of the domination of a negro majority over you; it is the question of the domination of a white man's minority over us that we are called upon by a just regard to our own rights and for constitutional liberty to consider. . . .

. . . If you can vote to occupy the rest of the session with public buildings, you can vote to occupy the rest of the session with the rights of American citizens. If you can vote that the expenditure for post-offices and custom-houses shall be in some measure equal in the different parts of the country, you can vote, if you care to, that a white man in Maine or in Kansas shall count at least a quarter part as much as a white man in Georgia or Alabama.

### The Fate of the Election Bill (1891)

The keynote of every Republican platform, the principle of every Republican union, is found in its respect for the dignity of the individual man. Until that shall become the pervading principle of the Republic, from Canada to the Gulf, from the Atlantic to the Pacific, our mission will not be ended. . . .

I believe that the great bulk of the business men of the North are, upon this question, sound to the core. I believe that they prefer liberty and honesty to ease and wealth. I believe that the great body of reformers and lovers of pure government in this land are to be found in the ranks of the Republican Party. But the overthrow of constitutional government in this country is due to the defection of the classes to which I have referred. . . .

Do they think, when they have introduced in the United States a clipped Constitution, a clipped manhood, a clipped suffrage, and a debased franchise, that clipped coinage and debased currency will not follow? . . .

While the suffrage is violated or debauched, no interest of the country is safe. If injustice lies at the foundation of our political power, justice will not long be found anywhere. The pestilence which has its origin in the hovel, fills the palace also with mourning. Where the poor man is deprived of his vote, the wealth of the rich man loses its value. The peaceful remedy which has just been defeated would have saved many a disaster that is to fall most heavily on the men upon whose blindness, or indifference, or cowardice, rests the blame of this defeat. The question will not down. Nothing is settled that is not right.

Sources: George Hoar, "Shall the Senate Keep Faith with the People?" Speech in
the Senate of the United States, Washington, n.p., August 20, 1890, 4–5, 10,

12–13, 17–18, 20; George F. Hoar, "The Fate of the Election Bill," *Forum*, April 1891, 127.

## Self-Made Men (1893)

### Frederick Douglass

This popular address echoed the self-made man gospel of the late nineteenth century. Douglass gave the speech scores of times between 1859 and 1893. "Self-Made Men" foreshadows the self-help message of Booker T. Washington. Indeed, Douglass once gave this speech at Washington's Tuskegee Institute. Also like Washington, Douglass sided with employers over racist unions, publishing editorials such as "The Folly, Tyranny, and Wickedness of Labor Unions" (1874).[10] Together with the Booker T. Washington documents (below), the following Douglass entry debunks the notion that self-help was inconsistent with action against injustice: Frederick Douglass, the consummate protester, was an advocate of self-help, just as Booker T. Washington protested injustice while advocating self-reliance. In this entry, Douglass emphasizes the work ethic but also demands justice: "Give the negro fair play and let him alone. . . . [But] do him justice in the present. Throw open to him the doors of the schools, the factories, the workshops, and of all mechanical industries." Douglass demanded secure property rights *and* opportunity, for these formed the bases of political and economic freedom. Booker T. Washington echoes these dual themes of justice and self-help (see entries below).

༒

It will be evident that, allowing only ordinary ability and opportunity, we may explain success mainly by one word and that word is WORK! WORK!! WORK!!! WORK!!!! Not transient and fitful effort, but patient, enduring, honest, unremitting and indefatigable work, into which the whole heart is put, and which, in both temporal and spiritual affairs, is the true miracle worker. Every one may avail himself of this marvelous power, if he will. . . . He who does not think himself worth saving from poverty and ignorance, by his own efforts, will hardly be thought worth the efforts of anybody else.

The lesson taught at this point by human experience is simply this, that the man who will get up will be helped up; and that the man who will not get up will be allowed to stay down. This rule may appear somewhat harsh, but in its general application and operation it is wise, just and beneficent. I know of no other rule which can be substituted for it without bringing social chaos. Personal independence is a virtue and it is the soul out of which comes the sturdiest manhood. But there can be no independence without a large share of self-dependence, and this virtue cannot be bestowed. It must be developed from within.

I have been asked "How will this theory affect the negro?" and "What shall be done in his case?" My general answer is "Give the negro fair play and let him alone. If he lives, well. If he dies, equally well. If he cannot stand up, let him fall down. . . ."

The nearest approach to justice to the negro for the past is to do him justice in the present. Throw open to him the doors of the schools, the factories, the workshops, and of all mechanical industries. For his own welfare, give him a chance to do whatever he can do well. If he fails then, let him fail! I can, however, assure you that he will not fail. Already has he proven it. As a soldier he proved it. He has since proved it by industry and sobriety and by the acquisition of knowledge and property. He is almost the only successful tiller of the soil of the South, and is fast becoming the owner of land formerly owned by his old master and by the old master class.

Source: Frederick Douglass, *Self-Made Men* (Carlisle, PA: Indian Print, 1893), 14–20.

### *Our Constitution Is Color-blind:* Plessy v. Ferguson *(1896)*

#### *John Marshall Harlan*

The disfranchisement of black voters (nearly all Republican) left the southern wing of the Democratic Party free to pass laws separating the two races wherever they might come into close contact: railroad cars, schools, public restrooms, restaurants, hotels, and so on. To get around the equal protection promised by the Fourteenth Amendment, the segregation laws adopted a "separate but equal" doctrine—the races might be separate, but their public accommodations and schools were theoretically equal. This was a fiction in the racist South, but it provided a constitutional defense.

When Louisiana enacted a law separating whites and "colored" on railroad cars, those opposed to the measure set up a test case. Homer Plessy (1858?–1925), a biracial man who was seven-eighths white and one-eighth black, tried to board a whites-only railroad car. Arrested for violating the law, Plessy fought and lost in the lower courts. Renowned lawyer Albion Tourgée appealed Plessy's case to the U.S. Supreme Court. The Court majority ruled that "separate but equal" laws did not violate the equal protection clause of the Fourteenth Amendment. This decision spurred the passage of more segregation measures, including the resegregation of the federal government under President Woodrow Wilson (1913).

Justice John Marshall Harlan (1833–1911) was a former slave owner turned civil rights champion. His dissent from the Plessy decision inspired later generation of civil rights lawyers and unites many of the documents in this reader.[11] An aide to NAACP lawyer Thurgood Marshall recalled: "Marshall had a 'Bible' to which he turned during his most depressed moments. . . . Marshall would read aloud passages from Harlan's amazing dissent. I do not believe we ever filed a major brief in the pre-Brown days in which a portion of that opinion was not quoted. Marshall's favorite quotation was, 'Our Constitution is color-blind.' It became our basic creed."[12]

℃℈

Mr. Justice BROWN, after stating the facts . . . , delivered the opinion of the court. . . .

A statute which implies merely a legal distinction between the white and colored races—a distinction which is founded in the color of the two races, and which must always exist so long as white men are distinguished from the other race by color—has no tendency to destroy the legal equality of the two races, or re-establish a state of involuntary servitude. . . .

So far, then, as a conflict with the fourteenth amendment is concerned, the case reduces itself to the question whether the statute of Louisiana is a reasonable regulation, and with respect to this there must necessarily be a large discretion on the part of the legislature. . . .

We consider the underlying fallacy of the plaintiff's argument to consist in the assumption that the enforced separation of the two races stamps the colored race with a badge of inferiority. If this be so, it is not by reason of anything found in the act, but solely because the colored race chooses to put that construction upon it. . . . The argument also assumes that social prejudices may be overcome by legislation, and that equal rights cannot be secured to the negro except by an enforced commingling of the two races. . . . If the civil and political rights of both races be equal, one cannot be inferior to the other civilly or politically. If one race be inferior to the other socially, the constitution of the United States cannot put them upon the same plane. . . .

Mr. Justice HARLAN dissenting. . . .

In respect of civil rights, common to all citizens, the constitution of the United States does not, I think, permit any public authority to know the race of those entitled to be protected in the enjoyment of such rights. Every true man has pride of race, and under appropriate circumstances, when the rights of others, his equals before the law, are not to be affected, it is his privilege to express such pride and to take such action based upon it as to him seems proper. But I deny that any legislative body or judicial tribunal may have regard to the race of citizens when the civil rights of those citizens are involved. . . .

The fundamental objection, therefore, to the statute, is that it interferes with the personal freedom of citizens. "Personal liberty," it has been well said, "consists in the power of locomotion, of changing situation, or removing one's person to whatsoever places one's own inclination may direct, without imprisonment or restraint, unless by due course of law." If a white man and a black man choose to occupy the same public conveyance on a public highway, it is their right to do so; and no government, proceeding alone on grounds of race, can prevent it without infringing the personal liberty of each. . . .

If a state can prescribe, as a rule of civil conduct, that whites and blacks shall not travel as passengers in the same railroad coach, why may it not so regulate the use of the streets of its cities and towns as to compel white citizens to keep on one side of a street, and black citizens to keep on the other? Why may it not, upon like grounds, punish whites and blacks who ride together in street cars or in open vehicles on a public road or street? Why may it not require sheriffs to assign whites to one side of a court room, and blacks to the other? And why may it not also prohibit the commingling of the two races in the galleries of legislative halls or in public assemblages convened for the consideration of the political questions of the day? Further, if this statute of Louisiana is consistent with the personal liberty of citizens, why may not the state require the separation in railroad coaches of native and naturalized citizens of the United States, or of Protestants and Roman Catholics? . . .

The white race deems itself to be the dominant race in this country. And so it is, in prestige, in achievements, in education, in wealth, and in power. So, I doubt not, it will continue to be for all time, if it remains true to its great heritage, and holds fast to the principles of constitutional liberty. But in view of the constitution, in the eye of the law, there is in this country no superior, dominant, ruling class of citizens. There is no caste here. Our constitution is color-blind, and neither knows nor tolerates classes among citizens. In respect of civil rights, all citizens are equal before the law. The humblest is the peer of the most powerful. . . .

In my opinion, the judgment this day rendered will, in time, prove to be quite as pernicious as the decision made by this tribunal in the Dred Scott Case. . . .

The arbitrary separation of citizens, on the basis of race, while they are on a public highway, is a badge of servitude wholly inconsistent with the civil freedom and the equality before the law established by the constitution. It cannot be justified upon any legal grounds. . . .

Source: *Plessy v. Ferguson*, 163 U.S. 537 (1896). Internal case citations have been omitted.

### Streetcar Company Opposes Segregation (1898, 1900)

This incident illustrates the "economics of discrimination"—the notion that business owners and employers have an incentive to hire the best employees and sell to all customers, regardless of race, and that racial discrimination is most effective when backed by state power. This theory permeates classical liberal thought and is present in Booker T. Washington's cautiously optimistic view that economics would "out" in the end: "there is little race prejudice in the American dollar."[13] Realism led Washington, Frederick Douglass, and Kelly Miller (below) to side with capital against labor, since labor unions refused to admit black members. The philanthropy of Julius Rosenwald and other wealthy capitalists further persuaded civil rights activists that the upper class was friendlier to African Americans. (On the construction of 5,500 Rosenwald schools for poor blacks in the South, see Peter Ascoli's biography of Rosenwald).[14]

While this episode was not *necessarily* representative of the "business community," it provides another way of examining the relationship between capitalism and race. In truth, there was never a free market operating so that capitalist forces *might* undermine racism, according to classical liberal theory. However, when state coercion did not prevent competition, the free market often worked in favor of blacks and immigrants. Several scholars have demonstrated how business and business-friendly courts undermined racism, but more research needs to be done.[15] The problem is that historians have started from a capitalism-causes-racism perspective and not considered alternative viewpoints.

In "The Political Economy of Segregation: The Case of Segregated Streetcars," economist Jennifer Roback offers a fascinating and provocative illustration of the "economics of discrimination."[16] Railway executives throughout the South opposed segregation because of the costs and trouble it imposed on their companies. This letter from the Augusta Railway and Electric Company lawyer illustrates a typical defense against enforcing an ordinance that mandated segregation on streetcars.

℘

1898

Col. D. B. Dyer. President Augusta Railway Company:

Dear Sir:—I beg to call your attention to the law requiring street railway companies to furnish separate transportation for white people and negroes. The commissioners of the village of Summerville beg that you will give this your attention at once, as the matter is specially urgent at this time. Yours respectfully.

T. I. HICKMAN,

Chairman Police Commission, Village of Summerville

[The president of Augusta Railway delayed, stating, "I know of no such law," but the village forced the company to post the following sign.]

"Notice to Conductors and Motormen:

All conductors, or other employees in charge of cars, are hereby required to assign all passengers to seats on the cars under their charge so as to separate the white and colored races as much as practicable.

This is in accordance with the law of the state; and the same law empowers you with police authority to carry out the above provision. You are therefore hereby directed to observe the above instructions so far as it is possible under all the circumstances to do so."

### 1900

Apparently, the company did not enforce the rule until two years later, after a black man allegedly murdered a white man on a streetcar.[17] A mob lynched the black man and cried for strict enforcement of the segregation law. Still, the streetcar company resisted, as evidenced by the following letter from Augusta Railway lawyer Boykin Wright to the village police commissioner stating the hardships such a rule imposed on the company and its customers.

ᘒ

May 18th 1900.

Hon. Tracy I. Hickman, Intendant of the Village of Summerville, City.

Dear Sir:—In the absence of Col. Dyer in New York, your letter of May 17th on the subject of the separation of the races in the street cars, has been referred to me for reply. . . .

As stated in my letter to the city attorney of Augusta, "the purpose of the Railway company is to meet every reasonable demand of the people, along the line of the proposed ordinance. The company shares with me the desire to do all in its power to win and deserve the good will of all our citizens, and to preserve harmony and amity between the races. If the city council and the village authorities will aid the Railway company in carrying out this or similar ordinances, the Railway company will do its part in trying to solve the difficult question in hand."

Every thoughtful man, certainly every deliberative body, called upon to consider this question will realize the difficulties presented, not only to the Railway company, but to the traveling public, in reaching a practical solution of the question. Travel is not uniform. Congestion at times is inevitable. The hauling of empty cars is expensive. Street transportation must be prompt and rapid. Delays are insufferable to the busy man. To haul regularly two cars over the broad expanse of sparsely settled territory covered by the lines of this Railway company in Augusta would be to nearly double the cost of transportation, and would be impracticable, and unreasonable, and, so far as we know, unprecedented. To know at all times when one car will be filled, or, when two will be required, would be to possess the powers of prophesy.

A passenger hurrying from his home to his business at a remote point would deem it intolerable to be passed simply because the seats of the car are filled when plenty of standing room remains in the aisle or between the seats. The same is true of most other passengers, male and female, white and colored, seeking to meet appointments. What shall the Railway company do? When that question is answered fairly and justly the Railway company will cheerfully respond. The proposed ordinance is an attempt to meet the question. It is but tentative. Any suggestion will be welcome.

Very truly yours,

BOYKIN WRIGHT

ℰℑ

**Soon the pages of the *Augusta Chronicle* filled with letters from indignant citizens complaining of the rule and the unintended consequences of separating the races: no space for tired white workers at the end of the day, separation of traveling companions (male and female), and the commingling of lower classes with "proper ladies" forced to sit in a confined area for whites.[18] There was no better illustration of the costs imposed on voters resulting from their "taste for discrimination."**

Sources: "Color Line on Trolley Cars," *Augusta Chronicle*, August 31, 1898, 5; "Must Have Separate Cars," *Augusta Chronicle*, May 20, 1900, 13.

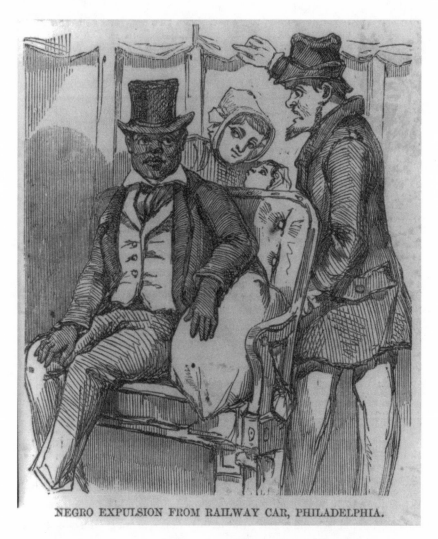

NEGRO EXPULSION FROM RAILWAY CAR, PHILADELPHIA.

"Negro Expulsion from Railway Car, Philadelphia." Segregation was an issue in the North and the South. Ultimately, the U.S. Supreme Court upheld streetcar segregation statutes in *Plessy v. Ferguson* (1896). (Library of Congress, Prints & Photographs Division, LC-USZ62–45698. This originally appeared in the *Illustrated London News* [1856].)

## Racism Corrupts Government (1898)

### Booker T. Washington

After the death of Frederick Douglass in 1895, Booker T. Washington became the most influential black leader in America until his own death in 1915. In *Up from Slavery* (1901), Washington recounted his rise from servitude to success. The book inspired many African Americans and white philanthropists with its message of hope based on self-help and self-made business success. As president of the National Negro Business League, Washington promoted the notion that markets were color-blind and capitalism was their best hope. Washington was right: southern blacks advanced further when marketplace competition prevailed than when state coercion blocked their chance to compete for jobs and business.[19]

Critics caricatured Washington as an "Uncle Tom" because he did not think the time was ripe for mass political agitation. Nevertheless, the "Wizard of Tuskegee" spoke out publicly against convict leasing and used his influence to get judges appointed who overturned peonage (debt slavery).[20] In *Bailey v. Alabama* (1908), the U.S. Supreme Court ruled that Alabama's peonage law was unconstitutional because it violated the Thirteenth Amendment ban on involuntary servitude. His 1912 magazine article "Is the Negro Having a Fair Chance?" answered in the negative.[21]

Washington addressed election fraud and inadequate schooling in the following letter to the Louisiana state constitutional convention. A loyal Republican, Washington placed many blacks in federal patronage jobs. Yet Washington recognized that this was not enough: without voting rights and an educated populace, both black and white, African Americans remained vulnerable to racist lawlessness.

ℭℌ

During the winter of 1898 a State Constitutional Convention assembled in New Orleans, La., for the purpose of passing a law which would result in disfranchising a large proportion of the Negro voters. Some of the members of the Convention were very anxious to pass a law that would result in the disfranchising of the Negro voters without disfranchising any portion of the whites. The passing of any such law seemed to me so manifestly unjust that I addressed an open letter to the Convention, which read as follows:

"To the Louisiana State Constitutional Convention:

. . . The Negro does not object to an education or property test, but let the law be so clear that no one clothed with State authority will be tempted to perjure and degrade himself, by putting one interpretation upon it for the white man and another for the black man. Study the history of the South, and you will find that where there has been the most dishonesty in the matter of voting, there you will find today the lowest moral condition of both races. First, there was the temptation to act wrongly with the Negro's ballot. From this it was an easy step to dishonesty with the white man's ballot, to the carrying of concealed weapons, to the murder of a Negro, and then to the murder of a white man and then to lynching. I entreat you not to pass such a law as will prove an eternal millstone about the neck of your children.

No man can have respect for government and officers of the law when he knows, deep down in his heart, that the exercise the franchise is tainted with fraud. . . .

I beg of you, further, that in the degree that you close the ballot box against the ignorant, you open the school house. More than one half of the people of your State are Negroes. No State can long prosper when a large percentage of its citizenship is in ignorance and poverty, and has no interest in government. . . . Let the very best educational opportunities be provided for both races; and add to this the enactment of an election law that shall be incapable of unjust discrimination, at the same time providing that in proportion as the ignorant secure education, property and character, they will be given the right of citizenship. . . ."

This letter was sent out through the Associated Press widely through the country. The leading papers of New Orleans as well as those in many other parts of the South indorsed my position editorially. The law that was finally passed by the Convention, while not as bad as when first presented, was not by any means the law that should have been enacted.

Source: Booker T. Washington, *The Story of My Life and Work* (Toronto: J. L. Nichols, 1901), 214–21.

## No Lynching Has an Excuse (1899, 1908, 1915)

*Booker T. Washington*

Washington also denounced lynching, which was the civil rights issue of the day. The following three editorials indicate how Washington became less accommodating and more strident in his criticism of those who did nothing to stop lynching.

છે

### 1899

Within a period of six years about 900 persons have been lynched in our Southern States. This is but a few hundred short of the total number of soldiers who lost their lives in Cuba during the Spanish-American war. If we would realize still more fully how far this unfortunate habit is leading us on, note the classes of crime, during a few months, which the local papers and Associated Press say that lynching has been inflicted for—they include "murder," "rioting," "incendiarism," "robbery," "larceny," "self-defense," "insulting women," "alleged stock poisoning," "malpractice," "alleged barn-burning," "suspected robbery," "race prejudice," "attempted murder," "horse stealing," and "mistaken identity," etc. . . .

The white man in the South has not only a serious duty and responsibility, but the Negro has a duty and responsibility in this matter. In speaking of my own people I want to be equally frank, but I speak with the greatest kindness. . . .

A large amount of the crime among us grows out of the idleness of our young men and women. It is for this reason that I have tried to insist upon some industry being taught in connection with their course of literary training. The time has come when every parent, every teacher and minister of the gospel, should teach with unusual emphasis morality and obedience to the law. . . .

. . . The Negro has among many of the Southern whites as good friends as he has anywhere in the world. These friends have not forsaken us. They will not do so; neither will our friends in the North. If we make ourselves intelligent, industrious, economical and virtuous, of value to the community in which we live, we can and will work out our own salvation right here in the South. In every community, by means of organized effort, we should seek in a manly and honorable way the

Booker T. Washington (1903). (Library of Congress, Prints & Photographs Division, LC-USZ62–49568.)

confidence, the co-operation, the sympathy of the best white people in the South and in our respective communities. With the best white people and the best black people standing together, in favor of law and order and justice, I believe that the safety and happiness of both races will be made secure.

### 1908

Within the past sixty days twenty-five Negroes have been lynched in different parts of the United States. . . .

One was publicly burned in open daylight in the presence of women and children, after oil had been poured upon his body, at Greenville, Tex., and reports state that a thousand people witnessed the spectacle in the open square of the town. One other victim was eighty years of age. How long can our Christian civilization stand this? . . .

It requires no courage for 500 men to tie the hands of an individual to the stake or to hang or shoot him. But young men and boys who have once witnessed or who have read in the papers of these exciting scenes of burnings and Lynches often get the idea that there is something heroic in attacking some individual in the community who is least able to defend himself. . . .

These lynches terrify the innocent, but they embolden the criminal. The criminal knows it is much easier to escape the mad fury of the mob than the deliberate vengeance of the law. But no man is so innocent that he can be safe at all times from the frenzy of the mob. . . .

Mob justice undermines the very foundation upon which our civilization rests, viz., respect for the law and confidence of its security. There are, in my opinion, two remedies—First of all, let us unite in a determined effort everywhere to see that the law is enforced, that all people at all times and all places see that the man charged with crime is given a fair trial.

Secondly, let all good citizens unite in an effort to rid the communities, especially the large cities, of the idle, vicious and gambling element. . . . In most cases it is this element that furnishes the powder for these explosions.

### 1915

As an American citizen, proud of his country and its history, I am shocked beyond measure to learn from your telegram of the lynching of two colored men and two colored women for whipping a policeman at Monticello, Ga.

You ask me for an expression of opinion. I can only say that I feel such acts of lawlessness are unfortunate and hurtful in the highest degree. They cast a blot upon our civilization. I feel there can be no excuse for such an outrageous and unlawful act. The community or State that permits such lawlessness is bound to suffer before the public opinion of the world and it is useless to invite and encourage immigration into any section of our country when such lawlessness is permitted.

Every such lynching keeps away hundreds, if not thousands of good people, who otherwise might be induced to settle in such States or communities. In my opinion, there is needed in every community and in every State law abiding men who will fearlessly stand for law and order. This is necessary in the interest of white people and black people.

Even as outrageous as the Monticello Lynches are, I cannot feel that the negro is the one most injured, but instead those guilty of perpetrating such outrages against law and order. I always condemn, as I now do, lawlessness on the part of my own people, but I have never felt that breaking the law on the part of one person justified other persons also in breaking the law.

We have gone a long way to lynching women for whipping a man, and I can but believe that the courts would have punished these people after regular and proper trial. The conscience of the American people, North and South, will be stirred by such offenses as the one here referred to, and I am glad to say there are brave and liberal men in all parts of the South, such as Gov. Emmet O'Neal of Alabama and others who represent a growing disposition to condemn and prevent the lynching of human beings.

Sources: Booker T. Washington, *Lynchings in the South* (1899; repr., Tuskegee, AL: Tuskegee Institute, 1901), 4–5, 7–8; Booker T. Washington, "Booker T. Washington Gives Facts and Condemns Lynchings in a Statement Telegraphed to the *New York World*" (Baltimore: n.p., 1908), 1–3; Booker T. Washington, "Booker T. Washington Declares No Lynching Has an Excuse," *New York World*, January 16, 1915, 4.


## Religion as a Solvent of the Race Problem (1908)

### Kelly Miller

Kelly Miller (1863–1939) was dean of Howard University's College of Arts and Sciences and helped established that school as the premier historically black university. Miller was a prolific writer whose syndicated columns reached five hundred thousand people weekly during the 1920s and 1930s. A staunch individualist, he aligned with neither the "radical" nor "conservative" camps. Miller denounced racial injustice while pledging loyalty to America. In his popular *Disgrace of Democracy* pamphlet, Miller condemned racial violence and asked, "The Negro, Mr. President, in this emergency [World War I], will stand by you and the nation. Will you and the nation stand by the Negro?"[22] Yet Miller was also an optimist who could see beyond race. In Kelly Miller's *History of the*

*World War for Human Rights*, he wrote: "The Negro is no longer a Negro, nor Afro-American, nor colored American, nor American of African descent, but he is American—simply this, and nothing more."[23]

Miller's emphasis on the role of religion in civil rights is worth noting, as it was a powerful force in "Christian civilization." Elsewhere he wrote, "A Christian is required by his creed to do right though the heavens fall. The practical statesman keeps the heavens from falling by doing right."[24] In this document, Miller discusses the impact of religion on black and white Americans.

∞

No people take a greater pride in their churches or give so large a share of their means to support them. The church is not merely a religious institution, but embraces all the complex functions of Negro life. It furnishes the broadest field for the exercise of talent, and is the only sphere in which the Negro has shown initiative and executive ability. Frederick Douglass began his public life as a local preacher in the A.M.E. [African Methodist Episcopal] Church, and if a wider career had not providentially opened up to him he doubtless would have risen to a position of ecclesiastical dignity and power.

In politics, education, and business the white man manages and controls the Negro's interests; it is only in the church that the field is undisputed. Upon the failure of the reconstruction governments the Negro politicians sought careers in the church as the most inviting field for the exploitation of their powers. The Negro preacher is a potential politician, whose natural qualities of organization and leadership being denied scope and exercise in the domain of secular activity, seek them in the religious realm. . . .

It was the consolation of religion that solaced and sustained the Negro slave under burdens as heavy as any that the human race has ever been called upon to bear. It was the manifestation of the religious spirit that gained for him the confidence and sympathy even of his oppressors, and played no small part in effecting his emancipation. If the Negro had remained a heathen, and had adhered to the repugnant religious rites of his ancestors, can any one believe that the Christian sentiment of this nation would have exerted itself so strongly in his behalf? Would a race of heathens have ever been incorporated into the body politic of this nation? . . .

A new people stand especially in the need of religious guidance. An old-established race, as history has often demonstrated, may exist for ages on the forms of faith after the vital spirit has departed. They are carried forward by the spiritual inertia acquired in a more virile and pious period. . . . The anchor-sheet of our own Republic was forged in the furnace of faith. It is absolutely essential for a people to begin right. The opening words of Genesis form the granite foundation of all true race building—"In the beginning, God. . . ."

The presence and promise of the Negro in the Western world is a striking fulfillment of that Scripture saying which is at once a beatitude and a prophecy: "Blessed are the meek for they shall inherit the earth." The Negro is not only preserved by his passive virtues, but he holds them as a lash over the conscience of the Anglo-Saxon, to scourge him to the observance of the requirements of the faith to which he avows allegiance. . . . The American Negro secured his first notion of the Christian religion from the Anglo-Saxon, but now, with acknowledged justice, denounces him bitterly for his failure to keep the precepts of the faith which he transmitted to others. . . .

A strong religious sanction can command amity among diverse races or enmity among kindred ones, and it will be so. The Apostle Paul found the new cult of grace sufficient to solve the ethnological problems of his day. For, through the eye of faith, he could discern neither "Jew nor Greek, Barbarian, Scythian, bond or free, but Christ is all and in all. . . ."

The solution of the race question depends upon the simple recognition of the Fatherhood of God and the Brotherhood of Man, and the application of the Golden Rule to the affairs of life. Let the Negro lay stress of emphasis upon the Ten Commandments and the white man upon the Golden Rule, and all will be well.

Source: Kelly Miller, "Religion as a Solvent of the Race Problem," in *Race Adjustment: Essays on the Negro in America* (New York: Neale, 1908), 137–39, 142, 145, 147, 151.

## Supreme Court Rules Residential Segregation Unconstitutional (1917)

*U.S. Supreme Court*

For the first fifteen years of its existence, the National Association for the Advancement of Colored People depended on Moorfield Storey in its highest-profile cases. Storey's legal briefs covered a full range of issues, from denial of voting rights to lynching. He also served as the NAACP's first president, from 1909 to 1915. Later, the NAACP turned to Louis Marshall, another prominent lawyer profiled in this collection.

The *Plessy v. Ferguson* case (1896) stimulated the passage of more segregation statutes. As African Americans migrated to the fast-growing cities, white politicians enacted laws prohibiting blacks from purchasing property in a majority-white neighborhood. The "separate but equal" rationale was that whites could not purchase property in a majority-black neighborhood. Storey challenged these laws by setting up a test case. He had William Warley, a black member of the Louisville, Kentucky, NAACP, purchase property from Charles H. Buchanan, a white businessman who opposed neighborhood segregation and agreed to Storey's plan. Because the law prohibited this interracial contract, Warley refused to pay and Buchanan sued. This set the stage for a legal challenge to housing segregation laws.

*Buchanan v. Warley* was a Supreme Court victory for Storey and local attorney Clayton B. Blakely. The Supreme Court overturned the residential segregation ordinance, making it a landmark case and a turning point for the Court's civil rights rulings. At the time, despite the protest of Booker T. Washington and others, "cities around the country stood on the brink of residential apartheid."[25] The Court accepted Storey's arguments, which were based on the Fourteenth Amendment (equal protection of the law) and denial of property rights. On this issue, the Court rejected the "separate but equal" doctrine of *Plessy v. Ferguson*. Although the decision was unanimous, progressive Justice Oliver Wendell Holmes wrote, but did not deliver, a dissent opposing property rights as a basis for civil rights. *Buchanan v. Warley* illustrates how economic liberty formed one basis for classical liberal challenges to unequal laws.

∾

Buchanan, [plaintiff], brought an action in the chancery branch of Jefferson circuit court of Kentucky for the specific performance of a contract for the sale of certain real estate situated in the city of Louisville at the corner of Thirty-seventh street and Pflanz avenue. The offer in writing to purchase the property contained a proviso:

"It is understood that I am purchasing the above property for the purpose of having erected thereon a house which I propose to make my residence. . . ."

This offer was accepted by the plaintiff.

. . . The defendant by way of answer set up the condition above set forth, that he is a colored person, and that on the block of which the lot in controversy is a part, there are ten residences, eight of which at the time of the making of the contract were occupied by white people, and only two (those nearest the lot in question) were occupied by colored people, and that under and by virtue of the ordinance of the city of Louisville, approved May 11, 1914, he would not be allowed to occupy the lot as a place of residence. . . .

The title of the ordinance is:

An ordinance to prevent conflict and ill-feeling between the white and colored races in the city of Louisville, and to preserve the public peace and promote the general welfare, by making reasonable provisions requiring, as far as practicable, the use of separate blocks, for residences, places of abode, and places of assembly by white and colored people respectively. . . .

The [plaintiffs] attack the ordinance upon the ground that it violates the Fourteenth Amendment of the Constitution of the United States, in that it abridges the privileges and immunities of citizens of the United States to acquire and enjoy property, takes property without due process of law, and denies equal protection of the laws. . . .

The right of the [plaintiff] to sell his property was directly involved and necessarily impaired because it was held in effect that he could not sell the lot to a person of color who was willing and ready to acquire the property, and had obligated himself to take it. . . . In this case the property rights of the [plaintiff] are directly and necessarily involved.

. . . This ordinance prevents the occupancy of a lot in the city of Louisville by a person of color in a block where the greater number of residences are occupied by white persons; where such a majority exists colored persons are excluded. This interdiction is based wholly upon color; simply that and nothing more. In effect, premises situated as are those in question in the so-called white block are effectively debarred from sale to persons of color, because if sold they cannot be occupied by the purchaser nor by him sold to another of the same color.

This drastic measure is sought to be justified under the authority of the state in the exercise of the police power. It is said such legislation tends to promote the public peace by preventing racial conflicts; that it tends to maintain racial purity; that it prevents the deterioration of property owned and occupied by white people, which deterioration, it is contended, is sure to follow the occupancy of adjacent premises by persons of color. . . .

The federal Constitution and laws passed within its authority are by the express terms of that instrument made the supreme law of the land. The Fourteenth Amendment protects life, liberty, and property from invasion by the states without due process of law. Property is more than the mere thing which a person owns. It is elementary that it includes the right to acquire, use, and dispose of it. The Constitution protects these essential attributes of property. . . .

The question now presented makes it pertinent to inquire into the constitutional right of the white man to sell his property to a colored man, having in view the legal status of the purchaser and occupant.

Following the Civil War certain amendments to the federal Constitution were adopted, which have become an integral part of that instrument, equally binding upon all the states and fixing certain fundamental rights which all are bound to respect. . . .

The statute of 1866, originally passed under sanction of the Thirteenth Amendment, and practically re-enacted after the adoption of the Fourteenth Amendment, expressly provided that all citizens of the United States in any state shall have the same right to purchase property as is enjoyed by white citizens. Colored persons are citizens of the United States and have the right to purchase property and enjoy and use the same without laws discriminating against them solely on account of color. . . . The Fourteenth Amendment and these statutes enacted in furtherance of its purpose operate to qualify and entitle a colored man to acquire property without state legislation discriminating against him solely because of color. . . .

That there exists a serious and difficult problem arising from a feeling of race hostility which the law is powerless to control, and to which it must give a measure of consideration, may be freely admitted. But its solution cannot be promoted by depriving citizens of their constitutional rights and privileges. . . .

It is urged that this proposed segregation will promote the public peace by preventing race conflicts. Desirable as this is, and important as is the preservation of the public peace, this aim cannot be accomplished by laws or ordinances which deny rights created or protected by the federal Constitution. It is said that such acquisitions by colored persons depreciate property owned in the neighborhood by white persons. But property may be acquired by undesirable white neighbors or put to disagreeable though lawful uses with like results.

We think this attempt to prevent the alienation of the property in question to a person of color was not a legitimate exercise of the police power of the state, and is in direct violation of the fundamental law enacted in the Fourteenth Amendment of the Constitution preventing state interference with property rights except by due process of law. That being the case, the ordinance cannot stand.

Source: *Buchanan v. Warley*, 245 U.S. 60 (1917). Internal case citations have been omitted.

## The Negro Question (1918)

*Moorfield Storey*

This speech circulated widely to "all Cabinet members, all state governors, the mayors of several cities, newspapers and periodicals, and selected prominent citizens; and it received even wider circulation in 1919."[26] *The Negro Question* summarizes Storey's view of the universality of civil rights, arguing that this was not solely a "Negro" problem, but one that also directly affected whites.

☙

Negroes are denied the protection which the law affords the lives and property of other citizens. If only charged with crime or even misdemeanor, they are at the mercy of the mob and may be killed and tortured with absolute impunity. In many States they cannot obtain justice in the courts. At hotels, restaurants and theatres they are not admitted or are given poor accommodation. In the public parks and public conveyances, even in the public offices of the nation, they are set apart from their fellow-citizens. The districts which they occupy in cities are neglected by the authorities, and of the money which the community devotes to education, a very small fraction is allotted to them, so that their schoolhouses and their teachers are grossly inadequate. . . .

But more dangerous and more wicked than neglect is the barbarous cruelty of lynching. I need not revive the figures of the past. What has happened within a year is enough. Since the United States entered the war a careful investigation shows that 219 Negro men, women and children have been killed and lynched by mobs. . . .

That you may realize what lynching is, let me give you instances. Dyersburg in Tennessee is a prosperous town of some 7,500 people, the county seat and a representative community of the better class. . . .

> The Negro was seated on the ground and a buggy-axle driven into the ground between his legs. His feet were chained together, with logging chains, and he was tied with wire. A fire was built. Pokers and flat-irons were procured and heated in the fire. It was thirty minutes before they were red-hot.

> His self-appointed executors burned his eyeballs with red-hot irons. When he opened his mouth to cry for mercy a red-hot poker was rammed down his gullet. Red-hot irons were placed on his feet, back and body, until a hideous stench of burning human flesh filled the Sabbath air of Dyersburg.

> Thousands of people witnessed this scene. They had to be pushed back from the stake to which the Negro was chained. Roof-tops, second-story windows and porch-tops were filled with spectators.

> Children were lifted to shoulders, that they might behold the agony of the victim. . . .

The Memphis *News-Scimitar* thus describes the scene: . . .

> Women scarcely changed countenance as the Negro's back was ironed with the hot brands. Even the executioners maintained their poise in the face of bloody creases left by the irons,—irons which some housewife had been using.

Three and a half hours were required to complete the execution. . . .

The Negroes are counted as voters in determining how many representatives the State shall have, but are not allowed to cast their own votes, so that each Democrat votes for himself and for one or more Negroes, and consequently exercises a much larger influence in the choice of President and Congress than the voter in Wisconsin or Massachusetts. In the latter States the voter casts one ballot, in the Southern States he casts two or three in effect. Remembering how small is the majority in the House of Representatives, it is clear that the policy of the country on all important questions like the incidence of taxation, as well as the administration of the laws by which the taxes are collected, is determined by men who cast votes which they have no right to cast. Men say that "the South is in the saddle" and the political situation which that phrase describes is due to the suppression of the Negro vote. . . .

I dwell on the facts to make you see that the suppression of the Negro vote does concern you. It takes away a large fraction of your voting power. . . .

We owe it to them—we owe it to ourselves—that while they are giving their lives abroad to make the world safe for democracy we should do our part to make this country safe for their kindred at home, or, to quote a better phrase, we should "make America safe for Americans."

Source: Moorfield Storey, *The Negro Question* (New York: NAACP, 1918), 3–4, 7–9, 20, 30.

## Notes

1. Charles J. McClain, *In Search of Equality: The Chinese Struggle against Discrimination in Nineteenth-Century America* (Berkeley: University of California Press, 1994), 12.

2. Morton Sosna, *In Search of the Silent South: Southern Liberals and the Race Issue* (New York: Columbia University Press, 1977), vii.

3. Ibid., 1.

4. Ibid., 5.

5. See, e.g., Margaret Levenstein, "African American Entrepreneurship: The View from the 1910 Census," *Business and Economic History* 24, no. 1 (1995): 106–22.

6. Republican Party Platform, 1888, http://americanpresidency.org (accessed July 6, 2007).

7. Thomas Adams Upchurch, *Legislating Racism: The Billion Dollar Congress and the Birth of Jim Crow* (Lexington: University Press of Kentucky, 2004), 129.

8. Benjamin Tillman, *Congressional Record,* February 26, 1900, 2245.

9. "The Political Future of the South," *New York Times,* May 10, 1900, 6.

10. Frederick Douglass, "The Folly, Tyranny, and Wickedness of Labor Unions," in *The Black Worker: A Documentary History from Colonial Times to the Present,* ed. Philip Sheldon Foner and Ronald L. Lewis (Philadelphia: Temple University Press, 1978), 178–79.

11. Harlan's opinion was not the first argument for colorblindness heard by the courts: in *Roberts v. City of Boston* (1849), Charles Sumner argued that the Massachusetts Declaration of Rights ("all men are born free and equal") rendered racial discrimination unconstitutional. Judge Shaw, however, held that segregated schools were allowed under a separate and equal–like ruling. See Andrew Kull, "Sumner and Shaw," in *The Color-Blind Constitution* (Cambridge, MA: Harvard University Press, 1992).

12. Charles T. Canady, "America's Struggle for Racial Equality," *Policy Review,* January–February 1998, 44.

13. Booker T. Washington, *The Negro in Business* (Boston: Hertel, 1907), 14.

14. Peter Max Ascoli, *Julius Rosenwald: The Man Who Built Sears, Roebuck and Advanced the Cause of Black Education in the American South* (Bloomington: Indiana University Press, 2006).

15. Robert Higgs, *Competition and Coercion: Blacks in the American Economy, 1865–1914* (New York: Cambridge University Press, 1977); Robert E. Weems, *Desegregating the Dollar: African American Consumerism in the Twentieth Century* (New York: New York University Press, 1998); David E. Bernstein, *Only One Place of Redress: African Americans, Labor Regulations, and the Courts from Reconstruction to the New Deal* (Durham, NC: Duke University Press, 2001); Paul D. Moreno, *Black Americans and Organized Labor: A New History* (Baton Rouge: Louisiana State University Press, 2006); Stephanie Capparell, *The Real Pepsi Challenge: The Inspirational Story of Breaking the Color Barrier in American Business* (New York: Free Press, 2007).

16. Jennifer Roback, "The Political Economy of Segregation: The Case of Segregated Streetcars," *Journal of Economic History* 46, no. 4 (1986): 893–917.

17. "Augusta Horrified by Brutal Murder," *Augusta Chronicle,* May 14, 1900, 1.

18. Roback, "Political Economy," 897, 901–3.

19. Higgs, *Competition and Coercion.*

20. Booker T. Washington, "To the Editor of the Southern Workman," February 18, 1886, University of Illinois Press, http://www.historycooperative.org/btw/ (accessed November 8, 2007); Pete Daniel, *The Shadow of Slavery: Peonage in the South, 1901–1969* (Urbana: University of Illinois Press, 1972).

21. Booker T. Washington, "Is the Negro Having a Fair Chance?" *Century Magazine*, November 1912, 46–55.

22. Kelly Miller, *The Disgrace of Democracy: Open Letter to President Woodrow Wilson* (Washington, DC: Howard University, 1917), 14.

23. Kelly Miller, *Kelly Miller's History of the World War for Human Rights* (Washington, DC: A. Jenkins, 1919), 553.

24. Kelly Miller, "White Methodists Succeed in Leaving Race out of Plan for Unity, Says Dr. Miller," *Chicago Defender*, September 14, 1935, 18.

25. Alexander M. Bickel and Benno C. Schmidt, *The Judiciary and Responsible Government, 1910–21* (New York: Macmillan, 1984), 792.

26. Robert L. Zangrando, *The NAACP Crusade against Lynching, 1909–1950* (Philadelphia: Temple University Press, 1980), 44–45.

## Recommended Reading

Daniels, Roger. *Asian America: Chinese and Japanese in the United States since 1850.* Seattle: University of Washington Press, 1988.

Eisenberg, Bernard. "Kelly Miller: The Negro Leader as a Marginal Man." *Journal of Negro History* 45, no. 3 (1960): 182–97.

Foner, Philip Sheldon, and Richard C. Winchester. *The Anti-Imperialist Reader: A Documentary History of Anti-Imperialism in the United States.* Vol. 1. New York: Holmes & Meier, 1984.

Harlan, Louis R. *Booker T. Washington: The Wizard of Tuskegee, 1901–1915.* New York: Oxford University Press, 1983.

Higham, John. *Strangers in the Land: Patterns of American Nativism, 1860–1925.* 2nd ed. New Brunswick, NJ: Rutgers University Press, 1988.

Hixson, William B. *Moorfield Storey and the Abolitionist Tradition.* New York: Oxford University Press, 1972.

Hurtado, Albert L., and Peter Iverson. *Major Problems in American Indian History: Documents and Essays.* 2nd ed. Boston: Houghton Mifflin, 2001.

Jones, Plummer Alston. *Libraries, Immigrants, and the American Experience.* Westport, CT: Greenwood, 1999.

Kull, Andrew. *The Color-Blind Constitution.* Cambridge, MA: Harvard University Press, 1992.

Leonard, Henry B. "Louis Marshall and Immigration Restriction, 1906–1924." *American Jewish Archives* 24, no. 1 (1972): 6–26.

Marshall, Louis. *Louis Marshall: Champion of Liberty; Selected Papers and Addresses.* Edited by Charles Reznikoff. Philadelphia: Jewish Publication Society of America, 1957.

McClain, Charles J. *In Search of Equality: The Chinese Struggle against Discrimination in Nineteenth-Century America.* Berkeley: University of California Press, 1994.

McFeely, William S. *Frederick Douglass.* New York: Norton, 1991.

Meier, August, and Elliott Rudwick. "Attorneys Black and White: A Case Study of Race Relations within the NAACP." *Journal of American History* 62, no. 4 (1976): 913–46.

Norrell, Robert. "Understanding the Wizard: Another Look at the Age of Booker T. Washington." In *Booker T. Washington and Black Progress: Up from Slavery 100 Years Later.* Edited by W. Fitzhugh Brundage. Gainesville: University Press of Florida, 2003.

Pfaelzer, Jean. *Driven Out: The Forgotten War against Chinese Americans.* New York: Random House, 2007.

Prucha, Francis Paul. *The Great Father: The United States Government and the American Indians.* Lincoln: University of Nebraska Press, 1995.

Przybyszewski, Linda. *The Republic According to John Marshall Harlan.* Chapel Hill: University of North Carolina Press, 1999.

Roback, Jennifer. "The Political Economy of Segregation: The Case of Segregated Streetcars." *Journal of Economic History* 46, no. 4 (1986): 893–917.

Roberts, Samuel K. "Kelly Miller and Thomas Dixon, Jr. on Blacks in American Civilization." *Phylon* 41, no. 2 (1980): 202–9.

Root, Damon W. "The Party of Jefferson: What the Democrats Can Learn from a Dead Libertarian Lawyer." *Reason,* December 2007. http://www.reason.com/news/show/123020.html (accessed July 8, 2008).

Rosenstock, Morton. *Louis Marshall, Defender of Jewish Rights*. Detroit: Wayne State University Press, 1965.

Rubin, Louis Decimus. *George W. Cable: The Life and Times of a Southern Heretic*. New York: Pegasus, 1969.

Sandmeyer, Elmer Clarence. *The Anti-Chinese Movement in California*. 1939. Reprint, Urbana: University of Illinois Press, 1991.

Sosna, Morton. *In Search of the Silent South: Southern Liberals and the Race Issue*. New York: Columbia University Press, 1977.

Sumner, William Graham. *On Liberty, Society, and Politics: The Essential Essays of William Graham Sumner*. Edited by Robert C. Bannister. Indianapolis: Liberty Fund, 1992.

Turner, Arlin. *George W. Cable: A Biography*. Baton Rouge: Louisiana State University Press, 1956.

Upchurch, Thomas Adams. *Legislating Racism: The Billion Dollar Congress and the Birth of Jim Crow*. Lexington: University Press of Kentucky, 2004.

Washington, Booker T. *The Booker T. Washington Papers*. Edited by Louis R. Harlan and Raymond Smock. Urbana: University of Illinois Press, 1972.

———. *Up from Slavery: An Autobiography*. Garden City, NY: Doubleday, 1901.

Wyllie, Irvin G. *The Self-Made Man in America: The Myth of Rags to Riches*. New Brunswick, NJ: Rutgers University Press, 1954.

Yarbrough, Tinsley E. *Judicial Enigma: The First Justice Harlan*. New York: Oxford University Press, 1995.

# 4

# Republicans and Race

*1921–1932*

THE ROARING TWENTIES were an ugly period in U.S. race relations. Lynching and mob violence continued to terrorize African Americans in the South, and occasionally the North and West (as witnessed by the bloody Tulsa race riot of 1921). The Ku Klux Klan revived in new form, attacking not only blacks but also Catholics, Jews, and immigrants. By the mid-1920s, the KKK had millions of members before disintegrating in the midst of scandal and counterattacks by opponents.

Above all, this was an era of paradox and pragmatism. Republicans passed an antilynching bill but relented when a Democratic filibuster stymied all other issues on the congressional agenda. President Warren Harding spoke courageously against southern racism, but Democratic victories in Congress limited his power to do more. President Calvin Coolidge signed the National Origins Quota Act (1924), which shut down immigration for decades to come. Yet, at the same time, Coolidge challenged the KKK and other nativist forces by espousing a classical liberal philosophy of civil rights in "controversial" venues, such as Howard University, the leading historically black college. As secretary of commerce, Herbert Hoover desegregated his agency's workforce and, as late as 1932, when Hoover ran for reelection, a majority of black voters supported his GOP ticket.

ↀ

## Warren Harding's Birmingham Address:
### Free the Black Voter (1921)

A president who touted a return to "normalcy" after World War I protested the "normal" state of affairs in the Deep South by delivering an address on racial equality in Birmingham. Harding's action, taken early in his administration, was a daring one; he told his audience he would speak frankly "whether you like it or not." Although militants were outraged at Harding's disavowal of "racial amalgamation" and "social equality" (southern euphemisms for racial intermarriage), the furious response of southern congressmen illustrates the subversive potential of Harding's speech. His administration's subsequent attack on the KKK and support for antilynching laws confirmed southern Democratic suspicions about the new Republican president. One historian writes that "Harding's Birmingham address was the most important presidential utterance on the race question since Reconstruction days and, regardless of motivation, required considerable courage."[1] Kelly Miller, however, chided Harding for believing there were "inescapable" and "eternal" differences between the races (that is, Harding was not sufficiently color-blind in his racial philosophizing). As Miller put it, "[T]he human race is moving toward unity, not diversity"—a forward-thinking belief that might not go down well with today's "diversity liberals" who espouse the old conservative belief in the "inescapable" nature of race.[2] The speech is followed by congressional reactions, both positive and negative.

### Harding's Speech

The World War brought us to full recognition that the race problem is national rather than merely sectional. There are no authentic statistics, but it is common knowledge that the World War was marked by a great migration of colored people to the North and West. They were attracted by the demand for labor and the higher wages offered. It has brought the question of race closer to North and West, and, I believe, it has served to modify somewhat the views of those sections on this question. It has made the South realize its industrial dependence on the labor of the black man and made the North realize the difficulties of the community in which two greatly differing races are brought to live side by side. I should say that it has been responsible for a larger charity on both sides, a beginning of better understanding; and in the light of that better understanding perhaps we shall be able to consider this problem together as a problem of all sections and of both races, in whose solution the best intelligence of both must be enlisted. . . .

Here, it has seemed to me, is suggestion of the true way out. Politically and economically there need be no occasion for great and permanent differentiation, for limitations of the individual's opportunity, provided that on both sides there shall be recognition of the absolute divergence in things social and racial. When I suggest the possibility of economic equality between the races, I mean it in precisely the same way and to the same extent that I would mean it if I spoke of equality of economic opportunity as between members of the same race. In each case I would mean equality proportioned to the honest capacities and deserts of the individual. . . .

On the other hand I would insist upon equal educational opportunity for both. This does not mean that both would become equally educated within a generation or two generations or ten generations. Even men of the same race do not accomplish such an equality as that. There must be such education among the colored people as will enable them to develop their own leaders, capable of understanding and sympathizing with such a differentiation between the races as I have suggested—leaders who will inspire the race with proper ideals of race pride, of national pride, of an honorable destiny; and important participation in the universal effort for advancement of humanity as a whole. . . .

The one thing we must sedulously avoid is the development of group and class organizations in this country. There has been time when we heard too much about the labor vote, the business vote, the Irish vote, the Scandinavian vote, the Italian vote, and so on. But the demagogues, who would array class against class and group against group have fortunately found little to reward their efforts. That is because, despite the demagogues, the idea of our oneness as Americans has risen superior to every appeal to mere class and group. And so I would wish it might be in this matter of our national problem of races. I would accept that a black man cannot be a white man, and that he does not need and should not aspire to be as much like a white man as possible in order for him to accomplish the best that is possible for him. He should seek to be, and he should be encouraged to be, the best possible black man, and not the best possible imitation of a white man.

It is a matter of the keenest national concern that the South shall not be encouraged to make its colored population a vast reservoir of ignorance, to be drained away by the processes of migration into all other sections. That is what has been going on in recent years at a rate so accentuated that it has caused this question of races to be, as I have already said, no longer one of a particular section. Just as I do not wish the South to be politically entirely one party; just as I believe that is bad for the South, and for the rest of the country as well, so I do not want the colored people to be entirely of one party. I wish that both the tradition of a solidly Democratic South and the tradition of a solidly Republican black race might be broken up. Neither political sectionalism nor any system of rigid group-ings of the people will in the long run prosper our country.

With such conventions one must urge the people of the South to take advan-tage of their superior understanding of this problem and to assume an attitude toward it that will deserve the confidence of the colored people. Likewise, I plead with my own political party to lay aside every program that looks to lining up the black man as a mere political adjunct. Let there be an end of prejudice and of demagogy in this line. Let the South understand the menace which lies in forcing upon the black race an attitude of political solidarity.

### Political Response

Democratic Senators today criticized President Harding for his speech in Bir-mingham yesterday dealing with the race question. . . .

Republican Senators, on the other hand, contended that the question was a national one, and one proper for consideration by the President and the Federal Government.

Senator [Pat] Harrison of Mississippi [Democrat], who has been continuously attacking the acts of the Administration, was the President's severest critic. . . .

"If the President's theory is carried to its ultimate conclusion, namely, that the black person, either man or woman, should have full economic and political rights with the white man and white woman, then that means that the black man can strive to become President of the United States, hold a Cabinet position and oc-cupy the highest places of public trust in the nation. It means white women should work under black men in public places, as well as in all trades and professions. . . ."

Senator [Tom] Watson of Georgia [Democrat] . . .

"Does the Governor of Alabama, who endorsed the President's lamentable speech think that Alabama should have a negro Governor instead of a white man like himself? Would he like to see the Supreme Court of Alabama filled with negro judges? Would he like to see negro bosses placed over white boys and white girls? Would President Harding be glad if his successor in the White House were to be a black man? Would the President like to see his Cabinet filled with negroes? . . ."

"I applaud the President's speech," said Senator [William] Calder of New York [Republican]. "It was a timely speech and right to the point."

Senator [Selden] Spencer of Missouri [Republican] said:

"The President, with characteristic force and dignity, uttered in the language of the statesmen what every man who believes in the Constitution of the United States accepts wholeheartedly. It is applicable to Alabama, as it is to Maine. To criticize the support of this Constitutional provision is nothing less than anarchy. The colored citizen has, as of right, equal political, economical and educational rights with the white citizen. It was a timely utterance of the President."

Sources: "Harding Says Negro Must Have Equality In Political Life," *New York Times*, October 27, 1921, 1, 11; "Praise and Assail Harding Negro Talk," *New York Times*, October 28, 1921, 4.

## Republican Lynching Bill Passes House (1922)

*Leonidas Dyer et al.*

Representative Leonidas P. Dyer (1871–1957) was a Republican congressman from St. Louis who witnessed the aftermath of the East Saint Louis riot of 1917, a horrible massacre of African Americans by whites. Many blacks from East Saint Louis fled across the Mississippi River to Dyer's district. Outraged by the riot, he crusaded for a federal antilynching bill to prevent and punish mob violence. In 1922, the Republican House passed the bill, "with Negroes cheering in the galleries and Southerners cursing on the floor."[3] The bill had the support of President Harding and Moorfield Storey, president of the NAACP, who provided the constitutional argument that state failure to act was a denial of equal protection of the law under the Fourteenth Amendment. Nonetheless, the bill died after a Democratic filibuster in the Senate. In later years (see chapter 5), the House would twice pass antilynching bills only to see them die in the Senate.

(*Above and opposite pages*) Two sides of a poster in support of the Dyer Anti-Lynching Bill (1922). District of Columbia Anti-Lynching Committee North Eastern Federation of Colored Women's Clubs, "A Terrible Blot on American Civilization." (Library of Congress, Rare Book and Special Collections Division.)

Classical liberals generally opposed federal interference with "states' rights" under the Constitution, but they also believed human beings formed government to protect "life, liberty, and property." Lynching was murder—and local

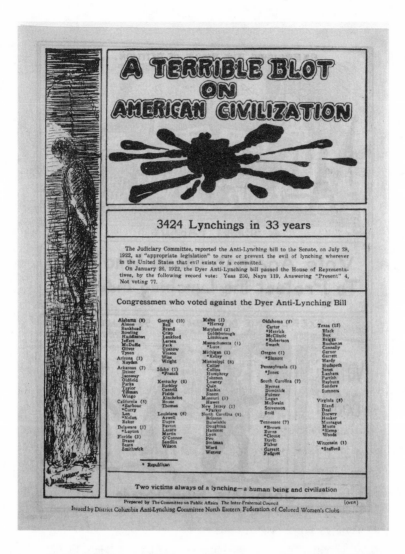

or state officials failed to punish the murderers not once but *thousands* of times. Thus, federal action was consistent with the classical liberal notion of justice.

This entry includes excerpts from congressional debate offering insight into both sides of this burning controversy.

&

Mr. [James] ASWELL [D-LA]. [T]his is a bill put forward by the Republican leaders for political purposes to satisfy the Negro agitator. It may have other purposes, but it is specifically intended to pretend to protect from mobs the assaulters of women. . . .

The criminal who would assault a woman is not easily deterred. He is deterred, if at all, only by knowing in advance that when captured he will meet certain and immediate death. By this bill, without protecting the criminal in fact, you would greatly increase the number of criminal assaults and resulting cases of mob violence. You would give courage to the criminal by leading him to believe that his chances to escape speedy death would be better. In some sections it would not be safe for a white woman to live. . . .

Then, when a black brute assaults a neighborhood girl, one we well know, a bright fascinating girl with infinite promise in which we all rejoice, when the brute assaults her, crushes out every spark of her hope into the unspeakable hell, men and boys will rush to the rescue to protect their own women from the peril of the monster at large among them. . . .

Mr. [Martin] ANSORGE [R-NY]. The opportunity is ours to put an end to the habit of lynching in this country. So long as Lynches are tolerated all the teachings from all the pulpits in all the churches are rank hypocrisy. The colored man shared equally the burdens and responsibilities of citizenship in the World War just won, and he should be guaranteed in practice as well as in print the equal protection of the laws. [Applause] . . .

Mr. [Finis] GARRETT [D-TN]. Mr. Speaker, this bill ought to be amended in its title to read: "A bill to encourage rape."

Mr. [Leonidas] DYER [R-MO]. Mr. Chairman and gentlemen of the committee, my interest in this legislation comes from Lynches that have occurred in my own State. My special attention to this matter came five years ago when at the very doors of my home occurred one of the most disgraceful Lynches and riots known to civilization. That occurred in the city of East St. Louis, Ill. I introduced a resolution at that time asking that the House of Representatives investigate that lynching and ascertain the cause and see if there was something we might do to make such disgraceful events scarce and impossible for the future. In that lynching and in that mob riot there were 100 and more people injured and killed—innocent men and innocent women.

Some of the most outrageous murders known to humanity took place at this time. Little children were taken away from their mother's arms and thrown into the fire. . . .

This legislation, if enacted into law, will cover cases of that kind, notwithstanding the statement made by some gentleman previous to the holiday recess that this legislation is aimed only at the Southern States, where Lynches have been promiscuous. Mr. Chairman, I may say in this connection that that thought never entered my mind in what I have done to secure this legislation. I want to make it so that Lynches of the kind that happened in East St. Louis, Ill., will not go unpunished to the fullest extent possible. [Applause] . . .

The charge has been made here, Mr. Chairman, that these Lynches are caused by attacks upon women, that they are the result of rape. That is as far from the truth as many of the other extravagant statements that have been made. . . . [Cites statistics]

I have the figures here of many years. I have the places, the dates, and the names of the people who were lynched. Let me call your attention here to the year 1918. Five of those lynched in that year were women. Two Negro men were burned at the stake before death, and four were burned after death. Aside from those burned at the stake three were tortured before death. In one case the victim's dead body was carried into town on the running board of an automobile and thrown into a public park, where it could be viewed by thousands of men, women, and children. . . .

. . . You gentlemen know, all of you know, that it is impossible to find a jury in the county where a lynching takes place that will indict in the first instance or convict in the second instance; but if it is brought into a Federal court you may bring your jury from other sections of the State far away from where the crime was committed. . . .

I have here the record of an incident taken from the Congregationalist and Advance of Atlanta, Ga., published August 8, in which is detailed the story of two men coming from a certain section of one of the Southern States, a Negro and a white soldier. They were upon the same ship, the Lincoln, I think it was, one of the transports which, I think, went down. When the ship was going down the Negro was rushing to save himself. He had secured a life belt. A young white soldier from his own section was there and he did not have any life belt. The Negro soldier took off his life belt and gave it to the white soldier. He then rushed back to find another, but before he could do so the ship went down. This paper publishes the statement that about the same time that event was taking place on the high seas, when this Negro soldier was saving the life of the white man, a lynching took place right down in that county, When the uncle of the Negro soldier was one of three who were lynched by white men. . . .

Mr. Chairman, in the name of justice, in the name of God and right, I trust we will do the thing that we ought to do and make lynching a crime against the United States of America. [Applause] . . .

Mr. [Hatton] SUMNERS [D-TX]. [I]f we could get a little more help from you people, exerted with the black people, to encourage them to run out the criminal element from among them while we work on the criminal element of the white people, instead of sending these Negro agitators down there to preach social equality among my people, you would aid more than you are aiding now. [Applause] We might just as well understand ourselves, gentlemen. That day never will come—there is no necessity for anybody mistaking it—that day never will come when the black man and the white man will stand upon a plane of social equality in this country, and that day never will come in any section of the United States when you will put a black man in office above the white man. [Applause] That never will happen. . . .

Mr. [John] TILLMAN [D-AR]. In the speeches so far made on this bill no proponent of the same has deplored the awful crime which provokes many Lynches. . . .

My good friend, Dr. [Simeon] Fess [R-OH], the imperial highbrow from Ohio [laughter], spoke for this measure on December 19, as did others, decrying lynching and not condemning assault upon women. . . .

This wretched bill and the conduct of its friends and proponents will multiply assaults upon women and thus increase materially the number of Lynches. . . .

. . . [A]ll through the South today a million sweet-faced Virginias with tablet and satchel go singing on their way to school, not knowing what lechery and outrage mean, pure as the lily's spotless leaf, but covertly watched by the vulture eyes of black criminals, ready and eager to assault and to ruin them. [Applause]

One potent influence that prompted many southern Members to vote for prohibition was to remove, if possible, from the Negro intoxicating liquor. It inflamed him and rendered him more liable to commit the crime for which Coleman [a black man] was hung, and I am afraid that some of the wets [opponents of

Prohibition] from the North are urging this legislation to even up with southern Members who supported prohibition.

The author of No. 13 [Rep. Dyer] is a stalwart wet.

The author of this bill represents the twelfth district of Missouri. In his district are the following wards in the city of St. Louis containing [43,113] Negro citizens. . . .

Mr. [Ira] HERSEY [R-ME]. Under the Dyer bill there is to its advocates no other road but Federal laws, United States marshals, Federal troops and the bayonet, civil war, and race riots. . . .

The SPEAKER. The question is on the passage of the bill.

The yeas and nays were ordered. . . . yeas 231, nays 119, answered "Present" 4, not voting 74.

Source: Leonidas Dyer et al., *Congressional Record,* December 19, 1921–January 26, 1922, 545–46, 548, 787–89, 798–99, 1011–12, 1024, 1795.

## Coolidge Denounces White Racism (1924)

### Calvin Coolidge

Historians often compare "Silent Cal" Coolidge (1872–1933) unfavorably with the activist presidents of the Progressive Era. A survey of academic historians conducted in 1983 found that they rated Theodore Roosevelt and Woodrow Wilson as "near great," with Coolidge among the "ten worst."[4] The Ku Klux Klan was the hot civil rights issue of the 1924 election: it was a national organization directing its hatred not only at blacks, but especially at Catholics and others deemed less than "100% American." Historians fault Coolidge for not denouncing the KKK by name during the campaign.[5] They fail to note that the Democratic candidate—segregationist John W. Davis—called upon Coolidge to speak when the president's son was dying from an infection—a two-month ordeal that devastated Coolidge. (Consider the irony: Davis is best known for defending segregation in the *Brown v. Board* case). Soon after his son's death, Coolidge spoke eloquently of religious and racial toleration before a parade of one hundred thousand Catholics honoring the Holy Name Society.[6] Klan leaders grumbled when the president refused to show up for their parade.[7]

Also compare Coolidge's strong denunciation of lynching with that of "progressive" presidents Theodore Roosevelt and William H. Taft. In a 1906 address, Roosevelt stated "the greatest existing cause of lynching is the perpetration, especially by black men, of the hideous crime of rape—the most abominable in all the category of crimes—even worse than murder."[8] In a 1909 message, Taft blamed lynching on "delays in trials, judgments, and the executions thereof by our courts."[9] By contrast, Coolidge made no excuses and urged Congress to punish the "hideous crime of lynching."[10]

In the following document, President Calvin Coolidge responds to a man who desired a lily-white government. The *Chicago Defender*, a leading black newspaper, praised Coolidge's rebuke with the front-page headline, "Cal Coolidge Tells Kluxer When to Stop."[11] Coolidge reprinted this letter in a collection of his presidential addresses.[12]

౾

My dear Sir:

Your letter is received, accompanied by a newspaper clipping which discusses the possibility that a colored man may be the Republican nominee for Congress from one of the New York districts. Referring to this newspaper statement, you say:

> It is of some concern whether a Negro is allowed to run for Congress anywhere, at any time, in any party, in this, a white man's country. Repeated ignoring of the growing race problem does not excuse us for allowing encroachments. Temporizing with the Negro whether he will or will not vote either a Democratic or a Republican ticket, as evidenced by the recent turnover in Oklahoma, is contemptible.

Leaving out of consideration the manifest impropriety of the President intruding himself in a local contest for nomination, I was amazed to receive such a letter. During the war 500,000 colored men and boys were called up under the draft, not one of whom sought to evade it. They took their places wherever assigned in defense of the nation of which they are just as truly citizens as are any others. The suggestion of denying any measure of their full political rights to such a great group of our population as the colored people is one which, however it might be received in some other quarters, could not possibly be permitted by one who feels a responsibility for living up to the traditions and maintaining the principles of the Republican Party. Our Constitution guarantees equal rights to all our citizens, without discrimination on account of race or color, I have taken my oath to support that Constitution. It is the source of your rights and my rights. I propose to regard it, and administer it, as the source of the rights of all the people, whatever their belief or race. A colored man is precisely as much entitled to submit his candidacy in a party primary, as is any other citizen. The decision must be made by the constituents to whom he offers himself, and by nobody else. You have suggested that in some fashion I should bring influence to bear to prevent the possibility of a colored man being nominated for Congress. In reply, I quote my great predecessor, Theodore Roosevelt:

" * * * [asterisk ellipsis in the original] I cannot consent to take the position that the door of hope—the door of opportunity—is to be shut upon any man, no matter how worthy, purely upon the grounds of race or color."

Yours very truly, etc.

Source: Calvin Coolidge, "Equality of Rights," in *Foundations of the Republic: Speeches and Addresses* (New York: Charles Scribner's Sons, 1926), 71–72.

## Coolidge at Howard University (1924)

### Calvin Coolidge

While the Ku Klux Klan was at its peak, President Coolidge countered it by speaking at Howard University, the historically black college; before a massive march of the Holy Name Society, a Catholic organization; and at a Jewish community center. In his Howard University commencement address (June 6), Coolidge preached Christian inclusiveness in his vision of a tolerant America.

છ૭

The accomplishments of the colored people in the United States, in the brief historic period since they were brought here from the restrictions of their native continent, can not but make us realize that there is something essential in our civilization which gives it a special power. I think we shall be able to agree that this particular element is the Christian religion, whose influence always and everywhere has been a force for the illumination and advancement of the peoples who have come under its sway. . . .

Calvin Coolidge delivers Howard University commencement address (1924). (Library of Congress, Prints & Photographs Division, LC-USZ62–111731.)

Those of you who are fortunate enough to equip yourselves for [leadership] have a special responsibility to make the best use of great opportunities. In a very special way it is incumbent upon those who are prepared to help their people to maintain the truest standards of character and unselfish purpose. The Negro community of America has already so far progressed that its members can be assured that their future is in their own hands. Racial hostility, ancient tradition, and social prejudice are not to be eliminated immediately or easily. But they will be lessened as the colored people by their own efforts and under their own leaders shall prove worthy of the fullest measure of opportunity.

The Nation has need of all that can be contributed to it through the best efforts of all its citizens. The colored people have repeatedly proved their devotion to the high ideals of our country. They gave their services in the war with the same patriotism. . . .

Among well-nigh 400,000 colored men who were taken into the military service, about one-half had overseas experience. They came home with many decorations and their conduct repeatedly won high commendation from both American and European commanders. . . .

. . . Whether in the military service, or in the vast mobilization of industrial resources which the war required, the Negro did his part precisely as did the white man. He drew no color line when patriotism made its call upon him. He gave precisely as his white fellow citizens gave, to the limit of resources and abilities, to help the general cause. Thus the American Negro established his right to the gratitude and appreciation which the Nation has been glad to accord.

Source: Calvin Coolidge, "Progress of a People," in *Foundations of the Republic: Speeches and Addresses* (New York: Charles Scribner's Sons, 1926), 31–36.

## The Negro and Capitalism (1924)

### Kelly Miller

**With a perceptive eye, Kelly Miller notes the unity of interests between black workers and capitalist employers. Color did not matter to the capitalist, as it did to the white workers and their labor unions, which excluded African Americans from skilled crafts. According to Miller, the growth of unions threatened blacks with further exclusion from the workplace and racial domination under American democracy.**

ᴄ⁄ᴐ

Where does the Negro stand in this nation-wide, yea world-wide issue between capital and labor? Logic aligns him with labor, but good sense arrays him on the side of capital. The race issue frustrates all of the conclusions of logic. The Negro is essentially a manual worker and, therefore, is vitally concerned in whatever advantages may accrue to the toiling world. He shares in every concession wrested from capital by the militant demands of labor. But the issue between the white and colored workman is sharper than that between capital and labor. Capital, white labor and the Negro constitute the eternal triangle of the industrial world. . . .

The capitalist has but one dominating motive, the production and sale of goods. The race or color of the producer counts but little. The work is listed with material assets as an instrument of production. A good engine and a good engineer are equally essential factors in the process of transportation. Manhood and mechanism are merged. There is little margin of favor between the white and black workman except as reflected in productive efficiency. There is no personal closeness or intimacy of contact between employer and employee. Race prejudice finds no room for manifestation. The capitalist is prone to a kind and generous attitude toward the black workman. The Negro is acceptable to him according to his merit and efficiency merely as a tool of production. There is also involved in this attitude the thought that, on the whole, the Negro may be a little cheaper than the white man, and is more easily manipulated.

The source of friction arises between the black and white workmen assigned to the same task at the same time. This implies racial equality which wounds the white man's sense of pride. If the capitalist shows race prejudice in his operations, it is merely the reflected attitude of the white workman. The colored man who applies at the office for skilled employment meets with one unvarying response from the employer: "I have no objection, but all of my white workmen will quit if I assign you a place among them."

In all the leading lines of industry the white workmen organize and either shut out the Negro or shunt him aside in separate lines with a lower level of dignity and compensation. The bricklayer must be white, the hod carrier may be black. The Negro may, indeed, bring the brick to the scaffold, but should he dare adjust it in its place on the wall, the white man would throw down his trowel with indignant protest.

In so far as the labor unions recognize the Negro, they are forced to do so by the attitude of capital. It seems easier to them to handle the black competitor through the union than to have him as a standing menace on the outside. The regulations of labor unions, however fair they may seem on their face, always work to the disadvantage of the Negro in practical applications. What boots the Negro carpenter to have a union card in his hand if the white workmen refuse to work with him? There is no practical advantage to the Negro in maintaining the same level of wages at the same craft, if at the same time the black man is not permitted to enter upon that craft.

The capitalist stands for an open shop which gives to every man the unhindered right to work according to his ability and skill. In this proposition the capitalist and the Negro are as one. . . .

The employing classes have been wonderfully helpful to the Negro by way of generous philanthropic contributions. They have built his schools and colleges and made the betterment of the race possible. Whenever a sharp issue is drawn between those who have, and those who have not, the Negro's instinct aligns him with wealth and power. It is also true that the capitalistic element at present possesses the culture and moral restraint in dealing with the Negro which the white workman misses. There is nothing in the white working class to which the Negro can appeal. They are the ones who lynch, and burn and torture him. He looks to the upper element for respect of law and order and the appeal to conscience.

But the laborers outnumber the capitalists more than ten to one, and under spur of the democratic ideal must in the long run gain the essential ends for which they strive. White labor in the South has already asserted its political power. Will it not also shortly assert its dominancy in the North and West, and indeed, in the nation? If the colored race aligns itself with capital, and refuses to help win the common battle of labor, how will it fare with him in the hour of triumph?

Source: Kelly Miller, "The Negro's Place in the Labor Struggle," in *The Everlasting Stain* (Washington, DC: Associated Publishers, 1924), 279–89.

## Silent Protest against Forced Sterilization: Buck v. Bell *(1927)*

*U.S. Supreme Court*

**In this infamous U.S. Supreme Court case upholding forced sterilization by the states, progressive Justice Oliver Wendell Holmes Jr. wrote, "Three generations of imbeciles are enough." Although this case did not deal with race per se, forced sterilization was based on the eugenic notion of inferior races and individuals. Pierce Butler (1866–1939), a classical liberal and the only Catholic on the Court, filed the sole dissent. As a rule, Butler did not believe in writing dissenting opinions, and his protest here was thus "silent." However, secondary sources suggest that Butler's Catholic Christianity and belief in individual freedom influenced his vote.[13] Butler was a Harding appointee.**

❧

Mr. Justice HOLMES delivered the opinion of the Court.

The judgment finds . . . that Carrie Buck "is the probable potential parent of socially inadequate offspring, likewise afflicted, that she may be sexually sterilized without detriment to her general health and that her welfare and that of society will be promoted by her sterilization." . . . We have seen more than once that the public welfare may call upon the best citizens for their lives. It would be strange if it could not call upon those who already sap the strength of the State for these lesser sacrifices, often not felt to be such by those concerned, in order to prevent our being swamped with incompetence. It is better for all the world, if instead of waiting to execute degenerate offspring for crime, or to let them starve for their imbecility, society can prevent those who are manifestly unfit from continuing their kind. The principle that sustains compulsory vaccination is broad enough to cover cutting the Fallopian tubes. Three generations of imbeciles are enough. . . .

Judgment affirmed.

Mr. Justice BUTLER dissents.

Source: *Buck v. Bell*, 274 U.S. 200 (1927). Internal legal citations have been omitted.

## Hoover Desegregates the Commerce Department (1928)

In 1913, Democratic president Woodrow Wilson ordered the segregation of government offices. Moorfield Storey and other officers of the NAACP protested, but Wilson responded: "[B]y putting certain bureaus and sections of the service in the charge of negroes we are rendering them more safe in their possession of office and less likely to be discriminated against."[14] Perhaps because he had spent most of his adult life outside the United States, Secretary of Commerce Hoover was uninterested in racial issues; moreover, thinking in terms of rigid classes violated his individualist philosophy. Hoover's Red Cross work during the Great Flood of 1927 opened his eyes to racism in the South. The following year he responded positively when the NAACP asked him to desegregate the Commerce Department. The following documents include Hoover's memo to a subordinate, a black newspaper editorial explaining how Hoover's short memo led to change, and southern responses. As a self-appointed spokesman for working-class whites, Senator Coleman Blease (D-SC) made a career of advocating segregation and mob violence directed at blacks. Blease engaged in a "bizarre death dance" to celebrate each lynching—his "grotesque gyrations" apparently mimicked the shaking body of a hanged man.[15]

ϟ

*Herbert Hoover*

March 13, 1928
Memorandum for Dr. Hill
Bureau of the Census
From: Secretary Hoover

I have complaints that there is segregation of colored workers going on in the Census Bureau. I would be glad to have a full report on this subject.

*Washington Sentinel*

For many years, in the past, by means of various kinds of subterfuges, Negro employees in the Census Bureau have been segregated by subordinate department heads. One of the most recent instances of this was the segregation of about twelve Negro employees in the Census Bureau, under the pretense that they were needed to compile certain statistics concerning the Negro population of the United States. These twelve employees, who made up the entire Negro contingent of this bureau, were placed in very inconvenient quarters under the supervision of a Negro chief clerk. The result desired was accomplished, and that was the segregation of all Negro employees in the Census Bureau of the Department of Commerce. . . .

But some people are not so easily fooled, and this case of segregation was brought to the attention of the Honorable Herbert Hoover, Secretary of Commerce, by a committee of colored men. Immediately Mr. Hoover began an investigation and ordered the twelve Negro employees redistributed throughout the bureau, and the Negro unit abolished.

Now southern newspapers and Southern Democratic senators are blowing hot over the violation of the "unwritten rule." And what is the "unwritten rule?" It is race prejudice, pure and simple, and that old Negro-hating policy of the white man to always impress the Negro that he is the inferior race, no matter if he is performing the same kind of work the white man performs, and with the same degree of efficiency. So the justice and fair play of Secretary Hoover has brought to light that there exists in governmental departments an "unwritten rule" to segregate Negro employees. Thanks to Secretary Hoover.

This is not the first time that Secretary Hoover has demonstrated that segregation is distasteful to him. During his administration of the flood relief work in

Arkansas, it was brought to his attention that Negroes [did not receive] proper care and attention and were being discriminated against, and that the number of Negro relief workers was inadequate. The Secretary met with the Colored Advisory Committee, which was appointed by his direction, and plans were made correcting these evils, and a larger force of Negro relief workers were put on to administer aid to the Negro flood victims. . . .

No, Mr. Hoover did not abolish segregation in the Census Bureau as a political move, but as a Christian act emanating from a heart filled with human kindness, for which the Negro people of this country are very grateful. And the Secretary is to be highly commended for having had the manhood to break down the "unwritten rule" of segregation of Negro employees in governmental departments.

*James Thomas Heflin (D-AL)*

Mr. Hoover seems to have a lot of sins to account for. He has taken a step right recently forcing whites and negroes to work side by side in the Commerce Department that will be repudiated by nearly every white man and woman in the country. . . .

What right has he to disturb the splendid segregation arrangement established in the Commerce Department by the Democratic Party, under which the negroes were working and getting along well in one section and the whites were working in another and pleased with the situation? . . . So Mr. Hoover comes now, in his effort to get delegates to a Republican National Convention, and is putting negro men and women in the offices to work alongside white women and girls. . . .

. . . the Senator from South Carolina [Mr. BLEASE] tells the story of humiliated white girls in the department coming here from the various States of this Union and being obliged to sit alongside buck negroes working in the department. Such a thing is a shocking outrage upon these fine American girls and a shame on any administration. . . .

God Almighty has made racial facts.

And you have no business, Mr. Hoover, to undertake to interfere with the handiwork of the Almighty. . . .

Just as the eagle is the king of all fowls, just as the lion is the king of all beasts, and just as the whale is the king of all the fishes of the seas, the white race is the superior race, the king race, the climax and crowning glory of the four races of black, yellow, red, and white. . . .

*Coleman Blease (D-SC)*

Mr. President, I send to the desk an article appearing in the Pittsburgh Courier of Saturday, April 21, 1928, which I ask that the clerk may read. . . .

"THE ANNOYING MR. BLEASE

The other day Secretary of Commerce Herbert Hoover, candidate for presidential nomination on the Republican ticket, abolished segregation of negro clerks in his department. That was a good move calculated to make Mr. Hoover more popular with the million or more negroes in the United States who can cast a ballot without fear of lynching. Now comes the annoying Senator Blease, elected to his office by a handful of people in South Carolina (because the bulk of the electorate down there is disfranchised), complaining against this action. . . ."

Mr. BLEASE. Mr. President, I understand that that newspaper is edited by a "nigger." I have no further comment to make on it.

Sources: Herbert Hoover to Dr. Hill, March 13, 1928, file "Census Bureau," Hoover Presidential Library, West Branch, IA; "Secretary Hoover Abolishes Segregation," *Washington Sentinel*, April 21, 1928, 1; *Congressional Record*, April 20–21, 1928, 6175, 6808.

## Racial Freedom on Campus (1922, 1926, 1928)

*Louis Marshall*

In one of the following documents, Marshall opposes quotas limiting the number of Jews entering Harvard University—a reminder that racial distinctions in admissions preceded affirmative action. In the early twentieth century, many colleges informally capped the number of Jews they would admit as students. In 1922, Harvard president A. Lawrence Lowell proposed an explicit quota of 15 percent: to limit anti-Semitism, he argued. Lowell explained that too many Jews could stir hatred and resentment among other students. This "for your own good" rationale stirred controversy and led Louis Marshall to speak out against the quota system. (Franklin Roosevelt, who served on Harvard's Board of Overseers, later said he supported quotas in college and government restricting the number of Jews and Catholics.)[16]

Marshall also opposed university-sponsored segregation on campus—an issue that reemerged in the 1990s with the spread of "multiculturalism." Nevertheless, he believed freedom of association meant that Christian (or Jewish) schools might retain their religious mission and character without violating the rights of others—a position he defended in the *Pierce v. Society of Sisters* (1925) case discussed in chapter 3.

ℰ𝒶

### End Quotas in College Admissions (1922)

June 17, 1922

To A. C. Ratshesky

I consider Dr. Lowell's letter . . . in every way offensive. It could not have been worse had it been written by the advocates of what the late Dr. Schechter called the Higher Anti-Semitism of Germany. He seems bent upon putting the burden upon the Jews of asking them to suggest plans which would enable him to carry out his discriminatory policies. I trust that we will not permit ourselves to be caught in any such trap. He has created the issue. He has insulted the intelligence of the American people. He has played with fire, and has given the sanction of his great office to what, after all, is a vulgar expression of Jew-baiting. He has made his bed. Let him lie in it. We, as Jews, will not admit the soundness of his premises. We must insist upon equality of right and of treatment. We cannot concede that there is any social aspect to the question which is entitled to consideration. The only tests that we can recognize are those of character and scholarship.

President Lowell's policy is that which prevailed in Russia in the days of the Czar, and that is now being practiced in Hungary. The *numerus clausus,* which is intended to deprive the Jews of Eastern Europe of the opportunity of obtaining a modern education, will never receive the acquiescence of any self-respecting American Jew. If President Lowell wishes to array himself on the side of these brutal persecutors, if the head of a great institution of learning which has hitherto rejoiced in the well-deserved reputation of intellectual breadth and freedom from prejudice, is willing to ally himself with the vilest of European politicians, let him do it. We shall not make the way easy for him to accomplish his disgraceful purposes.

### Private Discrimination in a Free Society (1926)
To Nathan D. Shapiro, October 28, 1926

I participated actively in the fight against the Oregon Compulsory Public School Law in the Supreme Court of the United States, for the purpose of establishing the principle that parents should have the right to control the education of their children and to send them to private schools as well as to public schools. [Marshall refers to his role in the *Pierce v. Society of Sisters* decision.] It would seem to follow from that principle that if any persons desire to establish private schools for the purpose of educating the children of their own religious faith or of their own social class, they would have the right to do so. Those who founded Adelphi Academy and who contributed to its endowment were Christians, just as they might have been Jews. I take it from the correspondence that as Christians they conduct Christian services at the opening of the classes, just as they might throughout the day if they saw fit to do so. They also have indicated a preference for those of their own religious beliefs. . . .

What right have we, as Jews, to criticize them for acting in accordance with their convictions or prejudices in that regard? What right would they have to criticize us as Jews if we established private schools and indicated that we did not consider it desirable that non-Jews should attend?

### The Evil of Segregation on Campus (1928)
To Paul Shipman Andrews [dean, College of Law, Syracuse University], December 12, 1928

For a variety of reasons, largely pressure of duties, I have failed to answer your kind letter of October 3, 1928, in which you asked permission to give my name to a law society about to be formed by members of the senior class of the Law College of Syracuse University "all of Jewish extraction. . . ."

This compulsory segregation of members of the same college class into distinct groups along religious or other lines, bodes ill to the public welfare. All of the members of these classes are Americans, all are engaged together under the same faculty in pursuing the study of law and equity, all are to become members of the same great profession, in the practice of which they are likely to have constant business relations, and yet the Christian students deliberately exclude their Jewish classmates from fellowship in societies devoted to the discussion of jurisprudential problems. If the Jewish students are to be thus arbitrarily discriminated against and were to accept the edict of inferiority and unfitness thus pronounced against them, and nothing is done to redress what is unquestionably a moral wrong of which they are the victims, I would not be true to myself and to the principles which I have advocated all my life were I, a Trustee of Syracuse University, to sanction by indirection what I consider to be an unspeakable disgrace.

For more than fifty years I have battled for the rights of man, for liberty, equality and fraternity, for the elevation of the human kind, for the overthrow of intolerance and oppression, and for an interpretation of the Constitution which, instead of making of it a mere collection of cold phrases, gives to it a living spirit. I had hoped that my name would at least feebly represent these ideals. Were I to consent at this late day that the young men in whom I am anxious to instil[*sic*] the ambition to stand in the fighting line against wrong and injustice of every kind, should meekly resign themselves under cover of my name to submit to the insults inflicted upon them, it would be pitiful.

Source: Louis Marshall, *Louis Marshall, Champion of Liberty: Selected Papers and Addresses*, ed. Charles Reznikoff (Philadelphia: Jewish Publication Society of America, 1957), 1:266–67, 272–73, 271. Reprinted from *Louis Marshall: Champion of Liberty*, © 1957 edited by Charles Reznikoff, published by the Jewish Publication Society, with the permission of the publisher.

# Notes

1. Robert K. Murray, *The Harding Era: Warren G. Harding and His Administration* (Minneapolis: University of Minnesota Press, 1969), 399–400.

2. Kelly Miller, *The Everlasting Stain* (Washington, DC: Associated Publishers, 1924), 125.

3. William B. Hixson Jr., "Moorfield Storey and the Defense of the Anti-Lynching Bill," *New England Quarterly* 42, no. 1 (1969): 74.

4. R. K. Murray and T. H. Blessing, "The Presidential Performance Study: A Progress Report," *Journal of American History* 70 (1983): 540.

5. Michael J. Klarman, *From Jim Crow to Civil Rights: The Supreme Court and the Struggle for Racial Equality* (New York: Oxford University Press, 2004), 107.

6. "100,000 Catholics Cheer Coolidge on Religious Liberty," *New York Times,* September 22, 1924, 1.

7. "Will Ask Congress to Review the Klan," *New York Times,* June 25, 1925, 6.

8. Theodore Roosevelt, "6th Annual Message," December 3, 1906, http://americanpresidency.org (accessed November 23, 2005).

9. William Howard Taft, "1st Annual Message," December 7, 1909, http://americanpresidency.org (accessed November 23, 2005).

10. Calvin Coolidge, "First Annual Message," December 6, 1923, http://americanpresidency.org (accessed October 10, 2006).

11. "Cal Coolidge Tells Kluxer When to Stop," *Chicago Defender,* August 16, 1924.

12. Calvin Coolidge, *Foundations of the Republic* (New York: C. Scribner's Sons, 1926).

13. Phillip Thompson, "Silent Protest: A Catholic Justice Dissents in *Buck v. Bell,*" *Catholic Lawyer* 43, no. 1 (2004): 125–48.

14. George C. Osborn, "The Problem of the Negro in Government, 1913," *Historian* 23 (1961): 339.

15. Bryant Simon, *A Fabric of Defeat: The Politics of South Carolina Millhands, 1910–1948* (Chapel Hill: University of North Carolina Press, 1998), 32.

16. Myron I. Scholnick, *The New Deal and Anti-Semitism in America* (New York: Garland, 1990); Frank Burt Freidel, *Franklin D. Roosevelt: A Rendezvous with Destiny* (Boston: Little, Brown, 1990).

## Recommended Reading

Bernstein, David E. *Only One Place of Redress: African Americans, Labor Regulations, and the Courts from Reconstruction to the New Deal.* Durham, NC: Duke University Press, 2001.

Danelski, David J. *A Supreme Court Justice Is Appointed.* New York: Random House, 1964.

Felzenberg, Alvin S. "Calvin Coolidge and Race: His Record in Dealing with the Racial Tensions of the 1920s." http://calvin-coolidge.org/html/calvin_coolidge_and_race.html.

Ferrell, Claudine L. *Nightmare and Dream: Antilynching in Congress, 1917–1921.* New York: Garland, 1986.

Hixson, William B., Jr. "Moorfield Storey and the Defense of the Anti-Lynching Bill." *New England Quarterly* 42, no. 1 (1969): 65–81.

Lisio, Donald J. *Hoover, Blacks, & Lily-Whites: A Study of Southern Strategies.* Chapel Hill: University of North Carolina Press, 1985.

Marshall, Louis. *Louis Marshall, Champion of Liberty: Selected Papers and Addresses.* Edited by Charles Reznikoff. Philadelphia: Jewish Publication Society of America, 1957.

Moreno, Paul D. *Black Americans and Organized Labor: A New History.* Baton Rouge: Louisiana State University Press, 2006.

Murray, Robert K. *The Harding Era: Warren G. Harding and His Administration.* Minneapolis: University of Minnesota Press, 1969.

Rosenstock, Morton. *Louis Marshall, Defender of Jewish Rights.* Detroit: Wayne State University Press, 1965.

Sobel, Robert. *Coolidge: An American Enigma.* Lanham, MD: Regnery, 1998.

Strum, Harvey. "Louis Marshall and Anti-Semitism at Syracuse University." *American Jewish Archives* 35, no. 1 (1983): 1–12.

Thompson, Phillip. "Silent Protest: A Catholic Justice Dissents in *Buck v. Bell.*" *Catholic Lawyer* 43, no. 1 (2004): 125–48.

Zangrando, Robert L. *The NAACP Crusade against Lynching, 1909–1950.* Philadelphia: Temple University Press, 1980.

# 5

# The Roosevelt Years

## 1933–1945

THE GREAT DEPRESSION and World War II transformed American politics as voters migrated en masse from the Republican to the Democratic Party. Franklin Roosevelt wielded great presidential power over a span of twelve years. Historians differ in their assessment of Roosevelt's civil rights record. Sympathetic interpreters emphasize the role of Eleanor Roosevelt, northern Democrats, and labor unions in promoting a civil rights agenda. They also note how FDR's judicial appointments and Department of Justice briefs paved the way for the court victories of the 1940s and 1950s.[1] Middle-of-the-road interpreters note the diverse responses of African Americans: younger, northern blacks migrated to the Democratic Party, while older, southern blacks would not vote for the "party of the Klan."[2]

With southern Democrats critical to his New Deal agenda of enlarging state power, Roosevelt remained silent on race and refused to back antilynching bills or other nondiscrimination measures. Despite FDR's silence on race, African Americans voted for the Democratic Party because the New Deal offered jobs to desperate people. However, those passionate about civil rights were far more critical of Roosevelt's record. The entries that follow highlight the continuing classical liberal critique of state-sponsored discrimination and inequality. The advent of war brought an additional critique of Japanese internment.

℘

# The Black Freedom Struggle

## *Jim Crow Restaurant in the House:*
## *The Right to Interracial Dining (1934)*

### *Oscar De Priest*

Oscar De Priest (R-IL) was the first black elected to Congress in the twentieth century (1929–1935). An opponent of the New Deal, De Priest secured an antidiscrimination provision in the Civilian Conservation Corps law and introduced an antilynching bill, but he is perhaps best known for making the Jim Crow restaurant in the House of Representatives a cause célèbre. De Priest gave a stirring speech that brought an unexpected outpouring of support for a House investigation and debate that lasted three months. The Republican minority lost, and the restaurant remained whites only. In November 1934, De Priest lost his reelection bid when Democrats swept many congressional districts; and black voters, desperate for government assistance, switched political parties.

ℰℳ

Mr. DE PRIEST On that day when my secretary went into the grillroom downstairs he was told by Mr. Johnson that by the orders of the Chairman of the Committee on Accounts he could not be served in that restaurant.

I read in the newspapers an interview where the Chairman of the Committee on Accounts said that no Negro had been served there and would not while he was here. I hope he was not quoted correctly. . . .

I want to say that if the chairman was quoted correctly in that article "that Negroes had not been served there before" he was mistaken. I have seen them there in the grillroom several times. In the last 5 years I think I have seen them there 50 times. . . .

The restaurant of the Capitol is run for the benefit of the American people, and every American, whether he be black or white, Jew or gentile, Protestant or Catholic, under our constitutional form of Government, is entitled to equal opportunities.

I introduced a resolution on the 24th of January, asking for an investigation of this ruling by the chairman of the committee. That resolution went to the Committee on Rules. The Committee on Rules has not acted as yet. I waited 30 legislative days, and then I filed a petition with the Clerk of this House to discharge the Committee on Rules and to bring the resolution to the floor of the House. That resolution calls for an investigation only. . . .

I am going to ask every justice-loving Member in this House to sign that petition, as that seems to be the only way it can be threshed out on the floor of the House. . . .

If we allow segregation and the denial of constitutional rights under the dome of the Capitol, where in God's name will we get them? . . .

I say to the Members of this House . . . this is the most dangerous precedent that could be established in the American Government. If we allow this challenge to go without correcting it, it will set an example where people will say Congress itself approves of segregation; Congress itself approves of denying 0.1 of our population equal rights and opportunity; why should not the rest of the American people do likewise? I have been informed that if I insisted on pressing this question it might hurt my usefulness down here. If I did not press it, I would not stay here very long. The people who sent me here would retire me next November, and they would rightly retire me because I should not be here if I did not stand up for a group of people who have always been on the square with this Government. I did not come here from a group of people who have committed treason against the Government; I did not come here from a group of people who are Communists or Socialists; I come here from the most loyal American citizens that we have.

. . . The secretary who works for me I have known for 40 years. He is a Christian gentleman, a great deal better Christian than I ever thought of being or ever expect to be. There certainly can be no fault found with his personal conduct. He has been in that restaurant dozens of times. Perhaps he needs it worse than any other man down here. You know the condition in Washington and I know it. The public restaurants outside do not serve Negroes, and you know it. . . .

. . . I have not imposed my society on any Member on either side of the House. I think every man has the right to select his own society. I would not say that, except that I received a letter from a Member of this Congress, which I am going to read into the Record. I would not do it if the gentleman had not published it himself first.

"Hon. Oscar De Priest,

House Office Building, Washington, D.C.

Dear Sir: I have your letter of the 7th instant enclosing House Resolution 236. I presume you desire a reply to this letter."

Which I did.

"I note the contents of the resolution and desire to state that I was raised among Negroes in the South and they have always been my personal friends. I work with them on my farm and pay them the same price that I pay white men for the same work. I treat them well and enjoy their confidence.

I am willing to allow them every right to which they are entitled under the Constitution and laws, but I am not in favor of social equality between the races."

And I do not give a damn about it, brother. It does not mean anything to me at all.

"If there are enough Negroes around the Capitol to justify a restaurant for them to patronize, I would have no objection to establishing a restaurant for their use."

That we do not want and we will not accept.

"I neither eat nor sleep with the Negroes, and no law can make me do so.

I think this explains my position clearly.

George B. Terrell, of Texas."

[Applause.]

. . . Nobody asked the gentleman to sleep with him. That was not in my mind at all. I do not know why he thought of it. [Laughter.] I am very careful about whom I sleep with. [Laughter.] I am also careful about whom I eat with; and I want to say to you gentlemen that the restaurant down here is a place where one pays for what one gets. If I go in there, sit down to a table, I pay for what I get, and I am not courting social equality with you. That does not mean anything in America. Social equality is something that comes about by an exchange of visits from home to home and not appearing in the same public dining room. . . .

Again, I ask every Member of this House who believes in a square deal, Democrats and Republicans alike, to sign this petition. I do not care where you live, you ought to be willing to give me and the people I represent the same rights and privileges under the dome of the Capital that you ask for yourselves and your constituents.

Source: Oscar De Priest, *Congressional Record*, March 21, 1934, 5047–49.

## Voice against Lynching (1937, 1940)

*Hamilton Fish*

Hamilton Fish (1888–1991) was best known as an anti–New Dealer (FDR mocked his opposition as "Martin, Barton, and Fish"). However, he was arguably one of the most important civil rights advocates in Congress from the 1920s to the 1940s. Fish took part in all three successful efforts by House Republicans, and a growing number of northern Democrats, to pass antilynching bills (1922, 1937, 1940), only to have them die at the hand of Democratic filibusters in the Senate.

Fish's interest in civil rights stemmed partly from his family history: his great-grandfather helped to abolish slavery in New York, and his grandfather certified ratification of the Fifteenth Amendment. During World War I, Fish volunteered to serve as an officer with the "Fighting 369th," a colored unit better known as the "Harlem Hellfighters." Fish's wartime experience made him passionate about civil rights.

Throughout the 1930s and 1940s, Fish denounced Roosevelt for his poor civil rights record. Before he spoke on the floor for civil rights legislation, white southern Democrats hurled "racial slurs and hate-inspired invectives" at the New York congressman.[3] Defenders of FDR often blame his poor record on the need to work with southern Democrats. However, even in his home state, FDR refused to encourage redistricting to allow African American representatives from Harlem. Nor did he speak out for mass repatriation of Jews from Nazi Germany, as Fish did repeatedly. Later, FDR accused Fish of delaying the call-up of troops with his amendment to ban discrimination in the military, but Fish stood firm and the amendment passed when he forced members of Congress to record their votes (the initial voice vote was against nondiscrimination).

In his memoir, Fish recalled: "While President Franklin Roosevelt told the American people that they had to fight a world war to protect democracy in Europe, he refused to support my efforts to extend the blessings of democracy to American blacks. Sadly, American blacks were learning what the people of Eastern Europe were to learn later: Roosevelt's lofty promises about freedom and democracy were empty. He never had any intention of fulfilling those promises, because his interest was not in defending principles, but in political aggrandizement; and when it served his cause to say one thing and do another, that is precisely what he did."[4]

❧

**1937**

Mr. FISH. I was here in 1922 when this House passed the Dyer antilynching bill by a vote of 2 to 1. There is nothing new or novel about a Federal antilynching bill. This issue has been discussed and debated in Congress for years as well as throughout the country. It is proper and right that this particular antilynching bill should be submitted to the House for vote and after due debate passed.

Let me say, as the American people are discussing the question of lawlessness arising from the illegal seizure of property through sit-down strikes, which we deplore, that human life is more important, and in this instance we are forced to have a Federal antilynching law, because in certain sections of the country prisoners are taken away from the constituted authorities and are mobbed and lynched, and the rule of the rope and the faggot prevails. This bill has to do with the protection of human life, guaranteed by the Constitution. But if there was no such provision in the Constitution, let me say to the Members of the House, because you are going to hear a great deal about the Constitution and the constitutionality of this bill, that the protection of the lives of American citizens, whether they be colored or whether they be white, is above and beyond the Constitution. To safeguard and protect the lives of American citizens is the main reason for the existence of government itself. The Constitution, however, specifically states that no person shall be deprived of life, liberty, or property without due process of law and that is the purpose of the Gavagan bill. . . .

Mr. [Lyndon] JOHNSON of Texas [Democrat]. Mr. Chairman, this bill is pernicious. Commendable in its purpose to suppress lynching, which no one condones and against which no one is more bitterly opposed than I, yet the means by which it attempts to eradicate this evil is revolting and shockingly illegal and unconstitutional.

Lynching and mob violence are indefensible, but they are no more indefensible than this bill, which is a reckless, arrogant, and illegal attempt upon the part of the Federal Government to usurp the lawmaking and the law-enforcing powers and agencies of the State governments. The bill does more than destroy State rights; it completely destroys State sovereignty, and makes the States, including all State and county officers, responsible, not to the State governments of which they are a part, and to which they have sworn allegiance, but responsible to the ukase of Federal officers, Federal courts, and Federal bureaucrats.

The despised force bill of reconstruction days was no more a wanton or reckless disregard of the inherent and exclusive rights of the States than this vicious measure. . . .

God save the Republic from legislation enacted for such a purpose. . . .

Mr. FISH. The gruesome lynching at Duck Hill, Miss., of two colored men taken out of the hands of the sheriff in broad daylight proves the immediate need for a Federal antilynching law. The victims had just pleaded not guilty when seized by a cowardly and brutal mob of lawless ruffians, armed to the teeth, who tortured and burned the two young Negroes to death by use of a blowtorch. It amounted to a rape of justice, liberty, civil rights, equal rights, human rights, and human lives and of the Constitution itself. Every member of the mob, amounting to 100, who, in defiance of the law and the courts, took part in this barbaric abomination should be apprehended, tried, and convicted to long terms in prison.

This is a typical lynching case, and the actual test of the ability of certain Southern States to protect colored citizens from violence is whether the members of the mob are arrested and convicted. If they are, then there is no real need for Federal antilynching legislation, but if not then even the southern Democrats should vote for the bill.

But, judging from past experience, I doubt if the members of this atrocious, bloodthirsty mob will be convicted and imprisoned; only time will tell. I am unwilling, however, to believe that intelligent, law-abiding southern people have any sympathy with rule by mob violence, torture, or with such bestial acts, and that they must see the need for Federal legislation.

### 1940

Mr. FISH. I also wanted to ask the gentleman from Illinois, if he had yielded, where the President of the United States stands on the antilynching bill. We know where the President of the United States stands on all racial and religious questions in foreign lands, but we should like to know where he stands on enacting

A young Hamilton Fish (1920), shortly after he left service with the "Harlem Hellfighters" and entered Congress to fight for antilynching bills and other civil rights legislation. (Library of Congress, Prints & Photographs Division, LC-DIG-npcc-03146.)

an antilynching bill at the present time in the United States of America. He has been strangely silent about that, a matter which vitally affects the security of some 13,000,000 colored people in America. One word from the White House and that bill would come flying through the Senate and be enacted into law. Day after day we hear about President Roosevelt's views affecting foreign lands, but when it comes to making democracy safe in America and safe for 13,000,000 colored people, he is strangely silent. The White House continues to be as silent as a tomb when the colored people ask for an endorsement of the Gavagan-Fish antilynching bill.

Sources: Hamilton Fish (R-NY) et al., *Congressional Record*, April 12–15, 1937, 3383, 3518, 3520, 3526; Hamilton Fish (R-NY), *Congressional Record*, March 18, 1940, 3026–27.

## No Time for Patience (1944)

*Rose Wilder Lane*

Rose Wilder Lane (1886–1968) was the daughter of Laura Ingalls Wilder, the famous author of the *Little House on the Prairie* series. Lane was also a popular fiction writer, but during the 1940s she turned to nonfiction, advocating individual freedom and denouncing state aggression in all its forms. Her greatest work, *The Discovery of Freedom* (1943), influenced an entire generation of classical liberals.

During World War II, she found a new literary home with the *Pittsburgh Courier*, the most widely read black newspaper in America. The newspaper coined the term "Double V"—victory over racism overseas and at home. A regular columnist for the Courier, she found an audience receptive to her classical liberal view that judging by skin color was wrong and doubly dangerous when sanctioned by the State. In the following column, Lane discusses the need to become impatient in the face of racism.

ℰℐ

I cannot say what I would do had I been an American called Negro during this still-continuing reactionary period that began with Reconstruction. But if today my skin darkened and some of my ancestors were known to have been African, I would still know:

That God does not make races or classes, but individual persons, all equally of the human race, and each one endowed with life and with inalienable liberty, which is self-control and responsibility. . . .

I would act as a human being and an American; not as a Negro. I would neither "pass" as a "white woman," nor think and behave as a "black woman." I would have no prejudice against anyone because of his pale skin or pale-face ancestors. I would judge others as I would be judged—by moral character, intelligence, tastes and talents and achievements.

I would know that all great Americans belong to all Americans; I would not exclude George Washington from me because our skins do not match, nor claim George Washington Carver as exclusively mine because our skins do. . . .

I would insist night and day that the government itself make no distinctions between American citizens. I would not be patient. Rome was not built in a day; neither was it built by men who waited for someone else to build it. I would vigorously resist tyranny in every form. I would protect my liberty, my rights, and those of any other person, wherever and whenever attacked or infringed.

Source: Rose Wilder Lane, "No Time for Patience," *Negro Digest*, May 1944, 43–45.

# World War II: Jewish Refugees and Japanese Internment

## The Problem of the Refugees (1939)

### H. L. Mencken

H. L. Mencken was one of the most prominent writers of the early twentieth century. A literary critic, editor of the popular *American Mercury*, and columnist for the *Baltimore Sun*, Mencken influenced an entire generation of writers with his piercing criticism of popular culture (Mencken wrote that the media catered to the tastes of uneducated "boobs"). He was also skeptical about the supposed munificence of government. Writers have characterized Mencken (1880–1956) as "the joyous libertarian" and "America's wittiest defender of liberty." His derogatory statements about Jews (and just about everyone else) should not overshadow Mencken's total, absolute commitment to individual liberty for all people. He embraced capitalism, thought "all government is evil," and favored individual freedom "up to the limit of the unbearable, and even beyond."[5]

When it came to racial freedom, Mencken's actions spoke as loudly as his words: he denounced lynching, even testifying before Congress on the matter. In 1917, Mencken praised Kelly Miller for his condemnation of violence against blacks before, during, and after the East St. Louis riot.[6] Moreover, Mencken was one of the few great authors to mentor and promote black writers: George Schuyler, "the black H. L. Mencken," was one of his few close friends (see entry below). Mencken also lambasted opponents of immigration: "Laws are passed," he wrote, "to hobble and cage the citizen of newer stocks in a hundred fantastic ways." Yet, "the fact that they [immigrants] increase is the best hope of civilization in America. They shake the old race out of its spiritual lethargy, and introduce it to disquiet and experiment. They make for a free play of ideas."[7]

In the following entry, Mencken advocates opening America to all Jewish refugees, at a time when President Franklin D. Roosevelt and Congress adhered strictly to immigration quotas, thus dooming many Jews to death in Nazi-occupied Europe. Indeed, Hitler taunted Roosevelt and the supposedly humane progressives in the West who kept the immigration doors shut to Jewish refugees.

 srchilly

The latest English scheme for "helping" the poor Jews of Central Europe involves parking them in England while arrangements are being made to admit them to the United States. The idea is to keep them there until the gradual unrolling of the present quota provides them with American passports, or the law is changed enough to let them in by larger squads. While they are enjoying the free air of England their expenses are to be met by their American friends. All the philanthropic English appear to offer is housing—carefully policed. There is no mention of jobs.

The best that may be said for this scheme is that it is measurably better than the one first proposed, which contemplated dividing the refugees between the inferno of British Guiana and the remote wilds of Tanganyika. . . .

It must be plain to any rational man that the new scheme only begs the question, and throws all responsibility for an ultimate solution into Uncle Sam's lap. It would be much more honest and much more humane to tackle the problem at once, and settle it without further ado. Either we are willing to give refuge to the German Jews, or we are not willing. If the former, then here is one vote for bringing them in by the first available ships, and staking them sufficiently to set them on their feet. That is the only way we can really help them, and that is the only way we can avoid going down into history as hypocrites almost as grotesque as the English.

To be sure, letting them in will stir up Ku Kluxers, and there may be outbreaks here and there of anti-Semitism. But outbreaks of that sort are much more likely to occur if the immigration is delayed indefinitely and yet constantly impends. The delay will only give the Ku Kluxers time to organize their holy war, and really alarm the booboisie. If the Jews are brought in at once it will be seen quickly that they can be absorbed without any strain, and so the old pals of Hugo Black will be stumped [Black was a former member of the KKK and a Roosevelt appointee to the U.S. Supreme Court]. Such idealists never flourish in the face of overt facts. Their whole metaphysic revolves around bugaboos.

I see no reason why the burden should be thrust upon [American Jews]: they have troubles enough already, and are probably doomed to more hereafter. The initiative should be taken by the so-called Christians who are now so free with weasel words of comfort and flattery, and so curiously stingy with practical aid. In particular, it should be taken by the political mountebanks who fill the air with hollow denunciations of Hitler, and yet never lift a hand to help an actual Jew.

Source: H. L. Mencken, "The Problem of the Refugees," *Baltimore Sun*, January 1, 1939, 6. Reprinted with the permission of the *Baltimore Sun*, permission conveyed through Copyright Clearance Center, Inc.

### Freedom Newspapers Denounce Japanese Internment (1942)

#### R. C. Hoiles

Raymond Cyrus Hoiles (1878–1970) ran seven newspapers nationwide, including what is now the *Orange County Register*. Hoiles and his editors judged issues based on how they corresponded to the principles of Christianity and classical liberalism—the touchstones of his Freedom Philosophy. The following passage is consistent with the policy statement that guided the Freedom Newspaper chain:

The Yardsticks of Morality . . . indicate several facts, uncontested by any Christian or Jew, of our acquaintance. They include:
1. That every man is born with certain inalienable rights.
2. That these rights are equally the birthright of all men, that they are the endowment of the Creator and not of any government.

Since we believe these facts are expressed in the Commandments, we do not believe any man has the moral right to curtail the rights of his brother. That is, no man has the right to initiate force against his brother.[8]

President Franklin D. Roosevelt ordered internment of the Japanese as a wartime measure. As early as 1925, he wrote in a newspaper column that the presence of Japanese in California was a "nightmare" that posed a further danger of racial intermarriage. Noting "repugnance" at the idea, FDR wrote, "The mingling of Asiatic blood with European or American blood produces, in nine cases out of ten, the most unfortunate results."[9]

✑

In this issue, we are reproducing a thoughtful article from the Christian Advocate, under the heading of "The Japanese Evacuation in Retrospect," written by Clarence Hall.

The Christian Advocate is performing a real Christian service by throwing light on this subject. It seems from the article that some of the acts were taken without having the facts at hand.

Few, if any, people ever believed that evacuation of the Japanese was constitutional. It was a result of emotion and fright rather than being in harmony with the Constitution and the inherent rights that belong to all citizens. . . .

We must realize, as Harry Emerson Fosdick so wisely said, "Liberty is always dangerous but it is the safest thing we have."

That, also, in reality, means that true democracy is always dangerous but it is the safest thing we have. If we are not willing to run any risks and cannot have faith in humanity and regard people innocent until they are proved guilty, we are on the road to losing our democracy.

We cannot help but believe that we would shorten the war and lose fewer lives and less property if we would rescind the order and let the Japanese return and go to work, until such time as we have reason, to suspect any individuals of being guilty of being disloyal to America.

Source: R. C. Hoiles, editorial, *Santa Ana Register*, October 14, 1942. Reprinted with the permission of the *Orange County Register*, © 1942.

## Their Fight Is Our Fight (1943)

*George Schuyler*

Dubbed the "black H. L. Mencken" because of his savage wit, George Schuyler (1895–1977) was one of the most widely read black authors and journalists of the mid-twentieth century. Difficult to peg politically, Schuyler was a staunch individualist and iconoclast. Married to a white woman, he believed racial intermarriage was a path to a color-blind society. He worked out this theme in a splendid satire on race relations, *Black No More* (1931). In the following essay, Schuyler uses his pen to oppose Japanese internment.

ℰⅈ⅃

All minority groups in the United States ought to be deeply concerned over the drive being conducted by viciously reactionary elements to take away the citizenship of native-born citizens of Japanese ancestry.

The Native Sons of California, a Fascist outfit, is fighting to have Japanese-Americans barred from voting, although the case has been thrown out of Federal courts twice. The California Assembly has just passed a bill authorizing the State to take over the farm equipment of Japanese-Americans which has been stored since these citizens were summarily and, I believe, unconstitutionally, placed in what the Nazis call "protective custody" solely on the basis of "race." The same Assembly passed on April 23 a bill which will strengthen the State's action in dismissing 80 civil service employees of Japanese ancestry solely because of "race."

The odious Congressman Rankin of Mississippi has introduced a bill in the House of Representatives providing for the incarceration of all persons of Japanese ancestry in this country for the duration of the war. A similar bill has been introduced in the Senate by Senator Tom Stewart of Tennessee. The California State American Legion has joined the Native Sons of the Golden West in a campaign to prevent those Japanese-American citizens now in concentration camps from ever returning to their homes on the Pacific Coast. . . . Recently in San Francisco, Lt. Gen. John L. DeWitt declared "A Jap's a Jap . . . it makes no difference whether he is an American citizen or not," which effectually killed plans afoot to return them to useful work on the Pacific Coast.

The drive to take away the citizenship of native-born Americans simply be-

San Francisco schoolchildren recite the Pledge of Allegiance (April 1942). Shortly after this, those of Japanese descent were sent off to internment camps. (Library of Congress, Prints & Photographs Division, LC-USZ62–42810.)

cause of "race" is in full swing. More ominous, the Native Sons of the Golden West has suggested that citizenship also be taken from Afro-American citizens. This is another reason why Negroes should be concerned about the mistreatment of Japanese-Americans. There has been talk of sending these citizens "back" to Japan (where most of them have never been) after the war. This is exactly what Senator Bilbo has been contending for the Afro-American citizens. . . . [See chapter 6 for further discussion of Senator Bilbo's extreme racism.]

We have seen how the Reds and Nazis have moved whole populations with callous disregard for their wishes or feelings, and we know of the annual shifts of hundreds of thousands of Africans to the gold and diamond mines of South Africa. There will be ample shipping after the war for such an enforced emigration. No one who is honest and knows the power of demagoguery and racial chauvinism will doubt that such a horror can happen here. . . .

Some colored folk have said we should remain indifferent because the Japanese-Americans have never championed our cause and sought to avoid us at all times. While this is not entirely true, it would make no difference if it were true. The point that is important is that we must fight with all our might against discrimination based on "race" or color, no matter who is involved. We are expending our money and lives, and undergoing privations, in order to save the Dutch, Belgians, Norwegians, Greeks, Russians, British, French and Chinese, and yet THESE people have never championed our cause. Indeed, some of them have been the worst exploiters of our people—in the past and are today. Our boys are also fighting to save such Neanderthals as Bilbo, Connally, Rankin, et al, and yet no one will contend that such "race-baiters" have ever championed our cause.

These Japanese-American citizens are NOT in concentration because of the commission of any crime against the state. The contention that 70,000 citizens among the millions of whites on the Pacific Coast constituted a danger is a fantastic falsehood. These people are the most industrious, thrifty and best behaved citizens in this country. Thousands of them are the offspring of American-born Japanese-Americans. Other thousands are the offspring of mixed marriages, many having blonde hair and blue eyes, and look no more Japanese than I do. They had farms, businesses, civil service jobs and professions. They sent their children to school and college and did all possible to measure up to American standards. They were put in concentration camps SOLELY because of "race," and the principle behind their jailing is exactly the same as that behind the jailing, torture and murder of the Jews under Hitler's jurisdiction.

Their fight is our fight . . . and the sooner we realize it the better.

Source: George Schuyler, "Views and Reviews," *Pittsburgh Courier*, May 29, 1943, 13.

## *Americans All!* Chicago Tribune Blasts Japanese Internment (1943, 1944)

### *Chicago Tribune*

*The Chicago Tribune* was a leading organ of classical liberalism under Colonel Robert R. McCormick (1880–1955).[10] Highly critical of Franklin Roosevelt's domestic and foreign policies, the newspaper exposed abuses at Japanese internment camps and questioned the whole enterprise of imprisoning people simply because of their race. The following two articles are among the many published by the Tribune during the war years.

დ

### 1943

The news that three American citizens of Japanese ancestry are to have jobs, at least temporarily, on the Curtiss Candy company farms near Marengo, Ill., is welcome. . . .

Japanese born abroad are not eligible for American citizenship, but those born under our flag are citizens by virtue of that fact, and as such are entitled to all the privileges and immunities of citizenship. The problem is an exceedingly difficult one. Tho there is no evidence to indicate that any of the native born have been disloyal it is only natural that these people are regarded with suspicion. It would be stupid to pretend that there is no prejudice against them, but it would be no less stupid to overlook the fact that discrimination against these people by the government would establish a precedent which could be turned against any minority of citizens at any time. If color and race are to be allowed to deprive men of their rights under the Constitution, the Civil war was fought in vain. . . .

THE TRIBUNE has assigned one of its reporters, Mr. Guy Gentry, to find out what has been done and what is being done to solve the problem. We believe that readers of this newspaper and particularly those who are deeply concerned for the preservation of civil rights, will follow the series of articles with close attention. Meanwhile we think that the spirit of tolerance which seems to be asserting itself in the Marengo neighborhood is a good augury. Once again we are finding that bigotry does not flourish on prairie soil.

### 1944

Japanese-Americans in the relocation center at Granada, Colo., have presented 11 demands on the war relocation authority, including a plea that they be given freedom to live and travel anywhere in the United States. . . .

. . . [The letter] said draft age Americans of Japanese ancestry had been responding to the call for military service and civilian responsibility to aid the war effort.

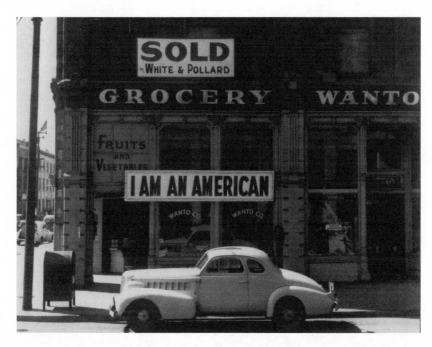

San Francisco business owned by a Japanese American (1942). Dorothea Lange took this photograph shortly after President Franklin D. Roosevelt ordered the evacuation and internment of Japanese Americans on the West Coast. (Library of Congress, Prints & Photographs Division, LC-USZ62–23602.)

**Want Right to Fight.**

These requests were made:

1. That equal opportunity for service and advancement in the military forces be offered Japanese-American draftees solely on the basis of individual merit and qualification.

2. That Japanese-Americans who are called to the colors no longer be assigned to segregated units.

3. That the right to travel and live wherever he chooses be restored.

**Ask Privileges Back.**

4. That evacuees be accorded all the rights and privileges which the Constitution gives them.

5. That any resettlement policy be coupled with adequate government protection and the economic means to start life anew.

6. That clarification be made regarding voting and residence status of Japanese-Americans who become of age in the centers.

7. That the right to become naturalized citizens be extended to alien Japanese.

8. That pending resettlement evacuees be accorded treatment befitting loyal Americans and that adequate wages be paid them.

**Want Public to be Enlightened.**

9. That vigorous effort be made by the government toward enlightening the "misinformed" American public with truth regarding the Japanese in America, and that the factual difference between the people of Japanese extraction who are loyal citizens of this country and the people in Japan be clearly presented.

10. That students of Japanese ancestry be freely admitted to all schools.

11. That the government establish adequate precautions so that the "sad" experiences of evacuation will never be repeated.

Sources: "Citizens of Japanese Ancestry," *Chicago Tribune*, May 7, 1943, 16; "Interned Japs Ask 11 'Rights'; Freedom Is One," *Chicago Tribune*, February 27, 1944, 11.

# Notes

1. Kevin J. McMahon, *Reconsidering Roosevelt on Race: How the Presidency Paved the Road to Brown* (Chicago: University of Chicago Press, 2004); Harvard Sitkoff, *A New Deal for Blacks: The Emergence of Civil Rights as a National Issue* (New York: Oxford University Press, 1978).

2. Nancy J. Weiss, *Farewell to the Party of Lincoln: Black Politics in the Age of FDR* (Princeton, NJ: Princeton University Press, 1983).

3. Hamilton Fish, *Memoir of an American Patriot* (Lanham, MD: Regnery, 1991), 33.

4. Ibid., 36.

5. Murray Rothbard, "H. L. Mencken: The Joyous Libertarian," *New Individualist Review* 2, no. 2 (1962): 15–27; Jim Powell, "H. L. Mencken: America's

Wittiest Defender of Liberty," *Freeman* 45, no. 9 (1995), http://www.fee.org/publications/the-freeman (accessed May 20, 2008).

6. H. L. Mencken, "Negro Spokesman Arises to Voice His Race's Wrongs," in *The Impossible H. L. Mencken: A Selection of His Best Newspaper Stories*, ed. Marion Elizabeth Rodgers (New York: Anchor, 1991), 186–91.

7. H. L. Mencken, "The Anglo Saxon," in *The Vintage Mencken*, ed. Alistair Cooke (1955; repr., New York: Vintage, 1983), 137.

8. Carl Watner, "To Thine Own Self Be True: The Story of Raymond Cyrus Hoiles and His Freedom Newspapers," in *I Must Speak Out: The Best of the Voluntaryist, 1982–1999* (San Francisco: Fox & Wilkes, 1999), 157.

9. Franklin D. Roosevelt, "The Average American and the Average Japanese Have Very Cloudy and Often Erroneous Points of View about Relations between the Two Countries," 1925, in *F.D.R., Columnist: The Uncollected Columns of Franklin D. Roosevelt*, ed. Donald Scott Carmichael (Chicago: Pellegrini & Cudahy, 1947), 57–58.

10. The "Colonel" comes from his service during World War I. Thereafter, he was known as "Colonel McCormick." Lisabeth G. Svendsgaard, "McCormick, Robert Rutherford," in *American National Biography Online*, http://www.anb.org/articles/16/16–02435.html (accessed July 29, 2008).

## Recommended Reading

Bradford, R. W. "A Politically Correct View of H. L. Mencken." *Liberty* 17, no. 2 (2003), http://libertyunbound.com/archive/03_02/bradford-mencken.html (accessed January 22, 2007).

Drinnon, Richard. *Keeper of Concentration Camps: Dillon S. Myer and American Racism.* Berkeley: University of California Press, 1987.

Fish, Hamilton. *Memoir of an American Patriot.* Lanham, MD: Regnery, 1991.

Friedman, Saul S. *No Haven for the Oppressed: United States Policy toward Jewish Refugees, 1938–1945.* Detroit: Wayne State University Press, 1973.

Kenneally, James J. "Black Republicans during the New Deal: The Role of Joseph W. Martin, Jr." *Review of Politics* 55, no. 1 (1993): 117–39.

Lane, Rose Wilder. *The Discovery of Freedom: Man's Struggle against Authority.* New York: John Day, 1943.

Mencken, H. L. *The Impossible H. L. Mencken: A Selection of His Best Newspaper Stories.* Edited by Marion Elizabeth Rodgers. New York: Anchor, 1991.

Michael, Robert. *A Concise History of American Antisemitism.* Lanham, MD: Rowman & Littlefield, 2005.

Powell, Jim. "H. L. Mencken: America's Wittiest Defender of Liberty." *Freeman* 45, no. 9 (1995), http://www.fee.org/publications/the-freeman (accessed May 22, 2008).

Rothbard, Murray. "H. L. Mencken: The Joyous Libertarian." *New Individualist Review* 2, no. 2 (1962): 15–27.

Rudwick, Elliott M. "Oscar De Priest and the Jim Crow Restaurant in the U.S. House of Representatives." *Journal of Negro Education* 35, no. 1 (1966): 77–82.

Schuyler, George S. *Black and Conservative: The Autobiography of George S. Schuyler.* New Rochelle, NY: Arlington House, 1966.

———. *Black No More: A Novel.* 1931. Reprint, New York: Modern Library, 1999.

———. *Rac(E)Ing to the Right: Selected Essays of George S. Schuyler.* Edited by Jeffrey B. Leak. Knoxville: University of Tennessee Press, 2001.

Smith, Richard Norton. *The Colonel: The Life and Legend of Robert R. McCormick, 1880–1955.* 1999. Reprint, Evanston, IL: Northwestern University Press, 2003.

TenBroek, Jacobus, Edward Norton Barnhart, and Floyd W. Matson. *Prejudice, War, and the Constitution.* Berkeley: University of California Press, 1954.

Watner, Carl. "To Thine Own Self Be True: The Story of Raymond Cyrus Hoiles and His Freedom Newspapers." In *I Must Speak Out: The Best of the Voluntaryist, 1982–1999,* 147–58. San Francisco: Fox & Wilkes, 1999.

Weiss, Nancy J. *Farewell to the Party of Lincoln: Black Politics in the Age of FDR.* Princeton, NJ: Princeton University Press, 1983.

# 6

# Classical Liberals in the Civil Rights Era

## 1946–1964

EVENTS MOVED SWIFTLY during the civil rights era. Federal courts ruled various forms of segregation unconstitutional, thus infuriating southern conservatives. A Republican Senate refused to seat a notorious racist, and subsequent congresses passed Civil Rights Acts protecting voting rights and overturning segregation. President Dwight D. Eisenhower played an instrumental role in the desegregation of Washington, DC (1953), and the *Brown v. Board* decision (1954). Eisenhower antagonized southern Democrats with his judicial appointments, his support of civil rights legislation (watered down by Senate majority leader Lyndon B. Johnson [D-TX]), and his order to send troops to Little Rock, Arkansas, where they enforced a federal court order desegregating public schools.[1] Later, President Lyndon B. Johnson moved with the times to sign the Civil Rights Act of 1964, a bill passed by a bipartisan congressional coalition over the opposition of southern Democrats. Yet racial freedom was too important to be left to politicians: the colorful baseball manager-owner Branch Rickey integrated the national pastime by signing Jackie Robinson to the Brooklyn Dodgers. Rickey's speech explaining why he signed Robinson is an inspiring exposition of the classical liberal creed.

Classical liberals believed state-sponsored discrimination was a problem. Federal laws that struck down such discrimination were not only constitutional but appropriate for achieving individual freedom from state interference.[2] White supremacy by government fiat violated classical liberal principles. On the other hand, classical liberals—Murray Rothbard, Ayn Rand, and Barry Goldwater—opposed laws that limited an individual's freedom of association or that required him (or her) to prefer one race over another.

185

⋖⋗

## Public Schools Breed Racism (1947)

*R. C. Hoiles*

**Mendez v. Westminster (1947) was a school desegregation case involving students of Mexican ancestry. Federal judge Paul McCormick, a Coolidge appointee, based his decision on strict construction of California law and on the Fourteenth Amendment's equal protection clause. R. C. Hoiles saw the larger picture: compulsory schooling resulted in the State empowering the worst in people, rather than letting them be free. Milton Friedman echoes this point in his essay below.**

⋖⋗

The rebuff to the Santa Ana School Board in its case before the Ninth U.S. Circuit Court of Appeals in their appealed segregation case should make the members of the Santa Ana board bow their heads in shame.

The Santa Ana School Board had for years been segregating Mexican pupils from other pupils. The Los Angeles Federal District Court ruled against the school boards in their practice of segregation. The board appealed the case to the Ninth U.S. Circuit Court.

The Ninth U.S. Circuit Court of Appeals unanimously ruled against the board of education. They denounced the practice of segregation as a "vicious principle" and denounced school trustees as violating their oaths of office.

It seems that the Santa Ana School Board knows no law except might makes right. The members of the board thought they had the power and they wanted to use it. They were not stopped because of their beliefs in Christian, moral and American principles; they had to be stopped by the court ruling against their desire to show their authority. The Fourteenth amendment to the constitution prevented them from continuing their un-American, un-Christian desires.

While all of the justices denounced this act of segregation, Justice William Denman in a separate opinion severely criticized the board members. He said, "In the instant case these Orange county trustees, public officers sworn to uphold the Constitution of the state of California, brazenly proclaimed their guilt in their discrimination in violation of the state educational laws.

"What is overlooked in the court's opinion (the majority opinion) is the fact that the appellants themselves declare they have violated the oaths of office and, in effect, say 'Well, what are you going to do about it.'

"Were the vicious principle sought to be established in Orange county followed elsewhere in scores of school districts, the adolescent minds of American children would become infected."

If the consciences of the Santa Ana board members had not been stultified, they would bow their heads in shame.

And yet we have as a member of this board a man that professes to be a disciple of Jesus Christ who holds a pulpit. We have another member that was a Sunday School teacher and another member a leader in the church. Yet, these men and women disobey the moral laws they profess to teach and have to be stopped by the policemen, the state.

It is little wonder that there is so much moral delinquency throughout our land when we have members of this type on the board of education responsible for the training of our children.

But that is the natural result of compulsory education. Men of this type are the kind that are usually on every board of education in the United States—self-seekers who want power; who want to appear to be leaders; who are willing to violate their oaths of office in order to let their will prevail.

If this rebuke is not evidence of the contention of this newspaper that the state cannot educate the youth of the land from a moral standpoint, and instead of retarding crime state education will increase it, then there is no such thing as evidence.

Source: "Santa Ana School Board Severely Criticized," *Santa Ana Register*, April 16, 1947. Reprinted with the permission of the *Orange County Register*, © 1947.

## Minority Report: Bilbo Must Go (1947)

*Styles Bridges and Bourke Hickenlooper*

The Republican minority on a special U.S. Senate committee investigating charges of voter intimidation condemned Senator Theodore Bilbo (D-MS), while the outgoing Democratic majority rationalized his vicious racism. Bilbo's inflammatory race baiting was so legendary, and infamous, that it gave rise to the term "Bilboism," used to describe the worst form of racial hatred. Bilbo's biographer describes "The Man" of Mississippi as a "Redneck Liberal": a loyal New Dealer eager to spend money on his constituents, but only those with white skin. A white supremacist, Bilbo advocated congressional spending to deport black Americans to Africa, an argument he made in *Take Your Choice: Separation or Mongrelization* (1947).[3] Bilbo's views were well known long before his expulsion from the Senate. In 1938, he said, "Move the whole 12,000,000 American Negroes back to the land of Africa. . . . We moved the Indians. . . . Then why can we not move the Negro in the same way?"[4]

ℰ∽

Mr. [Allen] Ellender [D-LA], from the Special Committee to Investigate Senatorial Campaign Expenditures, 1946, submitted the following [Majority Report, Democrats]:

While the record shows that in some respects Senator Bilbo's campaign oratory was crude and in poor taste as viewed by some, it is our opinion that these statements cannot and should not be reasonably construed as indicative of moral turpitude or as unconstitutional and illegal. Mississippi politics have always been heated, and the type of campaign oratory used by Senator Bilbo conforms to the custom prevalent in Mississippi for many years and to the wishes of the white citizenry of Mississippi regarding their candidate's position as evidenced by the returns in the primary, in which Senator Bilbo led his nearest opponent by nearly 40,000 votes. We consider it a highly dangerous precedent for the Senate of the United States to criticize one of its Members for conforming to the pattern desired by the electorate in his particular State. . . .

Minority Views of Mr. Bridges and Mr. Hickenlooper:

We feel that upon this record the conclusion that the primary campaign in Mississippi was illegally and unconstitutionally inflamed by advocacy of Senator Bilbo is inescapable. Assuming it to be a fact that white supremacy has long been the traditional pattern in Mississippi and perhaps many of the Southern States, nevertheless, the ordinary type of southern campaign oratory does not include the impertinent, illegal, and indiscreet type of speech consistently used by Senator

Bilbo during May and June 1946. In addition to the quotations admitted by Senator Bilbo, as outlined in the earlier portion of this report, the following relevant and contemptible language formed a part of his campaign speeches:

* * * [asterisk ellipses in the original] I think Fred Sullen's "friendly" warning to Mississippi Negroes is aptly stated: "Staying away from the polls on July 2 will be the best way to prevent unhealthy, and unhappy results."

* * * Congresswoman Clare Booth Luce is the greatest nigger lover in the North except Old Lady Eleanor Roosevelt. Yep, Old Lady Roosevelt is worse. . . . In Washington she forced our southern girls to use the stools and the toilets of darn syphilitic nigger women. . . .

Never to the knowledge of the undersigned has such vile, contemptible, inflammatory, and dangerous language been uttered in a campaign for the purpose of procuring nomination and election by an incumbent and Member of the United States Senate, sworn to uphold the Constitution. Where, as in the case of Senator Bilbo, it goes far beyond mere crudeness and strikes with disturbing force at the bastions of our national solidarity, such speech constitutes a corrupt and flagrant abuse of the right of free speech. It cannot be justified on the basis of expediency or tradition, and after the decision of the Supreme Court in Smith v. Allwright, the illegality of advocating exclusion of Negroes from the polls for reason of color or race is apparent. [*Smith v. Allwright* (1944) struck down the reconstituted "white-only primaries" of the Democratic Party in southern states.] The evidence presented to the committee clearly demonstrates that Senator Bilbo in his primary campaign in Mississippi has violated the Federal Constitution, the Federal Criminal Code, and the Hatch Act, and has aided, abetted, and urged the violation of these laws by officials of his own party in that State.

We also are of the opinion, based upon the inescapable conclusion, that must be drawn from the entire record, that Senator Theodore G. Bilbo by his own deliberate acts and upon his individual responsibility is guilty of such acts and conduct in connection with the 1946 primaries and election in the State of Mississippi as are contrary to sound public policy, harmful to the dignity and honor of the Senate, dangerous to the perpetuity of free government, and taint with fraud and corruption the credentials for a seat in the Senate presented by the said Theodore G. Bilbo.

Source: Styles Bridges (R-NH) and Bourke B. Hickenlooper (R-IA), in U.S. Congress, Special Committee to Investigate Senatorial Campaign Expenditures, Investigation of Senatorial Campaign Expenditures, 1946, *Report of the Special Committee to Investigate Senatorial Campaign Expenditures* [minority report], 80th Cong,, 1st sess., report no. 1, January 3, 1947, 9, 21–23.

## Speech to Unseat Senator Bilbo (1947)

*Robert Taft et al.*

Robert A. Taft (1889–1953) was the son of President William A. Taft and a U.S. senator from Ohio. The esteemed "Mr. Republican" supported congressional investigations that led to Bilbo's ouster from the Senate. Here Taft breaks a southern filibuster aimed at preventing the seating of any senators. *The Chicago Tribune's* front-page headline read: "G.O.P. Wins: Bilbo Kept Out."[5] Bilbo died of cancer later in the year.

⚬

**January 3**

The Secretary. The clerk will call the second name on the list.

The Chief Clerk called the name of Theodore G. Bilbo, of Mississippi.

Mr. [Glen] TAYLOR [D-ID]. Mr. Secretary, I send to the desk a resolution. . . .

The Chief Clerk read the resolution (S. Res. 1), as follows:

Whereas the Special Committee To Investigate Senatorial Campaign Expenditures, 1946, has conducted an investigation into the senatorial election in Mississippi in 1946, which investigation indicates that Theodore G. Bilbo may be guilty of violating the Constitution of the United States, the statutes of the United States, and his oath of office as a Senator of the United States in that he is alleged to have conspired to prevent citizens of the United States from exercising their constitutional rights to participate in the said election; and that he is alleged to have committed violations of [the Hatch Act]; and

Whereas the Special Committee To Investigate the National Defense Program has completed an inquiry into certain transactions between Theodore G. Bilbo and various war contractors and has found officially that the said BILBO, "in return for the aid he had given certain war contractors . . . received political contributions, accepted personal compensation . . . and that by his these transactions Senator BILBO misused his high office and violated certain Federal Statutes. . . ."

*Resolved,* That the claim of the said Theodore G. Bilbo to a seat in the United States Senate is hereby referred to the Committee on Rules . . . that until the coming in of the report of said committee, and until the final action of the Senate thereon, the said Theodore G. Bilbo be, and he is hereby, denied a seat in the United States Senate. . . .

Mr. TAYLOR. . . . Let me detail briefly the evidence against Mr. Bilbo. I shall consider first, because I believe it to be of first importance, the charge that Mr. Bilbo conspired to and did prevent duly qualified citizens from voting because of their race or color, in direct violation of the Constitution.

The contemporary news reports amply illustrate the type of activity in which Mr. Bilbo engaged. . . .

Time magazine of July 1, 1946, contained this account:

"Three of his four opponents * * * were campaigning hard. But Bilbo paid no heed. Instead he howled a warning, 'The white people of Mississippi are sitting on a volcano. * * * We are faced with a Nation-wide campaign to integrate the nigger with the social life of this country. . . . '

"I call on every red-blooded white man to use any means to keep the niggers away from the polls. If you don't understand what that means, you are just plain dumb."

An article by Harry Henderson and Sam Shaw in Collier's, July 6, 1946, quotes Mr. Bilbo, as follows:

> The poll tax won't keep 'em from voting. What keeps 'em from voting is section 244 of the constitution of 1890 that Senator George wrote. It says that a man to register must be able to read and explain the constitution or explain the constitution when read to him. * * * And then Senator George wrote a constitution that damn few white men and no niggers at all can explain. * * * . . .

Race hatred has always been the favorite theme of his repertoire, and we here in the Senate have often listened to his peculiar anthropological theories. . . . Invariably, they were couched in a language of violence; and if these were his accents on the Senate floor, what can we assume to have been his speech upon the hustings? . . .

Is the white robe and hood the uniform of a debating society? Is it the costume of a discussion group? Or is it the mask of the Ku Klux Klan, a secret organization which has committed more crimes under cover of darkness than any other organization in the Nation's history, an organization which from its inception has been dedicated to the oppression of Negroes, to an attempt to reduce them to the status of animals, to the denial of their franchise by beatings, bloodshed, torture, mayhem, threats, coercion, and murder?

Mr. BILBO has taken the solemn midnight pledge of membership in this organization. He has signed his name in blood to its tenets. In a recent radio speech, he admitted membership in the Ku Klux Klan. I quote him:

"I am a member of the Ku Klux Klan No. 40, called Bilbo, Bilbo Klan No. 40, Poplarvine, Miss." He said that he regarded his oath so conscientiously that "once a klansman, always a klansman. . . ."

[A filibuster ensues as Democrats try to tie up Senate business and seat Bilbo.]

Mr. THOMAS of Oklahoma. Since I started to read the report the Senate has been in constant disorder; apparently but few Members are paying any attention to the subject of the charges made against Senator BILBO, and few Senators are paying any attention to the findings of the majority of the committee. . . .

Mr. TAFT. I merely wanted to point out that the Senator was complaining that Senators were not listening to him. My answer to that is that the Senator is talking on wholly irrelevant matters which are not before the Senate at the time, and therefore Senators have a perfect right not to listen to the Senator from Oklahoma. . . .

Resort to a filibuster in such an important matter, for such a wholly inconsequential purpose, namely, to prevent the temporary postponement of this question until the Senate can organize itself, is so unjustifiable that it seems to me that if those who are conducting the filibuster, who are preventing the swearing in of 35 Senators from other States, are not willing to change their minds, they are going to face a complete change in the rules of the Senate. They are going to face a change which will bring about a majority cloture on all questions, and I think that will have the full support of the country.

We have shown today that two-thirds of the Senate desire that the Senate be organized without Mr. BILBO, and that the question of his prima facie right to a seat be considered immediately after that organization; yet, in spite of that, a few desire to thwart the will of the entire Senate.

### January 4

Mr. [Allen] ELLENDER [D-LA]. Senator BILBO has been one of the few Senators on this floor to speak his mind. He is a man who has the courage of his convictions. He has led the fight, on many occasions, against the antilynching bill. I helped him, as did many other Southerners. If he is to be condemned for that, so am I; for I helped him, as did the others. . . .

When the poll-tax bill was discussed before the Senate, Senator BILBO always spearheaded the movement to defeat the bill. . . .

Senator BILBO spearheaded the move to kill another bill, the so-called FEPC bill [Fair Employment Practices Commission]. I was with him in that move, which brought about a lively fight on the Senate floor. . . .

When it was disclosed that in a letter to a lady in New York he had addressed as "Dear Dago," reams of paper were utilized throughout the country to advertise that fact, to talk about and discuss it. Why? The reason why that was done was that for the past 4 or 5 years there has been a consistent effort made by many groups to build a case against Senator BILBO. . . .

Why should Life magazine, Time, and other publications have sent many editors and photographers to the State of Mississippi at great cost in order to follow the campaign of Senator BILBO? . . . if they should succeed in throwing him out, other Members of the Senate who share his views had better look out. . . .

The great Republican Party is now in power, and I was hopeful that it would make a good start. For many years it has been criticizing. . . .

I cannot help but express disappointment in many of my colleagues across the aisle who are insisting on the course which they are now pursuing. . . .

Unanimous-Consent Agreement as to Credentials of Senator-Elect from Mississippi, Etc

Mr. BARKLEY. The Senator-elect from Mississippi has advised me that he is compelled, in the interest of his health—and it may be in the interest of his life—to return immediately to New Orleans in order that the operation which Dr. Oschner desired to perform on the 26th of December, involving the removal of a larger portion of the lower jaw, two glands in the throat of the Senator-elect, and possibly a malignant growth in his cheek, may be completed at the earliest possible date. . . .

I ask unanimous consent that the credentials of the Senator-elect from Mississippi, Mr. Theodore G. BILBO, lie on the table without prejudice and without action until such time as he is able to return, in view of his physical condition. . . .

I also ask that the certificate of the Senator-elect from Mississippi lie on the table without prejudice and without action until such time as the official physician assigned to the Congress, Dr. Calver, certifies that he is able to return here. . . .

Mr. TAFT. There is unanimous approval of the agreement which he proposes.

Source: Robert Taft et al., *Congressional Record*, January 3–4, 1947, 7–11, 25, 77–78.

## A Negro Voter Sizes Up Taft: One View of Mr. Republican (1951)

### Zora Neale Hurston

Zora Neale Hurston (1891?–1960) was a brilliant writer best known for her literary contributions during the "Harlem Renaissance" of the 1920s and 1930s. Hurston explored African American folklore in *Mules and Men* (1935) and *Their Eyes Were Watching God* (1937). Her reputation declined in the late 1930s as left-wing writers objected to her apolitical fiction and her classical liberal ideology. During the 1940s and 1950s, Hurston eked out a living as a freelance writer for the *Saturday Evening Post* and other publications.

Hurston believed in the power of individual freedom, in both the creative and political realms. She refused to be a "race woman" and criticized those who took pride in group achievements, noting that only individuals merited praise. In her autobiography, *Dust Tracks on the Road* (1942), she wrote:

"Race Pride" in me had to go. And anyway, why should I be proud to be a Negro? Why should anybody be proud to be white? Or yellow? Or

Official U.S. Senate portrait of Robert A. Taft (1953). (http://www
.senate.gov/artandhistory/art/common/image/Painting_32_00030
.htm.)

red? After all, the word "race" is a loose classification of physical characteristics. It tells nothing about the insides of people. Pointing at achievements tells nothing either. Races have never done anything. What seems
race achievement is the work of individuals. The white race did not go
into a laboratory and invent incandescent light. That was Edison. The
Jews did not work out Relativity. That was Einstein. The Negroes did
not find out the inner secrets of peanuts and sweet potatoes, nor the
secret of the development of the egg. That was Carver and Just. If you
are under the impression that every white man is an Edison, just look

around a bit. If you have the idea that every Negro is a Carver, you had better take off plenty of time to do your searching. . . .

So Race Pride and Race Consciousness seem to me to be not only fallacious, but a thing to be abhorred. It is the root of misunderstanding and hence misery and injustice. I cannot, with logic cry against it in others and wallow in it myself. The only satisfaction to be gained from it anyway is, "I ain't nothing, my folks ain't nothing, but that makes no difference at all. I belong to such-and-such a race." Poor nourishment according to my notion.[6]

Politically, Hurston was an anti–New Deal Republican. Harshly critical of Roosevelt, she believed FDR was a false liberal who emphasized the State over the individual. In 1952, Hurston supported Senator Robert A. Taft for president because she shared what the *Indianapolis Star* called "Mr. Republican's" classic liberal belief that "the main purpose of government is to set men free and to keep them free, to give equal opportunity to all and special favor to none." Note her discussion of the showdown between Taft and Bilbo.

ℰↃ

"MISTER REPUBLICAN," otherwise known as Robert A. Taft, of Ohio, has an over-average chance to be chosen Elephant Boy of 1952. At a characteristic Taft gait, the senator has been moving up the field since 1936, until now he is in position to make his bid for the collar of roses. . . .

Taft has strong Negro backing in Ohio now. They no longer mention him politely as "Mister Robert A." He is "Senator Bob" now, and they take great pride in him. They admit now that his quiet manner fooled them. . . .

"Nobody else but Senator Bob could have thrown that Bilbo clean out of the Senate." With the gestures he made, you got the idea that Senator Taft had grabbed hold of his colleague from Mississippi and flung him bodily from the Senate chamber. "Don't let his quiet way fool you. That Senator Taft is a killer."

It is to be remembered that Senator Bilbo, "The Man," was re-elected to the Senate from Mississippi. For years he had amused himself by saying things from the Senate floor infuriating to Negroes. He was the sign and symbol of all that Negroes in general hated in American politics. Senator Taft, chairman of the Republican Policy Committee, personally took the lead, stood on the floor of the Senate and asked for a vote against Bilbo's taking the oath. The Senate upheld Taft's motion and their vote thus excluded Bilbo from his seat in the Senate. Needless to say, the Negroes all over the country rejoiced at this.

The Negroes of Ohio point with pride to Taft's long record on other measures affecting Negroes: antipolltax legislation, FEPC, consideration of the civil-rights bills, housing and rent programs, discrimination in selecting displaced persons for admission to the United States, withholding Federal education funds wherever racial discrimination was practiced, cloture, attempts to limit debate and break up filibustering, antilynch bills and, under the Taft-Hartley Law, a clause to protect Negroes' right to work regardless of the discriminatory union rules. In August, 1942, he voted to exempt all servicemen from poll taxes in national or congressional elections. This enabled many Negroes to vote for the first time in the South.

"Our Senator Taft's record is wonderful," an educated woman active in Ohio politics observed, "but I'm not sure that all of our people understand his motives. Senator Taft is not pro-Negro. He is not prowhite. He is not prolabor, nor promanagement. The man has some strange passion for justice. He would work just as hard to stop us tomorrow if he believed that we were oppressing anybody. And he will tell you so if you ask him. That gives what he does more weight with me. He is not trying to win our votes so much as he is trying to do what is right. . . ."

"Senator Taft," said the Indianapolis Star, "is a liberal in the traditional sense that Jefferson and Washington were liberal. He believes the main purpose of government is to set men free and to keep them free, to give equal opportunity to all and special favor to none. . . ."

We, as Negroes, will not find Taft a liberal in the sense we have been taking the word to mean, for Taft, I repeat, is not pro-anybody. Neither pro-Negro, prowhite, prolabor, promanagement or anything else. He is for the cause and the occasion when he believes it to be right. He states this carefully in four points in his My Political Credo:

1. The people and the individual retain true liberty.

2. All citizens are assured equal justice under law, that they may have life and liberty.

3. All citizens have equality of opportunity, particularly in their youth.

4. All citizens have a standard of living which will make happiness possible.

Therefore, it is as plain as white on rice that we, as Negroes, are included, provided we can disregard the intense political appeals to racial antagonism of the last few administrations, and see ourselves once more simply as citizens. You heard the man say "All." And from his record, when Taft says "all" he means all. . . .

Throughout the New Deal era the relief program was the biggest weapon ever placed in the hands of those who sought power and votes. If the average American had been asked flatly to abandon his rights as a citizen and to submit to a personal rule, he would have chewed tobacco and spit white lime. But under relief, dependent upon the Government for their daily bread, men gradually relaxed their watchfulness and submitted to the will of the "Little White Father," more or less. Once they had weakened that far, it was easy to go on and on voting for more relief, and leaving Government affairs in the hands of a few. The change from a republic to a dictatorship was imperceptibly pushed ahead.

Senator Taft has taken notice of this, "What concerns me is that people gradually come to accept limitations on freedom as the necessary incidents of government. They hear of outrageous treatment given to others with a kind of dull interest, instead of the fiery resentment such incidents would have aroused in the past. . . ."

Never mind that we have run off after strange gods like the rest of the nation. We, too, can see the light and be reasoned with. Let Taft come among us with his blunt truthfulness, his bag of facts and his reasoning, and tell us what he has to say.

Source: Zora Neale Hurston, "A Negro Voter Sizes Up Taft," *Saturday Evening Post*, December 8, 1951, 29, 150–52. Reprinted with the permission of Victoria Sanders & Associates, agents for the Zora Neale Hurston Estate.

## The Right to Play Interracial Tennis (1948)

*H. L. Mencken*

The struggle for racial freedom played out in every corner of American life, including sport. In 1947, for example, Jackie Robinson broke the color bar-

Portrait of Zora Neale Hurston (1938). (Library of Congress, Prints & Photographs Division, LC-USZ62-79898.)

rier in baseball. Yet segregation was still the law in the Jim Crow South, forcibly separating the races in ways both serious and absurd. Here H. L. Mencken savages the "relics of Ku Kluxry" that prohibited blacks and whites from playing—gasp!—tennis together on public courts.

❧

When, on July 11 last, a gang of so-called progressives, white and black, went to Druid Hill Park to stage an inter-racial tennis combat, and were collared and jugged by the cops, it became instantly impossible for anyone to discuss the matter in a newspaper, save, of course, to report impartially the proceedings in court. . . .

. . . Has the Park Board any right in law to forbid white and black citizens, if they are so inclined, to join in harmless games together on public playgrounds?

Again: Is such a prohibition, even supposing that it is lawful, supported by anything to be found in common sense and common decency?

I do not undertake to answer the first question, for I am too ignorant of law, but my answer to the second is a loud and unequivocal No. A free citizen in a free state, it seems to me, has an inalienable right to play with whomsoever he will, so long as he does not disturb the general peace. If any other citizen, offended by the spectacle, makes a pother, then that other citizen, and not the man exercising his inalienable right, should be put down by the police.

Certainly it is astounding to find so much of the spirit of the Georgia Cracker surviving in the Maryland Free State, and under official auspices. The public parks are supported by the taxpayer, including the colored taxpayer, for the health and pleasure of the whole people. Why should cops be sent into them to separate those people against their will into separate herds? Why should the law set up distinctions and discriminations which the persons directly affected themselves reject? . . .

It is high time that all such relics of Ku Kluxry be wiped out in Maryland. The position of the colored people, since the political revolution of 1895 [a Republican overthrow of one-party Democratic rule], has been gradually improving in the State, and it has already reached a point surpassed by few other states. But there is still plenty of room for further advances, and it is irritating indeed to see one of them blocked by silly Dogberrys. The Park Board rule is irrational and nefarious. It should be got rid of forthwith. . . .

In answer to all the foregoing I expect confidently to hear the argument that the late mixed tennis matches were not on the level, but were arranged by Communists to make trouble. So far as I am aware this may be true but it seems to me to be irrelevant. What gave the Communists their chance was the existence of the Park Board's rule. If it had carried on its business with more sense they would have been baffled. The way to dispose of their chicaneries is not to fight them when they are right.

Source: H. L. Mencken, "Equal Rights in Parks: Mencken Calls Tennis Order Silly, Nefarious," *Baltimore Sun*, November 9, 1948, 14. Reprinted with the permission of the *Baltimore Sun*, permission conveyed through Copyright Clearance Center, Inc.

# Let Freedom Ring! (1952)

## Archibald Carey Jr.

This political speech is included for its rhetorical importance. During the 1950s, the Republican Party still attracted a large share of the African American vote (one-third in presidential elections). Archibald Carey Jr. (1908–1981), a prominent minister and black Republican from Chicago, appeared before the Republican national convention and gave a stirring address on the urgent need to guarantee racial freedom to all Americans.[7] Martin Luther King Jr.'s "I Have a Dream" speech (1963) echoes the rousing finale of Carey's address (see King entry below). An obscure city councilman from Phoenix listened to Carey's speech and wrote praising him for being so "forceful" in his discussion of civil rights. The Arizonan was Barry Goldwater (see entry below).

ல

In the long history of America the Republican Party has been the party of freedom. It was the Republican Party that freed America of the blot of human bondage, by abolishing slavery. . . . And if the people are ever to be freed from the cruel burden of crushing taxes, the shameful blight of inequal treatment, the awful slaughter of undeclared wars and the confusion and corruption of government that confounds the people, and clouds our national honor, it will be the Republican Party that frees them again. . . .

As a Negro-American, I have been sorely disappointed, and millions of freedom-loving people of every race have been disappointed with me. We have heard [Democrats] promise an anti-lynch law and a Federal FEPC, to abolish the poll tax in national elections and end segregation in the Armed Forces. On critical roll calls most Republicans supported these measures, but still the anti-lynch law and FEPC remain pledges unfulfilled, the poll tax is not forbidden and segregation still exists in the Armed Forces. More irresponsible promises. When some Democrat cries, "The Dixiecrats did it," I answer—there is no Dixiecrat Party—only the Democrat. North and South, they're all Democrats and it is the Democrat Party that must account for its failure. The string of promises dangled before my people like a glittering necklace has been fashioned into a tight-fitting noose, strangling their freedom and their freedom of choice, and sometimes even their hopes. . . .

. . . The people turn to us, the Republicans, to get performance. Our destiny is at once, as simple but as solemn as that—to give performance and fulfillment to the great hopes which the people nurture in their hearts.

Foremost among these is the issue of human rights—the question of fair and equal treatment for every man, regardless of his race or his color, his religion or his national origin. Although many different races, religions and nationalities suffer discrimination, the matter comes to focus today upon the Negro-American. . . . The Negro-American aspires to first class citizenship and his vote will adhere to whichever party and nominee goes furthest to implement that aspiration. And there are millions of non-Negroes too—Jews, Catholics, Mexicans, Orientals and immigrants from the corners of the earth, whose major love is freedom, too. . . .

Sometimes I'm asked, "What does the Negro-American want?" The answer is, "Nothing special." Just what everybody else wants, nothing more—nothing less. We don't want any special cars to ride in or rooms to wait in. We don't want any special houses and blocks to live in or schools to go to. We don't want any special favors to put us ahead, or special agreements to hold us back. All we want is the right to live and work and play, to vote and be promoted, to fight for our country and hope to be President, like everyone else. More than that we do not ask, but with less than that we shall never be content.

We, Negro-Americans, sing with all other Americans:

My country, 'tis of thee,

Sweet land of liberty

Of thee, I sing

Land where my fathers died

Land of the Pilgrim's pride

From every mountain side

Let freedom ring!

That's exactly what we mean—from every mountain side, let freedom ring. Not only from the Green Mountains and White Mountains of Vermont and New Hampshire; Not only from the Catskills of New York; but from the Ozarks in Arkansas, from the Stone Mountain in Georgia, from the Great Smokies of Tennessee and from the Blue Ridge Mountains of Virginia—Not only for the minorities of the United States, but for the persecuted of Europe, for the rejected of Asia, for the disfranchised of South Africa and for the disinherited of all the earth—may the Republican Party, under God, from every mountain side, LET FREEDOM RING!

Source: Archibald Carey Jr. Republican National Committee, *Address of Honorable Archibald J. Carey Jr., Member of the Chicago City Council, to the Republican National Convention*, July 8, 1952, Chicago, Chicago Historical Society.


## Brown v. Board: *Not Just a "Black Thing" (1954)*

*American Jewish Congress*

From a classical liberal perspective, *Brown v. Board* was a mixed blessing. The unanimous Supreme Court decision struck down state-sponsored racial segregation but relied in doing so upon questionable social science rather than classical liberal principles.[8] Moreover, the court maintained the discretion to determine when racial discrimination was "reasonable"—thus leaving the door open to future government meddling in race. However, among the amicus curiae ("friend of the court") briefs, the one by the American Jewish Congress (filed in 1952) exemplified the classical liberal commitment to individual freedom, natural rights, and the difference between state-sponsored and private discrimination—it even imagined a world of only private schools, if merely for legal argumentation. Shortly thereafter, Frank Chodorov, George S. Schuyler, Milton Friedman, and Leonard Read argued for private schools to replace socialized education.[9] By the end of the twentieth century, these proposals for school privatization and choice had entered the mainstream and offered hope to minority youth trapped in failing government schools.[10]

⌘

Believing as we do that Jewish interests are inseparable from the interests of justice, the American Jewish Congress cannot remain impassive or disinterested when persecution, discrimination or humiliation is inflicted upon any human being because of his race, religion, color, national origin or ancestry. Through the thousands of years of our tragic history we have learned one lesson well: the persecution at any time of any minority portends the shape and intensity of persecution of all minorities. There is, however, an additional reason for our interest. The special concern of the Jewish people in human rights derives from an immemorial tradition which proclaims the common origin and end of all mankind and affirms, under the highest sanction of faith and human aspirations, the common and inalienable rights of all men. The struggle for human dignity and liberty is thus of the very substance of the Jewish tradition.

We submit this brief amicus because we are convinced that the policy of segregation has had a blighting effect upon Americans and consequently upon American democratic institutions. We believe that the doctrine of "separate but equal" has engendered hatred, fear and ignorance. We recognize in this triumvirate our greatest enemy in the struggle for human freedom. But our concern must not be construed as limited to minorities alone. The treatment of minorities in a community is indicative of its political and moral standards and ultimately determinative of the happiness of all its members. Our immediate objective here is to secure unconditional equality for Americans of Negro ancestry. Our ultimate objective in this case, as in all others, is to preserve the dignity of all men so that we may achieve full equality in a free society. . . .

The Fourteenth Amendment was intended to and did invalidate the gross discrimination of the Black Codes. It may be assumed, at least for the purposes of this case, that it did not lay upon the states the affirmative obligation to undo all the results of slavery. Thus, the Amendment did not reach whatever social inequality remained. Private individuals and institutions were free to discriminate as they chose.

Specifically, no question would have arisen under the Amendment in the area of education if the states had simply refrained from providing public schools. But if they did provide public schools, they were required to do so in a manner which did not cause unequal treatment. We pass over the question whether the Amendment would have been violated if the creation of public, racially-segregated schools had had no effect on the existing racial inequality. It is unnecessary to consider that question because, we submit, when government gives official sanction to pre-existing social inequality, its action comes a change in both the degree and the nature of the inequality and incorporates it into its own activities. This change takes place because once a social classification based on group inferiority is formally adopted by the state, the ensuing official inferiority in turn intensifies and deepens the social inequality from which it stems. As long as law is not called into play to shape conduct, gradual changes in attitude can bring about corresponding changes in conduct patterns. These changes, in turn, further the attitude changes. Once the law intervenes, however, gradual spontaneous change becomes impossible.

Suppose, for example, that Kansas did not maintain a public school system and had no laws requiring segregation in education. As already noted, privately operated schools would be free to segregate and even to exclude racial groups entirely. Those private groups, however, who rejected racial inequality would also be free to act according to their principles. Most important, those who opposed segregation would be able to change the situation gradually by persuading one school authority at a time to change its policy. Each success they achieved would demonstrate the feasibility of non-segregated schools and thereby increase their chances of success with other schools.

On the other hand, when the state places the policy of segregation in its laws, it freezes the social inequality in whose mold the laws are cast. More than that, the laws eliminate the free play of individualism and force all, without exception, to conform their conduct to the caste system. It is then no longer possible to urge gradual change or to attempt step-by-step improvement. The statute becomes a bulwark against dissentient opinion, persuasion and even economic pressure. . . .

Equality is impossible in a racially segregated grade school system. The inferior status in which it freezes the Negroes and the harmful effects which it has on them are the direct results of the fact that the state lends its power, resources and authority to the caste system. Under the principles of the Shelley case, supra, such use, or abuse, of state power is a violation of the Fourteenth Amendment. Regardless of where the doctrine of "white supremacy" originated, regardless of whether its tenets find explicit expression in state acts, and regardless of the avowed purpose of state-imposed racial segregation, that segregation is unconstitutional because, invoking "the full coercive power of government" [Shelley] it acts as no other force can to extend inequality, impede its elimination and incorporate it in the facilities which it provides for its citizens.

Respectfully submitted,

AMERICAN JEWISH CONGRESS,

Amicus Curiae,

HERMAN L. WEISMAN,

SHAD POLIER,

WILL MASLOW,

JOSEPH B. ROBISON,

Attorneys.

October 9, 1952

Source: American Jewish Congress, *Brief as Amicus Curiae, submitted for consideration in Brown v. Board of Education* (decided 347 U.S. 483).

## A Call from God: Christianity, Colorblindness, and Character (1956)

*Branch Rickey*

Branch Rickey (1881–1965) grew up in rural Ohio and earned a sports scholarship to Ohio Wesleyan University. A devout Methodist, Rickey played minor league baseball but refused to play on Sundays. Later, Rickey became general manager of the St. Louis Cardinals, where he pioneered modern baseball practices: the batting cage, radio broadcasts, and a "farm system" of minor league teams that boosted the Cardinals to World Series championships. Politically, Branch Rickey was an anti–New Deal Republican, but his primary concerns were God, baseball, and living the Golden Rule by treating everyone according to merit, regardless of race. In 1947, he signed African American player Jackie Robinson to the Brooklyn Dodgers, a move considered by many a landmark in civil rights history. Part businessman, part missionary, Rickey describes breaking baseball's color bar as a "call from God."

෴

Now I could talk at some length, of course, about the problem of hiring a negro ball player after an experience of 25 years in St. Louis, where at the end I

African American using the "colored entrance" of a movie theater in Mississippi (1939). (Library of Congress, Prints & Photographs Division, LC-USZ62–115416.)

had no stock at all in the club and no negro was permitted to buy his way into the grandstand during that entire period of my residence in St. Louis. The only place a negro could witness a ball game in St. Louis was to buy his way into the bleachers—the pavilion. With an experience of that kind in back of me, and having had sort of a "bringins up" that was a bit contrary to that regime, milieu, in St. Louis, I went to Brooklyn. . . .

Then I had to get the right man off the field. I couldn't come with a man to break down a tradition that had in it centered and concentrated all the prejudices of a great many people north and south unless he was good. He must justify himself upon the positive principle of merit. He must be a great player. I must not risk an excuse of trying to do something in the sociological field, or in the race field, just because of sort of a "holier than thou." I must be sure that the man was good on the field, but more dangerous to me, at that time, and even now, is the wrong man off the field. It didn't matter to me so much in choosing a man off the field that he was temperamental, righteously subject to resentments. I wanted a man of exceptional intelligence, a man who was able to grasp and control the responsibilities of himself to his race and could carry that load. That was the greatest danger point of all. . . .

A man of exceptional courage, and exceptional intelligence, a man of basically fine character, and he can thank his forbearers for a lot of it. He comes from the right sort of home, and I knew all this, and when somebody, somewhere, thinks in terms of a local athletic club not playing some other club because of the presence on the squad of a man of color. I am thinking that if an exhibition game were to be played in these parts against a team on whose squad was Jackie Robinson, even leaving out all of the principle of fair play, all the elements of equality and citizenship, all the economic necessities connected with it, all the violations of the whole form and conceptions of our Government from its beginning up to now, leave it all out of the picture, he would be depriving some of the citizens of his own community, some wonderful boys, from seeing an exhibition of skill and technique, and the great, beautiful, graciousness of a slide, the like of which they could not see from any other man in this country. . . .

The church has always, and it has been a tendency of the Christian church too to undertake to establish the equality of all men in the sight of God. And to the extent which that prevailed to that extent it became inevitable that all men should ultimately become free. That was the greatest force in the world—to give every man moral stature. Of course the Emancipation Proclamation by Lincoln made the southern negro slave free, but it never did make the white man morally free. He remained a slave to his inheritances. And some are even today.

I believe that a man can play baseball as coming to him from a call from God. . . .

Character is a great thing to have in an athlete, a team. It's a great thing. And when I wonder if there is any condonation, any explanation, anything that can be done to make an extenuating circumstance out of something that violates the right of a part of our citizenship throughout the country when I know that the Man of 1900 years ago spent His life and died for the sake of freedom—the right to come, to go, to see, to think, to believe, to act. It is to be understood, but it is too profoundly regretted. . . .

. . . I'm not sure, I'm not sure that legislators ought to drive against a prominent and very antagonistic minority. I'm not sure that they should drive F.E.C. [*sic*] too fast too far. I'm not sure that the 18th Amendment [Prohibition] might

Branch Rickey signing contract with Jackie Robinson (1950). (Reprinted by permission of National Baseball Hall of Fame Library.)

repeat itself. That you would have an organization of glued antagonisms that would be able to delay the solution of a problem that is now in my judgment fast being solved, and when you once gain an eminence you do not have to recede from it. The educational process is something. . . .

. . . I think, in due time with a sureness that will make possibly the very next generation wonder and look back, as I said that you quoted me in Cincinnati, I had forgotten that I had ever said it[,] look back with incredulity upon everything that was a problem to us today in this country, and will wonder what the issue was all about. I am completely color-blind. I know that America is—it's been proven Jackie—is more interested in the grace of a man's swing, in the dexterity of his cutting a base, and his speed afoot, in his scientific body control, in his excellence as a competitor on the field. America, wide and broad, and in Atlanta, and in Georgia, will become instantly more interested in those marvelous, beautiful qualities than they are in the pigmentation of a man's skin, or indeed in the last syllable of his name. Men are coming to be regarded of value based upon their merits, and God hasten the day when Governors of our States will become sufficiently educated that they will respond to those views.

Source: Branch Rickey, speech for the "One Hundred Percent Wrong Club" banquet, Atlanta, Georgia, January 20, 1956. Broadcast on WERD 860 AM radio. *Branch Rickey Papers*, Library of Congress, Manuscript Division, Washington, DC, http://memory.loc.gov/ammem/collections/robinson/branch.html (accessed October 26, 2006). Reprinted with the permission of Branch B. Rickey III.

## Capitalism and Discrimination (1962)

### Milton Friedman

In the mid-twentieth century, economists finally turned to discrimination as a topic worthy of scholarly treatment.[11] Social histories of the civil rights movement ignore the role the business community played in voluntarily desegregating the American economy. For more, see Robert Weems's *Desegregating the Dollar* (1998). Weems shows how African American "market specialists" were especially important in educating big business to the multibillion-dollar potential of the "Negro Market."[12]

One of the great economists of the twentieth century, Milton Friedman (1912–2006) won a Nobel Prize for his scholarly contributions to economic theory. Unlike most scholars, Friedman had a knack for explaining the virtues of individual freedom to a mass public. This essay is drawn from his popular book *Capitalism and Freedom*.

ℰↃ

We have already seen how a free market separates economic efficiency from irrelevant characteristics. . . . The purchaser of bread does not know whether it was made from wheat grown by a white man or a Negro, by a Christian or a Jew. In consequence, the producer of wheat is in a position to use resources as effectively as he can, regardless of what the attitudes of the community may be toward the color, the religion, or other characteristics of the people he hires. Furthermore, and perhaps more important, there is an economic incentive in a free market to separate economic efficiency from other characteristics of the individual. A businessman or an entrepreneur who expresses preferences in his business activities that are not related to productive efficiency is at a disadvantage compared to other individuals who do not. Such an individual is in effect imposing higher costs on himself than are other individuals who do not have such preferences. Hence, in a free market they will tend to drive him out. . . .

The man who exercises discrimination pays a price for doing so. He is, as it were, "buying" what he regards as a "product." It is hard to see that discrimination can have any meaning other than a "taste" of others that one does not share. . . .

. . . I believe strongly that the color of a man's skin or the religion of his parents is, by itself, no reason to treat him differently; that a man should be judged by what he is and what he does and not by these external characteristics. I deplore what seem to me the prejudice and narrowness of outlook of those whose tastes differ from mine in this respect and I think the less of them for it. But in a society based on free discussion, the appropriate recourse is for me to seek to persuade them that their tastes are bad and that they should change their views and their behavior, not to use coercive power to enforce my tastes and my attitudes on others. . . .

As already stressed, the appropriate recourse of those of us who believe that a particular criterion such as color is irrelevant is to persuade our fellows to be of like mind, not to use the coercive power of the state to force them to act in accordance with our principles. . . .

Segregation in schooling raises a particular problem not covered by the previous comments for one reason only. The reason is that schooling is, under present circumstances, primarily operated and administered by government. This means that government must make an explicit decision. It must either enforce segregation or enforce integration. Both seem to me bad solutions. Those of us who believe that color of skin is an irrelevant characteristic and that it is desirable for all to recognize this, yet who also believe in individual freedom, are therefore faced with a dilemma. If one must choose between the evils of enforced segregation or enforced integration, I myself would find it impossible not to choose integration.

. . . The appropriate solution is to eliminate government operation of the schools and permit parents to choose the kind of school they want their children to attend. In addition, of course, we should all of us, insofar as we possibly can, try by behavior and speech to foster the growth of attitudes and opinions that would lead mixed schools to become the rule and segregated schools the rare exception.

Source: Milton Friedman, "Capitalism and Discrimination," in *Capitalism and Freedom* (Chicago: University of Chicago Press, 1962), chap. 7. Reprinted by permission of the University of Chicago, © 1962 by The University of Chicago.

## A Negro Businessman Speaks His Mind (1963)

### S. B. Fuller

**Samuel B. (S. B.) Fuller (1905–1988) was a self-made African American entrepreneur who migrated from the South to Chicago, where he established a cosmetics conglomerate and branched out into other businesses. In this interview preceding the March on Washington, Fuller distanced himself from militant civil rights leaders and soon found himself boycotted by both black consumers and white southerners (who resented his buyout of a white-owned company). Nevertheless, Fuller remained an inspiration and mentor to other black businessmen. Here he alludes to the "other side" of race prejudice. The following article contained a photograph showing blacks and whites working together at Fuller's business. The caption read: "Mr. Fuller tells his supervisors to 'hire people on merit and not on the color of their skin.'"** [13]

☙❧

Q. How many employees do you have altogether?

A. We have on our direct payroll about 600 employees.

Q. How many of those are white?

A. About 20 per cent of them are white. And in our door-to-door selling, we have about 3,000 people selling and about 500 of those are white.

Q. Is there any friction? Do white persons seem to resent working for you?

A. No, the white people here are talking integration more than the colored people.

Q. What do you mean by that?

A. Here, in our organization, the white people are very sensitive about being treated as inferior in our organization. They are more concerned about discrimination than the Negroes are.

One thing that I find in my organization is this: If I don't watch very closely, the Negro bosses here will discriminate and hire all Negroes and no whites. I'm constantly watching them to see that they hire people on their merit and not on the color of their skin.

Q. Would you say, then, that racial discrimination is found among all races?

A. It is a universal human trait and people use it, if they can do so, at a profit. When it becomes unprofitable, they forget it.

Here in our organization, it pays the white people not to discriminate against the Negro, and they don't. But the Negroes will discriminate against the white people because they are trying to get the white people out of some of these well-paying jobs and put some Negroes in them. . . .

Q. Are the racial demonstrations doing any good?

A. The demonstrations have made the white man know that the Negroes are dissatisfied. But he knew that in the first place. Beyond that, I don't think they have done any good. In fact, they have done harm in the picture they give of Negroes. . . .

Q. Is getting ahead in business and industry, then, an essential part of the Negro's progress?

A. It is the really essential part. I think there's no other road that leads to progress. . . .

Q. What would be your advice today to a young Negro coming out of school?

A. My advice today is, first, go to school and get a good education. It's not up to the teacher to see that he gets it. It's up to the student. When a Negro child goes to school, he must concentrate on his work. Then, when he comes out of school, come out with something to offer, a talent that he can sell. . . .

Q. Is America, do you think, a good place for Negroes?

A. America is the best place for the Negro in the world. America is the best place for any man in the world. . . .

Q. What is the answer, then, to the Negro's future?

A. Work. And not only that: He must work and he must save his money and he must pool his money. If he wants integration, he must hire white people just as he wants white people to hire him.

Source: S. B. Fuller, "A Negro Businessman Speaks His Mind," *U.S. News & World Report*, August 19, 1963, 58–61. Copyright 1963 *U.S. News & World Report*, L.P. Reprinted with permission.

## "I Have a Dream": The Meaning of Words (1963)

*Martin Luther King Jr.*

In compiling an anthology, certain key documents are highly controversial. Do people with opposing viewpoints contest the document's meaning and appropriate it for differing ends? If so, how does the document "fit" the larger themes of the anthology?

No civil rights document is more hotly contested than Martin Luther King Jr.'s "I have a dream" speech, delivered August 28, 1963, at the Lincoln Memorial in Washington, DC. Classical liberal opponents of race preferences frequently cite the line

I have a dream that my four little children will one day live in a nation where they will not be judged by the color of their skin but by the content of their character.

Defenders of race preference fume at this appropriation of King's rhetoric and counter with lines that reflect the radical side of King:

In a sense we've come to our nation's capital to cash a check. When the architects of our republic wrote the magnificent words of the Constitution and the Declaration of Independence, they were signing a promissory note to which every American was to fall heir. . . . It is obvious today that America has defaulted on this promissory note, insofar as her citizens of color are concerned. Instead of honoring this sacred obligation, America has given the Negro people a bad check, a check which has come back marked "insufficient funds."

King emphasized "the fierce urgency of Now" and militantly rejected "the tranquilizing drug of gradualism." Clearly, these interpreters argue, King would support "benign" discrimination to redress past wrongs.

Who is right? Where does King's speech "fit" in relation to the classical liberal tradition of civil rights? Since he was assassinated in 1968, it is impossible to know what King's positions on race and liberty might be today. However, based on his philosophy at the time, the radical interpreters are correct: there is every reason to believe that King, like his associate Jesse Jackson, would have embraced massive government intervention, including preferences, for African Americans. The "dream" speech was short on specifics, but in *Why We Can't Wait* (1964) King advocated "compensatory or preferential treatment" for past discrimination against African Americans. He also proposed a "Bill of Rights for the Disadvantaged" that would offer government benefits to minorities and "the forgotten white poor."[14] On the other hand, these policy demands were means and not an end. The dream was a world that looked beyond the group distinction of race and into "the content of (individual) character." Thus, the King of 1968 would oppose a "diversity liberalism" that makes a fetish of skin color.[15] Contrary to the dream, diversity liberals plead, "Don't judge on individual merit or character but on the color of a person's skin" because it contributes to "diversity." Yet left-wing liberals cannot have it both ways—embracing the means but not the dream's end. If skin-deep diversity is the end, then there is no limit to the engineering of race relations. Skin color becomes a perpetual commodity traded in the marketplace of "diversity."

King was a social democrat who rejected the classical liberal vision of limited government. Yet King the speechmaker spoke to a national audience that did not accept his politics but was open (he hoped) to a reversal of Jim Crow. In reaching that audience, King understood the importance of words that resonated with

Americans across the political spectrum, words that rang true to the "American dream" as embodied in the Declaration of Independence. On that narrow score, King's dream "fit" the larger classical liberal tradition of civil rights. That is why the dream entered the American canon of speech. And that is why we remember the goal of judging a person's character and forget the lines that suggest a more radical King.

&

I am happy to join with you today in what will go down in history as the greatest demonstration for freedom in the history of our nation.

Five score years ago, a great American, in whose symbolic shadow we stand today, signed the Emancipation Proclamation. This momentous decree came as a great beacon light of hope to millions of Negro slaves who had been seared in the flames of withering injustice. It came as a joyous daybreak to end the long night of their captivity.

But one hundred years later, the Negro still is not free. One hundred years later, the life of the Negro is still sadly crippled by the manacles of segregation and the chains of discrimination. One hundred years later, the Negro lives on a lonely island of poverty in the midst of a vast ocean of material prosperity. One hundred years later, the Negro is still languished in the corners of American society and finds himself an exile in his own land. And so we've come here today to dramatize a shameful condition.

In a sense we've come to our nation's capital to cash a check. When the architects of our republic wrote the magnificent words of the Constitution and the Declaration of Independence, they were signing a promissory note to which every American was to fall heir. This note was a promise that all men, yes, black men as well as white men, would be guaranteed the "unalienable Rights" of "Life, Liberty and the pursuit of Happiness." It is obvious today that America has defaulted on this promissory note, insofar as her citizens of color are concerned. Instead of honoring this sacred obligation, America has given the Negro people a bad check, a check which has come back marked "insufficient funds."

But we refuse to believe that the bank of justice is bankrupt. We refuse to believe that there are insufficient funds in the great vaults of opportunity of this nation. And so, we've come to cash this check, a check that will give us upon demand the riches of freedom and the security of justice.

We have also come to this hallowed spot to remind America of the fierce urgency of Now. This is no time to engage in the luxury of cooling off or to take the tranquilizing drug of gradualism. Now is the time to make real the promises of democracy. Now is the time to rise from the dark and desolate valley of segregation to the sunlit path of racial justice. Now is the time to lift our nation from the quicksands of racial injustice to the solid rock of brotherhood. Now is the time to make justice a reality for all of God's children.

It would be fatal for the nation to overlook the urgency of the moment. This sweltering summer of the Negro's legitimate discontent will not pass until there is an invigorating autumn of freedom and equality. Nineteen sixty-three is not an end, but a beginning. And those who hope that the Negro needed to blow off steam and will now be content will have a rude awakening if the nation returns to business as usual. And there will be neither rest nor tranquility in America until the Negro is granted his citizenship rights. The whirlwinds of revolt will continue to shake the foundations of our nation until the bright day of justice emerges.

But there is something that I must say to my people, who stand on the warm threshold which leads into the palace of justice: In the process of gaining our rightful place, we must not be guilty of wrongful deeds. Let us not seek to satisfy our thirst for freedom by drinking from the cup of bitterness and hatred. We must forever conduct our struggle on the high plane of dignity and discipline. We must not allow our creative protest to degenerate into physical violence. Again and again, we must rise to the majestic heights of meeting physical force with soul force.

The marvelous new militancy which has engulfed the Negro community must not lead us to a distrust of all white people, for many of our white brothers, as evidenced by their presence here today, have come to realize that their destiny is tied up with our destiny. And they have come to realize that their freedom is inextricably bound to our freedom.

We cannot walk alone.

And as we walk, we must make the pledge that we shall always march ahead.

We cannot turn back.

There are those who are asking the devotees of civil rights, "When will you be satisfied?" We can never be satisfied as long as the Negro is the victim of the unspeakable horrors of police brutality. We can never be satisfied as long as our bodies, heavy with the fatigue of travel, cannot gain lodging in the motels of the highways and the hotels of the cities. We cannot be satisfied as long as the negro's basic mobility is from a smaller ghetto to a larger one. We can never be satisfied as long as our children are stripped of their self-hood and robbed of their dignity by a sign stating: "For Whites Only." We cannot be satisfied as long as a Negro in Mississippi cannot vote and a Negro in New York believes he has nothing for which to vote. No, no, we are not satisfied, and we will not be satisfied until "justice rolls down like waters, and righteousness like a mighty stream."

I am not unmindful that some of you have come here out of great trials and tribulations. Some of you have come fresh from narrow jail cells. And some of you have come from areas where your quest—quest for freedom left you battered by the storms of persecution and staggered by the winds of police brutality. You have been the veterans of creative suffering. Continue to work with the faith that unearned suffering is redemptive. Go back to Mississippi, go back to Alabama, go back to South Carolina, go back to Georgia, go back to Louisiana, go back to the slums and ghettos of our northern cities, knowing that somehow this situation can and will be changed.

Let us not wallow in the valley of despair, I say to you today, my friends.

And so even though we face the difficulties of today and tomorrow, I still have a dream. It is a dream deeply rooted in the American dream.

I have a dream that one day this nation will rise up and live out the true meaning of its creed: "We hold these truths to be self-evident, that all men are created equal."

I have a dream that one day on the red hills of Georgia, the sons of former slaves and the sons of former slave owners will be able to sit down together at the table of brotherhood.

I have a dream that one day even the state of Mississippi, a state sweltering with the heat of injustice, sweltering with the heat of oppression, will be transformed into an oasis of freedom and justice.

I have a dream that my four little children will one day live in a nation where they will not be judged by the color of their skin but by the content of their character.

I have a dream today!

I have a dream that one day, down in Alabama, with its vicious racists, with its governor having his lips dripping with the words of "interposition" and "nullification"—one day right there in Alabama little black boys and black girls will be able to join hands with little white boys and white girls as sisters and brothers.

I have a dream today!

I have a dream that one day every valley shall be exalted, and every hill and mountain shall be made low, the rough places will be made plain, and the crooked places will be made straight; "and the glory of the Lord shall be revealed and all flesh shall see it together."

This is our hope, and this is the faith that I go back to the South with.

With this faith, we will be able to hew out of the mountain of despair a stone of hope. With this faith, we will be able to transform the jangling discords of our nation into a beautiful symphony of brotherhood. With this faith, we will be able to work together, to pray together, to struggle together, to go to jail together, to stand up for freedom together, knowing that we will be free one day.

And this will be the day—this will be the day when all of God's children will be able to sing with new meaning:

My country 'tis of thee, sweet land of liberty, of thee I sing.

Land where my fathers died, land of the Pilgrim's pride,

From every mountainside, let freedom ring!

And if America is to be a great nation, this must become true.

And so let freedom ring from the prodigious hilltops of New Hampshire.

Let freedom ring from the mighty mountains of New York.

Let freedom ring from the heightening Alleghenies of Pennsylvania.

Let freedom ring from the snow-capped Rockies of Colorado.

Let freedom ring from the curvaceous slopes of California.

But not only that:

Let freedom ring from Stone Mountain of Georgia.

Let freedom ring from Lookout Mountain of Tennessee.

Let freedom ring from every hill and molehill of Mississippi.

From every mountainside, let freedom ring.

And when this happens, when we allow freedom to ring, when we let it ring from every village and every hamlet, from every state and every city, we will be able to speed up that day when all of God's children, black men and white men, Jews and Gentiles, Protestants and Catholics, will be able to join hands and sing in the words of the old Negro spiritual:

Free at last! Free at last!

Thank God Almighty, we are free at last!

Credit: Reprinted by arrangement with The Heirs to the Estate of Martin Luther King, Jr., c/o Writers House as agent for the proprietor New York, NY. Copyright 1963 Martin Luther King, Jr., copyright renewed 1991 Coretta Scott King.

## The Federal Bulldozer and "Negro Removal" (1964)

### Martin Anderson

In the 1950s and 1960s, city planners implemented ambitious, and ultimately disastrous, plans for "urban renewal." Planners sought to eliminate "blight" by replacing old neighborhoods with public housing projects and upscale commercial centers that would (in theory) produce higher tax revenue. The government crowded blacks and white immigrants into public housing projects that were "better for them." No one asked the intended beneficiaries—those living in "blighted" neighborhoods—whether they wanted to be removed from their homes and small businesses. Thus, a coalition of left-liberal planners and big-business interests colluded in one of the great tragedies of American city life.

Two very different authors saw the tragedy in the making and noted its racial overtones. Jane Jacobs (1916–2006) wrote *The Death and Life of Great American Cities* (1961), the most influential critique of urban planning ever written. Although Jacobs did not oppose all urban planning, she believed in a light hand, not the dictatorial policy of urban renewal. In *Death and Life,* she wrote:

Look what we have built with the first several billions: Low-income projects that become worse centers of delinquency, vandalism and general social hopelessness than the slums they were supposed to replace.

Middle-income housing projects which are truly marvels of dullness and regimentation, sealed against any buoyancy or vitality of city life. Luxury housing projects that mitigate their inanity, or try to, with a vapid vulgarity. Cultural centers that are unable to support a good bookstore. Civic centers that are avoided by everyone but bums, who have fewer choices of loitering place than others. Commercial centers that are lackluster imitations of standardized suburban chain-store shopping. Promenades that go from no place to nowhere and have no promenaders. Expressways that eviscerate great cities. This is not the rebuilding of cities. This is the sacking of cities.[16]

Martin Anderson's *Federal Bulldozer* (1964) offered a classical liberal critique with social science data to back up his contention that "only free enterprise" could do the job of providing the homes and businesses that ordinary people wanted. The government, Anderson argued, abused its constitutional powers of eminent domain by using it to benefit privileged private interests at the expense of poor people. Anderson's *Federal Bulldozer* reflects a classical liberal appreciation of individual freedom, the Constitution, decentralized power, and spontaneous order. In later years, the young free market business professor became an adviser to Republican presidents, including Ronald Reagan.[17] He is currently a fellow at the Hoover Institution.

In an excerpt from *Federal Bulldozer*, Martin Anderson makes his case for total repeal of all urban renewal laws. He later stated to a congressional subcommittee on small business that urban renewal is "unjust" because "private property is seized for private use, not public use." Moreover, "in my judgment, no businessman, no matter how small his operation, should be sacrificed for the esthetic pleasure or personal gain of anyone, no matter how rich, or how powerful, or how learned that person or those persons may be."[18] Decades later, urban planners continue their efforts to "renew" cities at the expense of the classical liberal values defended by Anderson and others.

ᘓ

During the last 15 years, notices similar to the following one have been received by hundreds of thousands of families and individuals living in cities throughout the United States.

The building in which you now live is located in an area which has been taken by the Boston Redevelopment Authority according to law as part of the Government Center Project. The buildings will be demolished after the families have been relocated and the land will be sold to developers for public and commercial uses, according to the Land Assembly and Redevelopment Plan presently being prepared.

The wording varies from city to city, but the meaning is clear: the house or apartment you live in is going to be taken by the government and destroyed. The government will then sell the cleared land to someone else for private development. Please move. This extraordinary action is just one of many evolving from a federal program whose scope has increased rapidly in recent years. This is the federal urban renewal program—damned by some, praised by many, and understood by very few. . . .

The public often takes it for granted that the people who are forced to move from their homes are well taken care of by the government authorities. It is commonly believed that these people move into better housing in better neighborhoods, and, by implication, are glad that they were forced to "better" themselves. On the contrary, a few private authorities have seriously questioned these conclusions, and they suggest that many of the families forcibly evicted drift into housing as bad as or worse than their original homes in neighborhoods that are also as bad or worse than their original neighborhoods. In addition they often have to pay higher rents. The factual evidence that would answer this question clearly is inconclusive at this time. Government statistics show a more optimistic picture than do private studies. But, although the question cannot be answered definitely, we shall see that there are certain indications which tend to support the gloomier view.

The federal urban renewal program also has some strong racial overtones. Approximately two thirds of the people who are forced out of their homes are Negroes, Puerto Ricans, or members of some other minority group. The problem of finding new homes is complicated for these people because of racial discrimination. The federal urban renewal program is sometimes privately referred to as the "Negro removal" program. The problems of finding new places to live are further complicated by the fact that most of the people who are forced to move have relatively low incomes, which limit them to a small number of homes and apartments in low-rent areas. Most of the people who are seriously affected by the program come from low-income, minority groups that, for various reasons, do not or cannot attempt to correct the injustices to which they are subjected.

By March of 1963 over 609,000 people had been forced to pack their belongings and leave their homes. There were some cases of intensive resistance, which often stopped the urban renewal program in a particular area, but many people appear to have reacted to their eviction notices without much outward indication of their indignation; in fact, many of them have appeared to welcome the program enthusiastically. It is doubtful that this combination of apathy and enthusiasm will long continue in the future. The amount of active resistance seems to be related to the level of ability, education, and income of the people who have to move. People with the knowledge to comprehend the full implications of what is happening and the ability and money to fight it, often resist bitterly. . . .

The basic premise on which the program was started and the one which maintains its intellectual momentum is that urban renewal eliminates slums, prevents the spread of blight, and revitalizes cities. It is much more likely that the federal urban renewal program shifts slums instead of removing them, and, in so doing, may actually encourage the spread of slums and blight. The people who move from the urban renewal area are not really helped by the operation of the program. Some receive payments for moving expenses and advice in finding new homes. But after they move, they still have the same incomes, the same social characteristics, and the same skin color. The only basic change is that they are now living in some other part of the city. . . .

The constitutionality of federal urban renewal was contested vigorously in the courts for years, primarily on the ground that it violated private property rights. However, in 1954 it was declared constitutional by the Supreme Court. In effect the Court stated that the concept of eminent domain—previously used only to acquire private property for public use—now could be employed in the federal urban renewal program to acquire private property from some individuals and then have this property sold by the government to other individuals for their private use.

This decision may have more serious results than many Americans realize, because it has significantly altered the traditional concept of private property rights in the United States. Private property may now be seized by the government and turned over to someone else for his private use; under the traditional concept of eminent domain, private property could only be seized by the government for public use. . . .

### Changes in Housing Quality for Low-Income, Minority Groups

It is sometimes charged and often assumed that the free working of a capitalistic society only benefits those of ability, that those who are poor and sometimes discriminated against because of their race cannot improve their living conditions. Many people believe that private enterprise cannot function effectively in this area and that public subsidy, in the form of the federal urban renewal program, is necessary and will be effective. Let's examine the record. In May 1963, the Office of the Administrator of the Housing and Home Finance Agency published a report entitled, Our Nonwhite Population and Its Housing: The Changes between 1950 and 1960. The essence of the report is that the members of this group enjoyed a very substantial increase in the quality of the housing they occupy. . . .

Who wants urban renewal? Certainly not the lower-income groups—they get displaced from their homes to make way for the modern apartments they cannot afford to rent. It is hard to know whether the middle class is much concerned with the changes that have occurred in the cities. Of course, they care somewhat; almost everyone would agree that a beautiful, clean city is preferable to an unattractive, dirty one. But their degree of concern can be determined by asking how much they would give up of what they have or hope to have in order to realize the goals of urban renewal. The achievement of these goals would make it necessary for people to allocate a much larger share of their income to someone else's housing and public facilities. There has been little indication of a strong desire to do this in the past, and it seems doubtful that their values will change significantly during the next ten to twenty years.

Then who is behind the tremendous push for urban renewal? Raymond Vernon, former Director of the New York Metropolitan Region Study, has speculated that the main stimulus for urban renewal comes from two elite groups—the wealthy elite and the intellectual elite. Both groups have strong economic and social attachments to the central city. And they are in a position to attempt to maintain these attachments despite the desires and wishes of the nonelite. Members of these elite groups include financial institutions, newspapers, department stores, owners of downtown real estate, academic intellectuals, city planners, city politicians, and others who have a strong stake in the maintenance and improvement of the city as they see it today.

In general, Vernon's proposition appears to be reasonable. There is a general feeling among the people of the United States that the federal urban renewal program is attempting to revitalize run-down areas of cities and help the people living in these areas. But our examination of what the program actually does indicates that it revitalizes run-down areas of cities primarily for the benefit of people who do not live in run-down areas. A hard, searching look should be taken at the following question: Is the federal urban renewal program effectively creating new urban communities consisting of people whose level of income is higher, whose skin is whiter, and whose social characteristics are more desirable than those of the former residents? . . .

It is recommended that the federal urban renewal program be repealed now. No new projects should be authorized; the program should be phased out by completing, as soon as possible, all current projects. The federal urban renewal program conceived in 1949 had admirable goals. Unfortunately it has not and cannot achieve them. Only free enterprise can.

Source: Martin Anderson, *The Federal Bulldozer* (1964; repr., New York: McGraw-Hill, 1967), 1–2, 7–9, 13, 208–9, 219, 230. From *The Federal Bulldozer*, reprinted by permission of Martin Anderson.

## Civil Rights Act Invades Private, State Spheres (1964)

### Barry Goldwater

The Civil Rights Act of 1964 posed a dilemma for classical liberals: several articles prohibited state or federal race discrimination, but other provisions prevented private individuals from discriminating in "public accommodations" or hiring. "Forced" racial equality in private places clashed with freedom of association. Some were also concerned that activist courts would turn the "plain meaning" of the act upside down, so that equality meant preference.

In the short term, Republicans made the Civil Rights Act possible by closing the Democratic filibuster and voting overwhelmingly for the final act, which contained antipreferential language. The party's presidential nominee, Senator Barry Goldwater (R-AZ), was a longtime member of the NAACP and Urban League (another civil rights organization). He had integrated the Arizona National Guard and supported desegregation of Phoenix public schools. However, Goldwater voted against the Civil Rights Act on classical liberal grounds. Thereafter, left-wing liberals preached that Republicans, conservatives, and classical liberals were "on the wrong side of civil rights," but the Left fails to note the consistent classical liberal opposition to governmental racial discrimination in any form. The Civil Rights Act overturned segregation but it also sanctioned continued government regulation of race. Subsequent events bore out the fear that the two provisions mentioned by Goldwater (below) would enable bureaucrats and judges to pervert the act so that equality meant treating members of certain government-designated groups more equally than others (on how this happened, see the Glazer entry in chapter 7).

℃℈

I am unalterably opposed to discrimination or segregation on the basis of race, color, or creed, or on any other basis; not only my words, but more importantly my actions through the years have repeatedly demonstrated the sincerity of my feeling in this regard. . . .

I realize fully that the Federal Government has a responsibility in the field of civil rights. I supported the civil rights bills which were enacted in 1957 and 1960, and my public utterances during the debates on those measures and since reveal clearly the areas in which I feel that Federal responsibility lies and Federal legislation on this subject can be both effective and appropriate. Many of those areas are encompassed in this bill and to that extent, I favor it.

I wish to make myself perfectly clear. The two portions of this bill to which I have constantly and consistently voiced objections, and which are of such overriding significance that they are determinative of my vote on the entire measure, are those which would embark the Federal Government on a regulatory course of action with regard to private enterprise in the area of so-called public accommodations and in the area of employment—to be more specific, titles II and VII of the bill. I find no constitutional basis for the exercise of Federal regulatory authority in either of these areas; and I believe the attempted usurpation of such power to be a grave threat to the very essence of our basic system of government; namely, that of a constitutional republic in which 50 sovereign States have reserved to themselves and to the people those powers not specifically granted to the Central or Federal Government.

Source: Barry Goldwater, "Civil Rights," *Congressional Record*, June 18, 1964, 14318–19.

## Notes

1. David A. Nichols, *A Matter of Justice: Eisenhower and the Beginning of the Civil Rights Revolution* (New York: Simon & Schuster, 2007).

2. Murray Rothbard, "The Negro Revolution," *New Individualist Review* 3, no. 1 (1963): 437.

3. Theodore Gilmore Bilbo, *Take Your Choice: Separation or Mongrelization* (Poplarville, MS: Dream House, 1947).

4. Theodore Bilbo, *Congressional Record*, January 21, 1938, 882–83.

5. William Moore, "G.O.P. Wins: Bilbo Kept Out," *Chicago Tribune*, January 5, 1947, 1. See also John Evans, "Negro Pastors Laud G.O.P. for Barring Bilbo," *Chicago Tribune*, January 6, 1947, 2.

6. Zora Neale Hurston, *Dust Tracks on a Road* (1942; repr., New York: HarperPerennial, 1996), 249–50.

7. According to a biographer, "Eisenhower appointed Carey a U.S. chief alternate delegate to the General Assembly of the United Nations (U.N.) in 1953. . . . There he worked on the Genocide Pact (1953) that made it an international crime to kill people because of their race, color, nationality, or religion." Eisenhower appointed him to various other civil rights posts, including chair of the President's Committee on Government Policy to enforce nondiscrimination in federal hiring. The GOP nominated him for a judgeship, but he did not obtain that position until he switched to the Democratic Party in 1964. David Michel, "Carey, Archibald

James, Jr.," in *African American National Biography*, ed. Henry Louis Gates Jr. and Evelyn Brooks Higginbotham, at Oxford African American Studies Center, http://www.oxfordaasc.com/article/opr/t0001/e2195 (accessed July 28, 2008).

8. F. A. Harper, "A Decree of Racial Inferiority," *Ideas on Liberty* 5, no. 5 (1955), http://www.fee.org/publications/the-freeman (accessed October 29, 2007).

9. Frank Chodorov, "A Really Free School System," *Freeman* 5, no. 1 (1954), http://www.fee.org/publications/*the-freeman* (accessed October 29, 2007); Milton Friedman, "The Role of Government in Education," in *Economics and the Public Interest*, ed. Robert A. Solo (New Brunswick, NJ: Rutgers University Press, 1955); George S. Schuyler, "The Case for Private School," *Freeman* 6, no. 3 (1956): 14–16; Leonard E. Read, "The Case for the Free Market in Education," *Freeman* 14, no. 9 (1964): 10–20.

10. Myron Lieberman, *Public Education: An Autopsy* (Cambridge, MA: Harvard University Press, 1993); Sheldon L. Richman, *Separating School and State: How to Liberate America's Families* (Fairfax, VA: Future of Freedom Foundation, 1995); R. K. Vedder, *Can Teachers Own Their Own Schools? New Strategies for Educational Excellence* (Oakland, CA: Independent Institute, 2000).

11. Gary Stanley Becker, *The Economics of Discrimination* (Chicago: University of Chicago Press, 1957); Milton Friedman, *Capitalism and Freedom* (Chicago: University of Chicago Press, 1962); Robert Higgs, *Competition and Coercion: Blacks in the American Economy, 1865–1914* (New York: Cambridge University Press, 1977); Thomas Sowell, *Markets and Minorities* (New York: Basic, 1981); Walter E. Williams, *The State against Blacks* (New York: New Press, 1982).

12. Robert E. Weems, *Desegregating the Dollar: African American Consumerism in the Twentieth Century* (New York: New York University Press, 1998).

13. S. B. Fuller, "A Negro Businessman Speaks His Mind," *U.S. News & World Report*, August 19, 1963, 60.

14. Martin Luther King Jr., *Why We Can't Wait* (New York: Harper & Row, 1964), 147, 152.

15. Tamar Jacoby, "Have We Abandoned Dr. King's Vision?" *Wall Street Journal*, January 19, 1998, A14.

16. Jane Jacobs, *The Death and Life of Great American Cities* (New York: Random House, 1961), 4.

17. Anderson wrote many other books, including a retrospective on the Reagan years, *Revolution* (San Diego: Harcourt Brace Jovanovich, 1988).

18. Martin Anderson, testimony before U.S. House, Small Business Committee, Subcommittee no. 5, *Small Business Problems in Urban Areas*, 89th Cong., 1st sess., June 7–12, 1965, 56.

## Recommended Reading

Beito, David T., Peter Gordon, and Alexander Tabarrok. *The Voluntary City: Choice, Community, and Civil Society.* Ann Arbor: University of Michigan Press, in association with Independent Institute, 2002.

Casey, Mary Fuller. *S. B. Fuller: Pioneer in Black Economic Development.* Jamestown, NC: Bridgemaster, 2003.

Chalberg, John C. *Rickey & Robinson: The Preacher, the Player, and America's Game.* Wheeling, IL: Harlan Davidson, 2000.

Friedman, Milton, and Rose D. Friedman. *Free to Choose: A Personal Statement.* New York: Harcourt Brace Jovanovich, 1980.

Goldberg, Robert Alan. *Barry Goldwater.* New Haven, CT: Yale University Press, 1995.

Goldwater, Barry M. *With No Apologies: The Personal and Political Memoirs of United States Senator Barry M. Goldwater.* New York: Morrow, 1979.

Lowenfish, Lee. *Branch Rickey: Baseball's Ferocious Gentleman.* Lincoln: University of Nebraska Press, 2007.

Mencken, H. L. *The Impossible H. L. Mencken: A Selection of His Best Newspaper Stories.* Edited by Marion Elizabeth Rodgers. New York: Anchor, 1991.

Morgan, Chester M. *Redneck Liberal: Theodore G. Bilbo and the New Deal.* Baton Rouge: Louisiana State University Press, 1985.

Patterson, James T. *Mr. Republican: A Biography of Robert A. Taft.* Boston: Houghton Mifflin, 1972.

Polner, Murray. *Branch Rickey: A Biography.* New York: Atheneum, 1982.

Taft, Robert A. *The Papers of Robert A. Taft.* Edited by Clarence E Wunderlin. Kent, OH: Kent State University Press, 1997.

Whalen, Charles W., and Barbara Whalen. *The Longest Debate: A Legislative History of the 1964 Civil Rights Act.* New York: New American Library, 1986.

White, Theodore H. *The Making of the President.* New York: Atheneum, 1965.

Wollenberg, Charles. "*Mendez v. Westminster:* Race, Nationality and Segregation in California Schools." *California Historical Quarterly* 53, no. 4 (1974): 317–32.

# 7

# Individualists in an Age of Group Discrimination

*1965–Present*

## Liberalism Turned Upside Down: The Group versus the Individual

CLASSICAL LIBERALS confronted a dilemma with the Civil Rights Act of 1964: several provisions struck down state-sponsored discrimination in the South. This was in keeping with the classical liberal tradition of civil rights—judicious use of federal law and court decisions was an acceptable means to end racial discrimination by the State. However, two sections (or "titles") mandated nondiscrimination in the private sector, forbidding discrimination in hiring or "public accommodations." This infringed upon the freedom of association that classical liberals also valued.

Sponsors of the Civil Rights Act mollified critics who feared that these two titles would lead to the government requiring racial discrimination in favor of preferred minorities. To allay such fears, and emphasize the colorblindness of the law, sponsors added section 703(j), stating: "Nothing contained in this title shall be interpreted to require any employer . . . to grant preferential treatment to any individual or to any group because of race, color, religion, sex, or national origin of such individual or group on account of an imbalance which may exist with respect to the total number of percentage of persons of any race, color, religion, sex, or national origin employed by any employer."[1] Section 706(g) required the government to show that an employer "intentionally" discriminated, rather than simply rely upon statistical underrepresentation as evidence of employment discrimination. This clear language had the backing of civil rights organizations, the Democratic and Republican leadership, and the *New York*

*Times*—it was understood to mean "colorblindness" by nearly every observer at the time. Furthermore, Senator Hubert Humphrey (D-MN) rejected the "bugaboo" of preferences (or "quotas"): "Title VII prohibits discrimination. In effect, it says that race, religion and national origin are not to be used as the basis for hiring and firing. Title VII is designed to encourage hiring on the basis of ability and qualifications, not race or religion." In a famous remark, he said, "If the senator [opposing the act] can find in Title VII . . . any language which provides that an employer will have to hire on the basis of percentage or quota related to color, race, religion, or national origin, I will start eating the pages one after another, because it is not in there."[2]

Thus, after the longest debate in history, Congress mandated nondiscrimination and opposed preferential treatment for any group. The sociologist Nathan Glazer accurately described the intent and language of the act:

> The Act could only be read as instituting into law Judge Harlan's famous dissent in Plessy v. Ferguson: "Our Constitution is color-blind." Again and again, one could read the sonorous phrases: no discrimination or segregation "on the ground of race, color, religion, or national origin" (Titles II and VI), "on account of his race, color, religion, or national origin" (Title III), "by reason of race, color, religion, or national origin" (Title IV), "because of such individual's color, religion, sex, or national origin" (Title VII). . . . The Act was understood as granting not group rights but individual rights.[3]

Yet the fear that federal regulation meant more discrimination came true as bureaucrats and judges turned the "plain meaning" of the act on its head. The move toward "group rights" began under Democratic president Lyndon B. Johnson, but solidified under Republican Richard M. Nixon. Revised Order No. 4 (below) and other actions taken by the Nixon administration enabled government agencies to subvert the Civil Rights Act. Nixon's embrace of racial preferences set the scene for debates over the meaning of equality, racial freedom, and group definition. The Democratic Party initially resisted Nixon's departure from color-blind law but soon saw the political benefits of supporting preferences for Democratic constituencies (blacks, Hispanics, and others). Despite its scholarly reputation for "backlash," the GOP establishment abandoned its classical liberal followers more often than not.[4] Nevertheless, by taking their case to the public, classical liberals made the intellectual, legal, and political case for nondiscrimination.[5]

Classical liberals also offered positive alternatives to racial discrimination, including school choice and welfare reform—two policies aimed at strengthening parents' involvement in their children's lives by offering uplift through civil society rather than the government. For insight into this uplifting vision of classical liberalism, readers may view Milton Friedman's popular *Free to Choose* television series at http://www.ideachannel.tv/, http://miltonfriedman.blogspot.com/, or read his book by the same title.[6] Ultimately, the pursuit of excellence is the only way for individuals to flourish. Individuals, not groups, need a "hand up," and better they get it from civil society (family, church, professional standards) than from a government that views them as members of voting blocs or, worse yet, symbols of group stereotypes. This is a theme that resonates in the writings of Anne Wortham, Stephen L. Carter, Stanley Crouch, Shelby Steele, and others.

இ

## *The Right to Interracial Marriage:*
## Loving v. Virginia *(1967)*

Government bans on interracial marriage were among the last barriers to racial freedom. As late as 1967, sixteen states made it a crime for black and white to marry. The prejudice against black-white marriages was so strong that only 4 percent of white Americans approved of the arrangement in 1958, the same year Richard Loving ("white") and Mildred Jeter ("Negro-Indian") married in the District of Columbia.[7] After returning to their native Virginia, the Lovings were convicted of violating the state's "Racial Integrity Act." In 1967, the U.S. Supreme Court ruled unanimously that such laws prohibiting interracial marriage were unconstitutional. Chief Justice Earl Warren (1891–1974) wrote the Court opinion. The date of the decision—June 12—is known as "Loving Day" and celebrated by mixed-raced couples (see www.lovingday.org).

Following the court opinion are comments from the amicus curiae ("friend of the court") briefs filed by the NAACP and thirteen U.S. Catholic Bishops. While the NAACP challenged Virginia's racist classifications with contrary science on the "fallacy of race," the argument that persuaded the Court was based on the Constitution and the natural right of marriage, not science. Echoing this view, the bishops, citing a Vatican statement, also emphasized God's law of non-discrimination. Once again, Christians split on civil rights: the Catholic brief upheld the right of interracial marriage while the lower-court judge pontificated that "Almighty God created the races white, black, yellow, malay and red, and he placed them on separate continents. And but for the interference with his arrangement there would be no cause for such marriages."

It is important to note that into the 1960s the NAACP argued that racial classifications of all kinds were irrelevant and dangerous—tools that government uses to discriminate against people. In 1961, for example, a New York attorney wrote NAACP attorney Robert L. Carter asking where the NAACP stood on a New York bill to repeal the legal requirement to state one's race on a marriage certificate (much like the "certificates of 'racial composition'" required by Virginia). Carter wrote:

> I cannot possibly see how the N.A.A.C.P. could do other than favor this bill since color designations on birth certificates, marriage licenses and the like can serve no useful purpose whatsoever. If we are prepared to accept the basic postulate of our society—that race or color is an ir-relevance—then contentions that race and color statistics are of social science value become sheer sophistical rationalization.[8]

Similarly, in 1965 the African American newspaper *Chicago Daily Defender* published an article reiterating the views of anthropology professor Morton H. Fried:

> What is the four-letter word that of all four-letter words has done the most damage?
> Race.
> "There is not now and there never was a white race or a black race; in the vocabulary of the laymen, the word 'race' is a nonsense term" [said Fried]. . . .
> Professor Fried . . . asks this: "Why is it so hard to give up this miserable little four-letter word that of all four-letter words has done the most damage?"[9]

☙

*Earl Warren and the U.S. Supreme Court*

MR. CHIEF JUSTICE WARREN delivered the opinion of the Court.

This case presents a constitutional question never addressed by this Court: whether a statutory scheme adopted by the State of Virginia to prevent marriages between persons solely on the basis of racial classifications violates the Equal Protection and Due Process Clauses of the Fourteenth Amendment. For reasons which seem to us to reflect the central meaning of those constitutional commands, we conclude that these statutes cannot stand consistently with the Fourteenth Amendment.

In June 1958, two residents of Virginia, Mildred Jeter, a Negro woman, and Richard Loving, a white man, were married in the District of Columbia pursuant to its laws. Shortly after their marriage, the Lovings returned to Virginia and established their marital abode in Caroline County. At the October Term, 1958, of the Circuit Court of Caroline County, a grand jury issued an indictment charging the Lovings with violating Virginia's ban on interracial marriages. On January 6, 1959, the Lovings pleaded guilty to the charge and were sentenced to one year in jail; however, the trial judge suspended the sentence for a period of 25 years on the condition that the Lovings leave the State and not return to Virginia together for 25 years. He stated in an opinion that:

> Almighty God created the races white, black, yellow, malay and red, and he placed them on separate continents. And but for the interference with his arrangement there would be no cause for such marriages. The fact that he separated the races shows that he did not intend for the races to mix. . . .

The two statutes under which appellants were convicted and sentenced are part of a comprehensive statutory scheme aimed at prohibiting and punishing interracial marriages. The Lovings were convicted of violating 20-58 of the Virginia Code:

> Leaving State to evade law. If any white person and colored person shall go out of this State, for the purpose of being married, and with the intention of returning, and be married out of it, and afterwards return to and reside in it, cohabiting as man and wife, they shall be punished as provided in

20-59, and the marriage shall be governed by the same law as if it had been solemnized in this State. The fact of their cohabitation here as man and wife shall be evidence of their marriage.

Section 20-59, which defines the penalty for miscegenation, provides:

Punishment for marriage. If any white person intermarry with a colored person, or any colored person intermarry with a white person, he shall be guilty of a felony and shall be punished by confinement in the penitentiary for not less than one nor more than five years. . . .

Virginia is now one of 16 States which prohibit and punish marriages on the basis of racial classifications. Penalties for miscegenation arose as an incident to slavery and have been common in Virginia since the colonial period. The present statutory scheme dates from the adoption of the Racial Integrity Act of 1924, passed during the period of extreme nativism which followed the end of the First World War. The central features of this Act, and current Virginia law, are the absolute prohibition of a "white person" marrying other than another "white person," a prohibition against issuing marriage licenses until the issuing official is satisfied that the applicants' statements as to their race are correct, certificates of "racial composition" to be kept by both local and state registrars, and the carrying forward of earlier prohibitions against racial intermarriage. . . .

There can be no question but that Virginia's miscegenation statutes rest solely upon distinctions drawn according to race. The statutes proscribe generally accepted conduct if engaged in by members of different races. Over the years, this Court has consistently repudiated "[d]istinctions between citizens solely because of their ancestry" as being "odious to a free people whose institutions are founded upon the doctrine of equality." Hirabayashi v. United States, 320 U.S. 81, 100 (1943). At the very least, the Equal Protection Clause demands that racial classifications, especially suspect in criminal statutes, be subjected to the "most rigid scrutiny," Korematsu v. United States, 323 U.S. 214, 216 (1944), and, if they are ever to be upheld, they must be shown to be necessary to the accomplishment of some permissible state objective, independent of the racial discrimination which it was the object of the Fourteenth Amendment to eliminate. Indeed, two members of this Court have already stated that they "cannot conceive of a valid legislative purpose . . . which makes the color of a person's skin the test of whether his conduct is a criminal offense." McLaughlin v. Florida, supra, at 198 (STEWART, J., joined by DOUGLAS, J., concurring).

There is patently no legitimate overriding purpose independent of invidious racial discrimination which justifies this classification. The fact that Virginia prohibits only interracial marriages involving white persons demonstrates that the racial classifications must stand on their own justification, as measures designed to maintain White Supremacy. We have consistently denied the constitutionality of measures which restrict the rights of citizens on account of race. There can be no doubt that restricting the freedom to marry solely because of racial classifications violates the central meaning of the Equal Protection Clause.

These statutes also deprive the Lovings of liberty without due process of law in violation of the Due Process Clause of the Fourteenth Amendment. The freedom to marry has long been recognized as one of the vital personal rights essential to the orderly pursuit of happiness by free men.

Marriage is one of the "basic civil rights of man," fundamental to our very existence and survival. Skinner v. Oklahoma, 316 U.S. 535, 541 (1942). See also Maynard v. Hill, 125 U.S. 190 (1888). . . . The Fourteenth Amendment requires that the freedom of choice to marry not be restricted by invidious racial discriminations. Under our Constitution, the freedom to marry, or not marry, a person of another race resides with the individual and cannot be infringed by the State.

### NAACP

Classification by race based upon non-existent racial traits does not serve any valid legislative purpose but merely continues a classification of Americans as superior and inferior in contradiction to the American concept of equality.

### U.S. Catholic Bishops

Thirteen Catholic bishops stated to the Court that they were "committed to the proposition that 'with regard to the fundamental rights of the person, every type of discrimination, whether social or cultural, whether based on sex, race, color, social condition, language or religion, is to be overcome and eradicated as contrary to God's intent.' (Vatican Council II, Pastoral Constitution on the Church in the Modern World.)"

Sources: *Loving v. Virginia,* 388 U.S. 1 (1967). Case citations and footnotes have been omitted. Brief of the National Association for the Advancement of Colored People as Amicus Curiae, submitted for consideration in *Loving v. Virginia,* 14, reprinted in *Landmark Briefs and Arguments of the Supreme Court of the United States,* vol. 64, ed. Philip B. Kurland and Gerhard Casper (Washington, DC: University Publications of America, 1975), 904; 13; Brief of John J. Russell, et al. as Amicus Curiae, submitted for consideration in *Loving v. Virginia,* 3, reprinted in *Landmark Briefs and Arguments,* 930.

## *Revised Order No. 4 (1971)*

### *U.S. Department of Labor*

In the early 1960s, Presidents John F. Kennedy and Lyndon Johnson issued executive orders prohibiting employment discrimination by federal contractors. The orders also required contractors to take "affirmative action" to assure that there was no such discrimination in hiring. Originally, affirmative action meant "aggressive recruitment" and hiring "without regard to race."[10] But, from a variety of motives, President Richard M. Nixon launched a plan to impose racial preferences on the construction industry, where unions had kept African Americans out of the skilled trades. Nixon's Department of Labor then issued Revised Order No. 4 requiring all federal contractors to set hiring "goals" if certain minority groups were "underutilized." Thus affirmative action became "goal" oriented, and "goals" quickly translated into "employment quotas" as understood by both supporters and opponents.[11] In short, Revised Order No. 4 was a landmark regulation that upset years of progress toward the classical liberal goal of a limited, race-neutral state.

In retrospect, one of the ironies of affirmative action was the strong opposition of Democrats to race preferences or even racial classification. As I have written elsewhere: "When the EEOC [Equal Employment Opportunity Commission] argued for racial reporting in August 1965, there was an uproar among liberals and civil rights groups. Racial classification, however 'benign,' smacked of Jim Crow. Clarence Mitchell of the National Association for the Advancement of Colored People (NAACP), declared that 'the minute you put race on a civil service form . . . you have opened the door to discrimination.' He feared the use of racial categories would 'put us back fifty years.'" Given the commitment to colorblindness, the Civil Rights Commission instructed agencies to avoid "the placing of a question on race or national origin on any application."[12] Democratic opposition remained strong through the Nixon years. The comptroller general under Lyndon Johnson opposed what became Revised Order No. 4 on the grounds that it encouraged employers to discriminate. Congressional Democrats lined up against Nixon's proposed order and his other minority-only programs.[13] As late as 1973, Representative Edward Koch (D-NY) opposed race preferences in the Small Business Administration, stating: "Just as I am opposed to quotas at the university level for either students or teachers or in any job or profession, I am opposed to quotas in the Small Business Administration."[14] Although Democrats later embraced race preferences, the Republican Party was the first to lose its classical liberal "soul," during and after the Nixon years (see Ward Connerly entry below).

ɞ

Purpose of affirmative action program.

An affirmative action program is a set of specific and result-oriented procedures to which a contractor commits itself to apply every good faith effort. . . . An acceptable affirmative action program must include an analysis of areas within which the contractor is deficient in the utilization of minority groups and women, and further, goals and timetables to which the contractor's good faith efforts must be directed to correct the deficiencies and, thus to achieve prompt and full utilization of minorities and women, at all levels and in all segments of its work force. . . .

For each job title, the total number of incumbents, the total number of male and female incumbents, and the total number of male and female incumbents in each of the following groups must be given: Blacks, Spanish-surnamed Americans, American Indians, and Orientals. . . .

"Underutilization" is defined as having fewer minorities or women in a particular job group than would reasonably be expected by their availability. . . .

Establishment of goals and timetables.

(d) Goals should be specific for planned results, with timetables for completion.

Development or reaffirmation of the equal employment opportunity policy.

(1) Recruit, hire, train, and promote persons in all job titles, without regard to race, color, religion, sex, or national origin, except where sex is a bona fide occupational qualification.

Source: U.S. National Archives and Records Administration, Office of the Federal Register, Code of Federal Regulations, Title 41—Public Contracts and Property Management, chapter 60, sec. 2.10–2.20.

## Affirmative Discrimination: "Orwellian Nightmare" of Group Rights (1975)

### Nathan Glazer

By the 1970s, "affirmative action" had erupted into a controversy over the meaning of racial equality. Harvard sociologist Nathan Glazer (1924– ) entered the fray with the first comprehensive critique of racial preferences. In clear, compelling prose Glazer explained how bureaucrats and racial interest groups had hijacked the Civil Rights Act of 1964. Within ten years, the antipreferential provisions of the act had become a "nullity" to officials charged with enforcing the law. Glazer's social analysis vindicated those classical liberal critics who feared that government regulation of employment would lead to the "Orwellian nightmare [where] 'all animals are equal, but some animals are more equal than others.'"

Glazer's book also emphasized the classical liberal struggle to get beyond racial distinctions. For over a century, liberals had agitated for individual rights and the equal application of the law to all Americans, regardless of race. After 1964, left-liberals abandoned individualism for the pottage of "group rights." In a passionate closing, Glazer urged Americans to return to an earlier understanding of the Constitution and the Civil Rights Act in which "the individual is the measure."

In later years, Glazer changed his views because he feared that blacks would never perform at the same level as other Americans.[15] Their exclusion from the professional elite, however merited by qualifications, was simply intolerable.

Glazer therefore urged restriction of racial preferences to blacks only. Glazer's reversal did not undermine his earlier reasons for opposing affirmative action. His 1975 book stands as a tour de force for advocates of individual freedom and the rule of law.

ↄ

One place to begin is with the Civil Rights Act of 1964. In the wake of the assassination of President Kennedy and the harrowing and violent resistance in the South to the exercise of simple political rights by blacks, the nation decided, in an act of sweeping power, to finally fulfill the 100-year-old promise of the Emancipation Proclamation. The Act dealt with the right to vote (Title I), to use places of public accommodation (Title II), with the desegregation of public facilities (Title III), with the desegregation of public education (Title IV), with the expansion of the powers of the Commission on Civil Rights (Title V), with nondiscrimination in Federally assisted programs (Title VI), and, most significantly for employment discrimination, with equal employment opportunity. . . . The Act was understood as granting not group rights but individual rights. Two provisions, among others, were inserted in Title VII to protect individual rights. . . .

"Affirmative action" originally meant that one should not only not discriminate, but inform people one did not discriminate; not only treat those who applied for jobs without discrimination, but seek out those who might not apply. This is what it apparently meant when first used in executive orders. In the Civil Rights Act of 1964, it was used to mean something else—the remedies a court could impose when some employer was found guilty of discrimination, and they could be severe. The new concept of "affirmative action" that has since emerged and has been enforced with ever greater vigor combines both elements: It assumes that everyone is guilty of discrimination; it then imposes on every employer the remedies which in the Civil Rights Act of 1964 could only be imposed on those guilty of discrimination.

Affirmative action has developed a wonderful Catch-22 type of existence. The employer is required by the OFCC [Office of Federal Contract Compliance] to state numerical goals and dates when he will reach them. There is no presumption of discrimination. However, if he does not reach these goals, the question will come up as to whether he has made a "good faith" effort to reach them. The test of a good faith effort has not been spelled out. . . .

There is a simple solution to Catch-22: proportional hiring, quotas; and every employer worth his salt knows that is the solution that the EEOC and the OFCC and the rest of the agencies are urging upon him, while they simultaneously explain they have nothing of the sort in mind. . . .

Against the argument that, whatever the moral or legal faults or these procedures, they are socially good, I would make three points:

First, they became institutionalized and strengthened at a time when very substantial progress had been made, and was being made, in the upgrading of black employment and income, a progress that had, oddly enough, taken place without benefit of such extreme measures. Second, it is questionable whether they reach in any significant way the remaining and indeed most severe problems involved in the black condition. And third . . . , they threaten a desirable, emergent pattern of dealing with ethnic differences. . . .

The Department of Labor, apparently, was the organization which decided that the "affected" or "protected" classes should consist of Negroes, Spanish-surnamed Americans, Native Americans, and Orientals. It is a strange mix. Why just these and no others? We understand why Negroes and American Indians—they have been the subjects of state discrimination, and the latter group has been, in a sense, a ward of the state. Puerto Ricans, perhaps, are included because we conquered them and are responsible for them. We did not conquer most of the Mexican Americans. They came as immigrants, and why they should be "protected" more than other minorities is an interesting question. Other Spanish-surnamed Americans raise even more difficult questions. Why Cubans? They have already received substantial assistance in immigration and have made as much progress as any immigrant might expect. Why immigrants from Latin America, aside from Puerto Ricans, who must also be included among the "protected," "assisted"—and, of course, therefore counted—classes? Why Oriental Americans? They have indeed been subject in the past to savage official discrimination, but that is in the past. Having done passably well under discrimination, and much better since discrimination was radically reduced, it is not clear why the government came rushing in to include them in "affirmative action"—unless it was under the vague notion that any race aside from the white must be the victim of discrimination in the United States. . . .

Thus the nation is by government action increasingly divided formally into racial and ethnic categories with differential rights. The Orwellian nightmare " . . . all animals are equal, but some animals are more equal than others . . ." comes closer. Individuals find subtle pressures to make use of their group affiliation not necessarily because of any desire to be associated with a group but because groups become the basis for rights, and those who want to claim certain rights must do so as a member of an affected or protected class. New lines of conflict are created, by government action. New resentments are created; new turfs are to be protected; new angers arise. . . .

For ten years now, we have drifted in another direction, certainly in some ways an easier one to understand, and in some ways even easier to institute. Let us number and divide up (some of) the people into their appropriate racial and ethnic groups, and let equality prevail between them and the "others." But this has meant that we abandon the first principle of a liberal society, that the individual and the individual's interests and good and welfare are the test of a good society, for we now attach benefits and penalties to individuals simply on the basis of their race, color, and national origin. The implications of the new course are an increasing consciousness of the significance of group membership, an increasing divisiveness on the basis of race, color, and national origin, and a spreading resentment among the disfavored groups against the favored groups. If the individual is the measure, however, our public concern is with the individual's capacity to work out an individual fate by means of education, work, and self-realization in the various spheres of life. Then how the figures add up on the basis of whatever measures of group we use may be interesting, but should be no concern of public policy.

This, I believe, is what was intended by the Constitution and the Civil Rights Act, and what most of the American people—in all the various ethnic and racial groups that make it up—believe to be the measure of a good society. It is now our task to work with the intellectual, judicial, and political institutions of the country to reestablish this simple and clear understanding, that rights attach to the individual, not the group, and that public policy must be exercised without distinction of race, color, or national origin.

Source: Nathan Glazer, *Affirmative Discrimination: Ethnic Inequality and Public Policy* (New York: Basic, 1975), 43, 58–59, 69–70, 73–75, 220–21. Footnotes and internal citations have been omitted. Reprinted by permission of Basic Books, a member of the Perseus Books Group.

# *Bakke*: The Civil Rights Act Means What It Says (1978)

### *John Paul Stevens*

In this landmark case, the Supreme Court divided three ways on whether the Civil Rights Act and the Constitution allowed racial preferences in college admissions. Four justices ruled that the Civil Rights Act prohibited such discrimination, four justices allowed it to compensate for past discrimination, and one justice stated that promoting "diversity" (among other factors) might allow colleges room to discriminate in the future, but not in this case, which involved explicit quotas. The result: a tortured decision that encouraged institutions to wrap their discriminatory practices in the new mantle of "diversity."

ᘓ

MR. JUSTICE STEVENS, with whom THE CHIEF JUSTICE, MR. JUSTICE STEWART, and MR. JUSTICE REHNQUIST join, concurring in the judgment in part and dissenting in part.

Allan Bakke challenged petitioner's special admissions program, claiming that it denied him a place in medical school because of his race in violation of the Federal and California Constitutions and of Title VI of the Civil Rights Act of 1964. The California Supreme Court upheld his challenge and ordered him admitted. If the state court was correct in its view that the University's special program was illegal, and that Bakke was therefore unlawfully excluded from the Medical School because of his race, we should affirm its judgment, regardless of our views about the legality of admissions programs that are not now before the Court. . . .

Both petitioner and respondent have asked us to determine the legality of the University's special admissions program by reference to the Constitution. Our settled practice, however, is to avoid the decision of a constitutional issue if a case can be fairly decided on a statutory ground. . . .

[The Civil Rights Act of 1964] provides:

"No person in the United States shall, on the ground of race, color, or national origin, be excluded from participation in, be denied the benefits of, or be subjected to discrimination under any program or activity receiving Federal financial assistance."

The University, through its special admissions policy, excluded Bakke from participation in its program of medical education because of his race. The University also acknowledges that it was, and still is, receiving federal financial assistance. The plain language of the statute therefore requires affirmance of the judgment below. . . .

Petitioner contends, however, that exclusion of applicants on the basis of race does not violate Title VI if the exclusion carries with it no racial stigma. No such qualification or limitation of 601's categorical prohibition of "exclusion" is justified by the statute or its history. The language of the entire section is perfectly clear. . . .

The legislative history reinforces this reading. The only suggestion that [section] 601 would allow exclusion of non minority applicants came from opponents of the legislation and then only by way of a discussion of the meaning of the word "discrimination." The opponents feared that the term "discrimination" would be read as mandating racial quotas and "racially balanced" colleges and universities, and they pressed for a specific definition of the term in order to avoid this possibility. In response, the proponents of the legislation gave repeated assurances that the Act would be "colorblind" in its application. Senator Humphrey, the Senate floor manager for the Act, expressed this position as follows:

"[T]he word 'discrimination' has been used in many a court case. What it really means in the bill is a distinction in treatment . . . given to different individuals because of their different race, religion or national origin. . . .

"[I]f we started to treat Americans as Americans, not as fat ones, thin ones, short ones, tall ones, brown ones, green ones, yellow ones, or white ones, but as Americans. If we did that we would not need to worry about discrimination. . . ."

In unmistakable terms the Act prohibits the exclusion of individuals from federally funded programs because of their race. As succinctly phrased during the Senate debate, under Title VI it is not "permissible to say 'yes' to one person; but to say 'no' to another person, only because of the color of his skin."

Source: *University of California Regents v. Bakke*, 438 U.S. 265 (1978). Internal legal citations have been omitted.

### A Decision against Meritorious Achievement (1978)

*Anne Wortham*

**A graduate of Booker T. Washington's Tuskegee Institute, Anne Wortham**

(1941–) became a media researcher and, later, a professor of sociology at Illinois State University. She wrote for classical liberal journals, including the *Freeman*, and produced a book on black racism.[16] The *Bakke* decision offended Wortham because the Court held that achievements were "gifts from the State," rather than the result of individual merit. Since 1966, the self-described "individualist liberal" has published articles exposing the violation of individual rights required by civil rights policy. She is currently compiling an anthology of her essays on individualism.

ᗡᘓ

For blacks like me, the supreme irony of having to contend with affirmative action measures is that we grew up in a tradition which prepared us for precisely the opposite—that tradition which measured achievement in terms of merit as evidenced by one's skill, knowledge, experience, interest and attitude. It was, we were told, "the American way"—the practical expression of our culture's devotion to human individuality. Now, we are told that virtue lies not in such aspirations as color-blindness and meritorious achievement, but in the social good of implementing race-conscious programs to remedy the effects of racism.

As I contemplate the Bakke decision, my mind is crowded with reminders of all that went into my adherence to "the American way." I hear my father's repeated admonitions to his five children that we grow up to be independent, self-supporting citizens. I see him working long hours and sacrificing to provide for our education, determined that he would do so despite Jim Crow and without outside assistance. I hear this self-educated man, who at one period made a salary of only $50 a week, telling us that our education was his investment in the future. "I don't want my girls to work as domestics or my boys to be ditch diggers," he would say. And always there was the reminder we hear from him to this day: "Remember, your record follows you."

The society he was preparing me for was one in which merit was the basis of achievement. It was also one in which racial discrimination and prejudice were prevalent; but in addressing this issue, black fathers like mine taught their children a rule of thumb taken from the words of Booker T. Washington:

"Any individual who learns to do something better than anybody else—learns to do a common thing in an uncommon manner—has solved his problem, regardless of the color of his skin. . . ."

"In the long run, the world is going to have the best, and any difference in race, religion, or previous history will not long keep the world from what it wants. . . ."

[Lyndon] Johnson challenged those who might offer the counterclaim that if other Americans could overcome their disadvantages without special equality-of-result legislation, so could Negroes. [In a famous Howard University commencement address], he cited a long list of statistics indicating the gap between the opportunities of Negroes and whites and said:

> The Negro, like these others [white minorities], will have to rely mostly upon his own efforts. But he just cannot do it alone. For they did not have a cultural tradition which has been twisted and battered by endless years of hatred and hopelessness, nor were they excluded—these others—because of race or color—a feeling whose dark intensity is matched by no other prejudice in our society.

This distorted view of black history supported by biased research, statistical "explanations," and a great deal of ignorance has now been made "official" by the 1978 Supreme Court. With the memory of past discrimination so fresh in my mind, I am profoundly resentful that I, along with every other American, must bear the burden of this new stereotype of my race—that I cannot overcome the circumstances of my forefathers on my own and in my own way; that the only way I can compete with a white person is by weighing him down with penalties for the sins of his race and the government against my race. What an insult to me—and, oh what injustice to the innocent white person! Neither of us is responsible for the cultural heritage that stretches across the centuries behind us; yet both must be burdened by it. I am branded as incapable of walking through the gates of opportunity on my own, and he is branded as the source of my incapacity.

But I protest! It was not legislative decree but my parents who brought me to the starting line of a life of productivity, achievement, liberty and happiness. Oh, the richness of that which was handed to me and to other black children of an earlier time—that time of discrimination and prejudice and segregation. . . .

Now I find that I was fueled by the spirit and meaning of those aspirations ["excellence, wisdom and greatness"] only to have the Supreme Court stamp my racial identity as the symbol by which my fellowmen are to judge my achievements as gifts from the State.

Source: Anne Wortham, "A Decision against Meritorious Achievement," *Freeman* 28, no. 10 (1978): 611–15. Reprinted with the permission of the publisher, Foundation for Economic Education.

## Government Is the Problem, Not the Solution (1985)

*Walter Williams*

Along with fellow economist Thomas Sowell, Professor Walter Williams (1936– ) is one of the most popular classical liberals who happens to be African American. Williams published *The State against Blacks* (1982) and later became a syndicated columnist and national commentator on radio and television. Here Williams calls for the Reagan administration to abandon "numbers-based privileges and benefits" and help blacks by removing government regulations that hamper minorities (and others) from advancing in life.

Despite the high hopes of classical liberals, President Ronald Reagan never delivered on his promise of "color-blind law." From this perspective, the administration's civil rights record was mixed at best. On the one hand, Reagan's Department of Justice applied a race-neutral yardstick to civil rights enforcement.[17] Yet, Reagan also embraced quotas and set-asides for minority business owners.[18] Despite the pleas of his attorney general, Reagan refused to repeal the executive orders mandating affirmative action. Encouraged to discriminate, large corporations accepted racial preference as "the cost of doing business" in America. In short, despite their "colorblind rhetoric," Reagan and his fellow Republicans often said one thing and did another.[19] Thus it is not surprising that the GOP abandoned classical liberal activists such as Ward Connerly (see his entry below).

☙

In a very real sense the civil rights struggle, envisaged by its founders and millions of American supporters, is over and *won*. Black people are no longer lynched, no longer denied access to the judicial process of impartial hearings, speedy trials, and jury service. Black people are no longer denied access to public schools and colleges because of race. Black people are no longer denied access to the political arena. . . .

Today's new civil rights movement is not a push for the kind of legal equality firmly expressed by the plaintiffs in *Brown* who said, "That the Constitution is color-blind is our dedicated belief." In regard to school assignment, plaintiffs said, "If you have some other basis . . . any other basis, we have no objection. But just do not put in race or color as a factor."

By contrast, the new civil rights vision holds that the Constitution is color conscious. The position of the High Court is that racial discrimination in order to achieve certain social objectives is a form of compensatory justice. This sentiment is expressed not only by rulings of the Supreme Court, but by one of its members, Justice Thurgood Marshall, who said, "You guys have been practicing discrimination for years. Now it is our turn. . . ."

The immorality of numbers-based privileges and benefits is readily realized when we recognize that government *cannot* give a special advantage to one person without simultaneously giving a special disadvantage to another. Thus, when under government pressure a university sets aside a certain number of seats for blacks, of necessity the policy reduces the number of seats open to other people. A white who was denied entry as a result did not own slaves, nor was he responsible for Reconstruction abuses suffered by blacks [i.e., Ku Klux Klan violence]. By the same token, the policy does nothing for the blacks who *were* slaves *and* suffered the abuses of Reconstruction.

In effect, numbers-oriented policy says we should help individual *A* (a black of today) by punishing *B* (a white of today) for what individual *C* (a white of yesterday) did to individual *D* (a black of yesterday). That is a warped criterion for social justice, especially if we accept the principle of individual accountability.

This rejection of numbers-based racial policy on factual, equity, and efficiency grounds is not the same thing as saying there are no problems of race and there is nothing government can do about it. . . .

The socioeconomic game of life is not fair. The U.S. Civil Rights Commission would be wise in pressing government at all levels to make the game fair. There are numerous laws and regulations at every level of government that systematically rig the economic game against certain people according to their personal characteristics. Among them are: minimum wage laws, occupational licensure laws, business licensing laws, health and safety laws, and many others. These laws adversely affect many Americans, but they exact a disproportional effect on blacks because of their special history in the United States, namely, that blacks were the last major ethnic group to become urbanized and receive the franchise. When they did, many of the traditional avenues to upward socioeconomic mobility had been closed by powerful vested interest groups using the coercive powers of government.

I propose that the U.S. Civil Rights Commission launch an attack on these and other laws that rig the economic game and we keep on playing the game—made fair.

Source: Walter Williams, *Selected Affirmative Action Topics in Employment and Business Set-asides*, Hearing of the United States Commission on Civil Rights, March 6–7, 1985, 1:9–10, 18–19.

## Role Models: Frederick Douglass, Branch Rickey, and Other Omni-Americans (1991)

### Stanley Crouch

It is impossible to place a label on the iconoclastic Crouch (1945– ), except perhaps "Crouchian." An independent-minded individualist, Crouch is best known for his jazz criticism and syndicated columns on race. Like Clarence Thomas, he was swept up in the riptide of black nationalism but later rejected separatism entirely. Crouch's vision of America is one of "Omni-Americans" of all races interacting to achieve their individual best. Their achievements are the cultural possession of all Americans. Role models cross racial lines: just as "white" Americans may be inspired by a black individual's achievements, so too have black Americans been inspired by white accomplishments.

In the following essay, Crouch harkens back to the individualist philosophy of Zora Neale Hurston and Frederick Douglass. All three saw that race was a "decoy" that distracted us from pursuing individual excellence. Crouch uses the examples of Douglass, Rickey, and others to illustrate the inspirational power of "Omni-Americanism" (a term coined by fellow jazz critic Albert Murray).[20] In a telling passage, he relates how his mother exposed him to role models of all races: "The Afro-American tradition of which I speak is a continuation of what we learn from the life of Frederick Douglass, whose career makes it possible to see that all Americans, regardless of point of social origin, are capable of producing those who will do remarkable things." According to Crouch, Douglass and other great "Negroes" cannot be "reduced to mere racial heroes. They are symbols of great American achievement against extraordinary odds." Moreover, they—and all other "remarkable" individuals—belong to everyone.

ℰℛ

The battle with so-called "white middle-class standards" that we still hear discussed when the subjects ranging from school performance to rap records are addressed is itself a distortion of the goals of the Civil Rights Movement. This battle would lead us to believe that there are differences so great in this society that we should actually accept a separatist vision in which the elemental necessity of human identification across racial, sexual, and class lines would be replaced by the idea that people from various backgrounds can identify only with those from their own groups. Such a conception avoids King's idea that people should be judged by the content of their character and not by the color of their skin or, if we extend that to include sex, by gender.

The nature of ethnic nationalism and of gender antagonism that has polluted so much contemporary discussion misses the point of the March on Washington in symbolic terms—that this culture is usually bettered when we have as many people as possible intelligently interacting, when quality takes precedence over point of social origin, class, race, sex, nationality, and religion. Those who came forward in the late sixties and began to trumpet the idea that there were two Americas—one black, one white—not only ignored all of the regional complexities of North, South, Midwest, Southwest, and West, but of Catholic and Protestant, Christian and Jew, as well as all of the variations that break down inside such large categories as white, black, Hispanic, Jew, and American Indian. Now those benumbing simplifications have pulled feminism into the task of making the white male the same thing that he is inside the cosmology of the Nation of Islam: the source of all evil.

This simplification is at odds with the realities of human interaction within our society, and it suggests that those removed from the proverbial seats of power are invariably limited in their freedom to be inspired. We can see that quite easily if we look at something like the controversy at Harvard, where the demand has been raised that a tenured black female be hired by the Law School. No one can be disturbed by a first-class black female professor's being hired by the department, but the argument that has begun to vibrate with hysteria about such matters implies a fundamental inferiority on the part of black female students. If we were to listen to the activists, we would conclude that black females are so incapable of identifying across racial lines that they cannot look at Sandra Day O'Connor on the Supreme Court and feel that there is a place for them in the American legal profession, perhaps one of extraordinary import someday.

Nothing in my own experience or in the experience of Afro-Americans I have met or read about corroborates the idea that, to any significant extent, people of color are capable of being inspired only by their own race or sex. To suggest that is to distort the heroic engagement that defines Negro history, a good measure of which has always been about struggling with any exclusive conception of human possibility or human identification. Yet we are now supposed to wolf down the idea that if a black child is looking at Kenneth Branagh's remarkable film of Shakespeare's Henry V, he or she will not be intrigued by the insights into the problems of power and struggle, of class and cultural clash, but will only be bored or feel left out because the work is something written by "a dead white man about dead white people." In its very provincialism and its racist conception of culture, such an idea opposes the richness of the best of Afro-American culture, regardless of class.

It is due to the distortions of people such as James Baldwin that we have come to believe in far too many instances that black people are such victims of racism that they are as limited as they are purported to be in the most provincial superstitions, those irrational undergirdings of discrimination. Having been born December 14, 1945, in Los Angeles, California, I can say that the people in my community, which was not so much blue-collar as blues-collar, were forever encouraging all of us to aspire to the very best that we could achieve and were always at war with any idea that would result in our accepting the ethnic limits encouraged by the traditions of segregated thought. Though my mother was a domestic worker who earned sometimes no more than $11 a day and often worked six days a week, she was always cutting out editorials for me to read, bringing home books that her employers either gave her or loaned, and wasn't above forcing me against my will to watch Laurence Olivier's Richard III when it came on, or doing the same thing when Orson Welles's Macbeth was shown nightly on The Million Dollar Movie, which I had to keep looking at until I came to understand what they were saying.

My blues-collar mother wasn't being pretentious or exhibiting the effects of having been brainwashed by a Eurocentric conception of cultural values. I was never given the impression that I was looking at some great white people strutting some great white stuff. That wasn't the idea at all. My mother knew that Olivier was a great actor and that Shakespeare was a great dramatist. She wanted me to know and experience those facts. She also told me about Marian Anderson, Duke Ellington, Jackie Robinson, and anybody else who represented exemplary achievement. The same was true in public school, where we read Julius Caesar aloud in class, saw films about Marian Anderson and Jackie Robinson, read Dickens, and so on. We were constantly taught that great significance was not the franchise of any single group and that we were supposed to identify with the best from whomever and wherever in the world it happened to come. We were not allowed to give any excuses for poor performance either. If we had come up with some so-called cultural difference excuse, we would have been laughed at, if not whacked on the boody, for disrespecting the intelligence of the teacher. Our teachers were tough and supportive. They knew well that the best way to respect so-called minority students was to demand the most of them.

It is not that the adults of my childhood were naive about racial matters. They knew that excellence and bulldog tenacity were the best weapons against the dragons of this society. That was the point of telling us about the struggles of the Andersons and the Robinsons. But the worst thing that you could be within that community at that time was a racist, no matter how obvious the social limitations were. Adults would say to you, "Boy, the lowest thing you can be is a man who spends all his time hating somebody he doesn't even know. You know, if you want to hold a man down in a hole full of mud, you got to get down there in that mud with him, which will make you just as dirty as the man you say you don't like because he's so damn filthy." Those Negroes I grew up under were always quick to tell you that there were just two kinds of people in the world: those who tried their best to be good and those who didn't care about being bad. They were true democrats, perhaps because they had learned the hard way what it meant when you submitted to the superstitions of discrimination. Those adults were just as proud of Branch Rickey as they were of Jackie Robinson, for each symbolized the will and the discipline necessary to expand the idea of democracy into the arena of practice.

The Afro-American tradition of which I speak is a continuation of what we learn from the life of Frederick Douglass, whose career makes it possible to see that all Americans, regardless of point of social origin, are capable of producing those who will do remarkable things. As Albert Murray points out in *The Omni-Americans,* a book all should read who really wish to know something about this country, the embodiment of the nineteenth-century self-made man is Douglass. Lincoln, the self-made Midwesterner, easily saw that. After Lincoln met with Douglass, the Great Emancipator told his secretary that, given Douglass's beginnings as a slave and his present achievements, he was probably "the most meritorious man in the United States." Murray also observes that Harriet Tubman is surely the best example of the pioneer woman, what my grandmother meant when she complimented someone on having "shit, grit, and mother wit." Yet neither of them can be reduced to mere racial heroes. They are symbols of great American achievement against extraordinary odds.

When we address the richness of our heritage, we will understand our national heritage in the context of Western civilization to the degree that we will acknowledge it for what it is—an astonishing gathering of information from the entire world, a gathering that had its impact at least partially because of the fight against provincialism that fresh information from other cultures demanded. The experiment that is American democracy is an extension of the ideas of the Magna Carta and the Enlightenment and is also a social development of the New Testament's motion away from the idea of a chosen people. That is why a reduction of the meaning of Western civilization to "the story of dead white men" and racist exploitation distorts the realities of the ongoing debate that has lifted our social vision beyond the provincial, whether that lifting meant the debate over slavery or women's suffrage or anything else that has hobbled this country's freedom to benefit from its human resources. . . .

. . . We must get back to the grandest vision of this society, which is that all exemplary human endeavor is the heritage of every person. It is the combination of one's ethnic and human heritage that is the issue. Every ethnic group has a heritage of its own and is also heir to symbols of inspiration as different as Michael Jordan and William Shakespeare. All people are heir to everything of wonder that anyone has produced, regardless of race, gender, and place. Anyone who would deny any person identification with the vastness of that marvelously rich offering of human achievement is not truly speaking as an American.

Source: Stanley Crouch, "Role Models," in *Second Thoughts about Race in America*, ed. Peter Collier and David Horowitz (Lanham, MD: Madison, 1991), 54–57, 63. Reproduced with permission of Madison Books, permission conveyed through Copyright Clearance Center, Inc.

## Being the Best: The Case
## for Excellence (1991)

### Stephen L. Carter

Some of the most thought-provoking commentaries on race have come from independent-minded writers on the left who remain committed to aspects of the classical liberal tradition. Although law professor Stephen L. Carter (1954– ) supports affirmative action at the starting gate of higher education, he opposes racial preferences in determining success beyond college admissions. In the following essay, Carter argues that advocates of race preferences have become obsessed with "the group" to the point of rejecting individual merit and excellence. Carter argues that such an attitude discourages blacks from pursuing excellence. "Being the best" takes a back seat to being the "best black" qualified for a job or award. Carter terms this the "best black syndrome." This condescending policy handicaps blacks in the professional world, where a "market test" sorts out the excellent from the mediocre.

By equating skin color with "diversity," black leaders offered a new definition of "merit" that is false and dangerous. Peddling diversity to the elites has led to intense group pressure among blacks to silence dissenters. If being black advances the group's "point of view"—a thing of value marketed to the outside world—then dissenters are race traitors to be purged. Carter writes: "A purge is, in its essence, a denial of the right to think. It punishes those who disagree with the established view or with a newly minted view being made into the established one."²¹ This race obsession is anti-intellectual and mocks the old motto of the United Negro College Fund (UNCF) that "a mind is a terrible thing to waste."

Classical liberals (and others) will find Professor Carter's other writings on civility, the importance of voluntarism, the need for dissent, and Christianity well worth reading. A regular columnist for *Christianity Today* and author of books on all of these topics, Carter's philosophy might be characterized as "contrarian Christian liberal."²²

ℭℌ

### Silencing Dissent

. . . Enormous progress has been made in the struggle for equality, but the problems that remain, particularly those related to drugs and education, often seem insurmountable. All too few new ideas are being generated, and some of the old ones—such as the need for widespread systems of racial preference in college admission and employment—seem increasingly irrelevant, yet are defended with a desperation that often turns to virulence.

I worry about what messages we are sending to these kids who will one day be the leaders of our community and our country. In particular, I worry about the message conveyed by the righteous fury that many of the current leaders of the black community direct toward dissenters from the traditional civil rights agenda—especially when the dissenters are black and when the agenda involves preferences. Racially conscious affirmative action, I fear, has become for some powerful voices in black America a kind of shibboleth and, like other shibboleths, has come to be used as a convenient device for separating friends from enemies. (We are not debatable.) And on college campuses, the rallying cry of "diversity" has become a shibboleth, too; and any person of color who does not agree that the reason to hire more people of color is to liberate the voices that racism has stifled, to represent the special perspective that people of color bring, evidently sacrifices his or her birthright. As an intellectual struggling to escape from the box of other people's preconceptions, I find the development of a loyalty test particularly distressing.

The word shibboleth has come into contemporary dialogue as a reference to a thing that is beyond criticism. I am using the word, however, in its original sense, as recounted in chapter 12 of the Book of Judges, which tells the story of the defeat of the Ephraimites at the hands of the Gileadites. After being put to rout, the Ephraimites found their retreat cut off by the Gileadites, who had prudently garrisoned the escape routes. Anyone desiring to pass was asked whether he was an Ephraimite, and if he denied it:

> Then they said unto him, Say now Shibboleth: and he said Sibboleth: for he could not frame to pronounce it right. Then they took him, and slew him at the passages of Jordan: and there fell at that time of the Ephraimites forty and two thousand.

Thus, to be true to its origins, shibboleth should be used as a metaphor for a test that determines who is a genuine member of a group. The shibboleth must always be pronounced correctly, with careful attention to every nuance; those unable to say it right are outsiders who warrant destruction.

Thus, when I say that affirmative action has become a shibboleth for many of the most powerful voices in black America, I mean that there is now a correct way to talk about racial preferences—as simple justice, the minimum a racist society ought to offer the victims of its oppression, a sine qua non of our progress as a people—and an incorrect way—as unfair, illicit, denigrating, counterproductive, or unnecessary. Group membership is determined by the tale one chooses: a black person (or, nowadays, an African-American) who tells the wrong tale—who mispronounces the shibboleth—is a traitor and an outsider. And traitors are much worse than adversaries; for every nation hates most the betrayer from within. In the black community, our response to the dissent that we label treason is often painfully straightforward: the dissenters face ostracism, expulsion, official death. We purge them.

Purges are never pretty. They are not meant to be. The more ruthless and complete the campaign in which one's opponents are eliminated, the more emphatic the warning sent to those who might dissent in the future: Beware, the message reads. See how we deal with those who deny the official word. Don't get on the wrong side, or you could be next. . . .

### Merit and Excellence

And a sensible way to start, so it seems to me, is to say that with all the various instances in which race might be relevant, either to the government or to individuals, it will not be used as an indicator of merit—no one will be more valued than anyone else because of skin color. The corollary is that everyone's merit would therefore be judged by the same tests, and if the tests in question are unfair (truly unfair . . . , and not just exclusionary), then they will be swept away and replaced with something else.

It is that last step, I think, that is often missed in debates over qualifications for admission or employment. No matter how bad one might think current standards are, some standard will be used, either explicitly or implicitly. My argument is that the standard should be explicit, and that once it is selected, everyone should be required to meet it. And yet, in a nation with the turbulent racial history of this one, one must wonder: Somewhere along the way, has there been an error of analysis? Were the nationalists right—is this path to the profession simply a lure to get us to give up on true freedom? Mario Baeza, a member of New York's legal elite who also happens to be black, has put the dilemma this way: "You go to law school, you study like crazy, and you have to continually wonder, Am I adopting a way of thinking that could be used to enslave me?" This possibility lies very near the core of the diversity movement, which counsels people of color against what is usually termed surrender of their identity in the cause of success. The same possibility, albeit put in far less sophisticated terms, motivates those black children who tell other kids that studying and even going to class is acting white. Why else, the nationalists demanded back in the 1960s, would whitey have made the opportunity of higher education available? Clearly, the power structure has something in mind, and whatever it is . . . cannot possibly be good for people who are black.

All of which returns us to the matter of academic and professional standards. There, too, it is whispered (and sometimes shouted) that people of color are victims of a plan—of the centuries of affirmative action favoring white males, for example, or at least of the virulent societal racism that has held us in a subordinate status. When one challenges racial preferences on the ground that they sometimes result in the admission or employment of people not as good (as well prepared, as professionally capable) as some who are turned away or even on the ground that preferences call into question the legitimate achievements of very smart and very capable people of color, the modern vision of affirmative action quickly turns the challenge back on itself: the standards by which these judgments are made, the

Stephen L. Carter. (Courtesy Elena Siebert.)

standards that black people are often less able than white people to meet, are said to lack objectivity, to import cultural bias, or simply to be racist. The idea that even if all of this is true, we should aim to meet and beat them anyway—that we should put ourselves beyond criticism on this ground, as well as on the ground of our leaders' conduct—is quickly dismissed as irrelevant, or as a smokescreen, or as naive, or even as thinking white.

But what it really is, is thinking like a professional. To rise to the pinnacle of professional success, a black person must function in an integrated world, but to do so is no more a betrayal of one's birthright than it is for white people to do the same thing. As Mario Baeza has put it, resolving his own dilemma, "I'm integrated, but I've never tried to be white. That's not what I aspire to in life."

The professional world is competitive, now more than ever, and has little time or space for argument over what should count as standards of achievement. In the professions, unlike the campuses, there is a market test: one either performs well enough to justify one's compensation or one does not. And it is because successful professionals know this, I think that many of them have grown impatient with the argument over affirmative action for hiring and advancement in their fields.

"I've made it because I'm good," said [a corporate executive Carter quoted in an unexcerpted part of the book], and that, at bottom, is what all professionals, black or white, must believe in order to succeed. . . .

One must be very careful about the leveling that is implicit in the conversational habit that affirmative action has become. Elite educational institutions, after all, owe their existence in part to a belief that some people are smarter and more likely to achieve. This, I take it, is just the reason that people of color are beating so hard on the doors to get in. So I wince when I hear supporters of preferences talk blithely of tossing out the window standards of excellence—for college entry grading, hiring, or promotion—that might actually be rational. Sometimes the argument is that the standards are the playthings of white males, manipulated by this amorphous set for their own advantage. Sometimes the argument is that standards are not possible. Sometimes the argument is that meritocracy is itself a bad idea.

My own view is that the traditional justification for accepting a concept of merit is correct: standards of excellence are a requisite of civilization. To say instead that excellence cannot be judged is to say that excellence is not possible. To, say that excellence is not possible is to say, really, that nothing is better than anything else. And if nothing is better than anything else, then the entire project of human progress is a joke. But it isn't a joke. There is such a thing as excellence; there is such a thing as civilization. We live in a world of brilliant scientific discoveries, remarkable acts of moral and spiritual courage, profound literary achievements, and outstanding professional performances. We live in a world that cares about excellence, needs it, and should not be afraid to judge it. . . .

To think about the future is also to reflect on the past. If we as a people were not defeated by slavery and Jim Crow, we will not be beaten by the demise of affirmative action. Before there were any racial preferences, before there was a federal antidiscrimination law with any teeth, our achievements were already on the rise: our middle class was growing, as was our rate of college matriculation—both of them at higher rates than in the years since. Black professionals, in short, should not do much worse without affirmative action than we are doing with it, and, thrown on our own resources and knowing that we have no choice but to meet the same tests as everybody else, we may do better.

Source: Stephen L. Carter, *Reflections of an Affirmative Action Baby* (New York: Basic, 1991), 101–2, 228–32. Reprinted with permission of BasicBooks, a member of the Perseus Books Group.

## Freedom Liberalism: Shattering the Icons of Race (1998)

*Shelby Steele*

Shelby Steele (1946– ) is another writer who defies left versus right thinking on race. Steele describes himself as a "classical liberal focusing on freedom and the power of the individual."[23] His mixed parentage (black father, white mother) made him realize that whites and blacks were not monolithic groups. (Steele also married a white woman.) It is worth noting how many classical liberals married people of other races: Frederick Douglass, George Schuyler, Mildred Loving, Shelby Steele, Ward Connerly, and Clarence Thomas. Perhaps George Schuyler was right when he argued that interracial marriage was one way to overcome racial prejudice on both sides of the color barrier.[24] Frederick Douglass put it this way: "In affairs of this nature [love], who is to decide the why and the wherefore?"[25] Who but the individual? Some critics disparage those black Americans who marry outside their race, yet praise Mildred Loving's Supreme Court victory allowing individual Americans to marry the person they love, regardless of race (see "The Right to Interracial Marriage" above). The new racialists want doors open so that they may shut them on individuals who then choose that freedom—a theme that permeates Steele's work.

A professor of literature at San Jose State University, Steele burst on the scene with his best-selling *The Content of our Character: A New Vision of Race in America* (1990), winner of the National Book Critics Circle Award. Steele became a senior fellow at the Hoover Institution and has written several more thought-provoking books: *A Dream Deferred: The Second Betrayal of Black Freedom* (1998), *White Guilt: How Blacks and Whites Together Destroyed the Promise of the Civil Rights Era* (2006), and *A Bound Man: Why We Are Excited about Obama and Why He Can't Win* (2008).

Why did the long civil rights movement, driven by the classic liberal goal of individual freedom, result in a "culture of preference"? Why did so many

Americans fight to open the doors of freedom and then return to the usual pattern of thinking in terms of group rights? Steele's books explore this critical question. According to Steele, educated white elites (academic, political, professional) developed "iconographic racial reform" to "fend off" white stigma and offer privileges to blacks as members of a group that had shamed white America. These racial preferences failed to help black individuals who lacked the necessary skills to "get along" in life. By expecting little of black Americans, white policy makers felt good about themselves ("At least they are sensitive to the problem"), while black power brokers took what they could get from this "culture of preference." In the following excerpt from *A Dream Deferred*, Steele explains how we got here and then challenges us to live up to the classical liberal principles that destroyed the first "racial world" of slavery and segregation.

℘

Racial oppression imposes nonindividuality on its victims, tells them they will achieve no self, no singularity, that will ever supersede the mark of their race. This surely is the opposite of happiness, this confinement of the self inside a color. The early civil rights movement—grounded in freedom-focused liberalism—saw the mark of race as anathema to freedom, to the individual, and to the pursuit of happiness. It wanted freedom from racial determinism. Therefore, it was a struggle *for* the black individual and *against* his or her race as a political determinism. This was how the great movement sought to bring blacks into the difficulty of a true and unencumbered pursuit of happiness. . . .

Just when the idea of the individual might have taken hold, the idea of interventionism came in its place—and with it specimenization, helplessness, contingency, and overreliance on white moral obligation. This is where the black individual lost out to the nation's need to redeem itself. And this is also where we became essentially a *sociological people* with a sociological identity, a group moving from the dehumanization of oppression to the deindividualization of the remedies for it. . . .

The conspicuous extravagance of President Johnson's Great Society, the drama and scope of its almost wild assault on poverty, was not primarily about ending poverty. Of course, no one would have objected had poverty been conquered. But I don't believe the *will* to conquer it was what gave the Great Society its frenetic energy. This came from a kind of denial—a reflexive insistence that the United

States was *not* the shameful country that the civil rights victories had shown it to be. The Great Society *screamed* that the stigma of whites was not true, that they were actually a fair and compassionate people who would now "end poverty in our time." But this grandiosity was primarily a measure of the shame that stigmatization had delivered.

The Great Society was America's first rather hysterical wrestling with racial stigma. It may have involved an abundance of good intentions, but its ulterior motivation of fending off stigma turned it into a hyperbolic, contrived, and ineffective exhibition of racial and social virtuousness.

I worked in four separate Great Society educational programs in the late sixties and early seventies, and they were all very exciting, though no small part of this excitement was the fact that we didn't really know what we were doing. Our mission was simply to be "innovative," but this only meant rejecting the traditional ways of doing things, whether that way made sense or not. (I believe that the Great Society helped launch the trend of wanton educational "innovation" that so injured American schools in the seventies and eighties.) The trick to "innovation" was simply to stigmatize the traditional way of doing things with the shames of America's past—racism, repression, intolerance, rigidity, exclusion, "mechanized" learning, "rote learning" (that is, repression), and so on. Against these heavy stigmas, any idea that was deferential to the "oppression" of students—whether racial, ethnic, patriarchal, or simply the result of a repressive and mechanized society—and that licensed students to a relief from traditional expectations, was "innovative" *and* socially virtuous. By the magic of this formula we could think of ourselves as socially committed, innovative educators, even though the majority of us were teaching without any training and many among us had only a few more years of education than did our students. We needed a formula.

And so did the Great Society. It, too, did not know what it was doing and so needed a formula by which it could seem innovative and virtuous *without having to accomplish anything.* From its inception the Great Society was defined by ulteriority: It was infinitely more accountable to its ulterior goal of fending off a shameful stigma than to its announced goal of "ending poverty in our time." So it created a chimera of exciting good works through the magic of deference and license. Ask less, excuse from principle, stigmatize tradition, mock the difficult struggle for mastery. And at the end of the day everyone could claim "at least" to have been *well-intentioned* even if nothing had been accomplished. And this claim was entirely the point of everything, because the true "war" of the Great Society was not against poverty: It was against stigma.

Because the Great Society was largely stigma-driven, it gave America its first clear example of what I will call *iconographic* racial reform—reform that exists for what it represents rather than for what it does. Iconographic programs and policies function as icons of the high and honorable motivations that people want credit for when they support these reforms. And this representation of high motivation is the true reason for their existence. The announced goals of these programs and policies will be very grand, the better to represent their high virtuousness, yet vague so that their inevitable failures will not be held against them. (Today any program with "diversity" as a goal is an example.) Supporters of iconographic policies are primarily concerned that these policies function as icons of their high motivations, not whether they achieve anything or whether they mire those they claim to help in terrible unintended consequences. Societies go to this kind of policy when they need an iconography with which to fend off stigmatization. So there is always an inverse relationship between stigma and icon. They will be literally two sides of the same coin.

In the area of race, iconographic policies are based on deference and license because these themes give whites and American institutions the imagery with which to dissociate from the stigma that says they are racist and oppressive. Virtually all American institutions of any size, public or private, have "diversity programs," regardless of whether they achieve anything or whether they are even constitutional. Iconographically they represent a dissociation from America's historical shame that wins the institution at least a *look* of moral authority. We say, "At least they are sensitive to the problem" (America's racism), and so we give them credit for decency. This is the credit they need in order to do business in a shamed society. . . .

But this language of racial kitsch [promoting "diversity"] is hardly innocent. Like any other political kitsch, it is a corruption of power. It is a manipulation that makes the use of an undemocratic power seem no more than an innocent necessity. Kitsch allows the university admissions officer to say that he is not using a preference that racially discriminates against poor and hardworking Asians and whites in favor of better-off and underperforming blacks; rather he is pursuing diversity. Society has never voted to give him the power to discriminate racially, nor would the university administration go to its board of trustees and ask for the power to discriminate against Asians and whites. The 1964 Civil Rights Bill expressly prohibits exactly this kind of racial discrimination. Yet, because the kitsch of diversity answers the stigma of racism, he can tell himself that he is acting against racism even as he discriminates against Asians and whites *solely* on the basis of their race. He practices racism to escape the stigma of racism. . . .

Political correctness is essentially a demagoguery of kitsch. It is a series of empty and banal words and ideas that iconographically oppose the racist and sexist stigma and, thus, license people to circumvent the normal avenues to power. Under a kitschy word like "inclusion" you can hire only women for two years, or set up an executive lounge only for blacks, or reject all Asians after a certain cutoff, or lower the bar three hundred SAT points for blacks, or set aside 30 percent of city contracts for minorities, and so on. Because the kitsch of "inclusion" has no evil, actions in its name can be only good. . . .

And yet the stigmatization of whites as racist remains so powerful that it keeps this culture alive well past the time when it has clearly lost respect (and despite the fact that it has never enjoyed wide support). One of the greatest failures of the culture of preference is that, for all its deference and preference, it was unable to lift the stigma from whites and American institutions. Corporate America is more vulnerable to stigma than ever before. The Republican Party avoids more than approaches legislation to end group preferences. And, more important, people across the country who truly disapprove of preferences simply remain silent. One wonders if Proposition 209 would have passed if people had been required to publicly declare their vote. ["Prop 209" repealed racial preferences in California. See the Connerly and Brown entries below.] It very likely passed not because Californians are racist, but because they genuinely dislike group preferences and were given the opportunity to vote that sentiment *without threat of stigma*. Many who dislike preferences, in and out of public life, look hopefully to the Supreme Court not only because it can declare them unconstitutional but because, in doing so, it can spare everyone from stigmatization. . . .

. . . The United States has simply become habituated to fighting stigma with iconography. When someone says, "I'd be against preferences except I don't know what we'd put in their place," he or she is really saying that without preferences "I would have no iconography with which to fight off stigma. I would have nothing to separate myself from the evil the stigma accuses me of, so it would look to all the world that I was synonymous with it. I would simply be seen as a racist."

It was a discipline of principle that finally saved the United States from that first racial world, which was erected around slavery and segregation. The true American identity, I believe, is simply the profoundness of our relationship to democratic principles *despite* our many failings and duplicities. It is as though every catastrophe of principle only drives the point home more deeply that these principles are all we have. Of course they offer no shelter from stigma. But then, the culture of preference with its elaborate iconography doesn't either. The United States has to accept its past as proof of its need for principles today. We all *know* what is right and fair and democratic. No stigma should make us afraid of this.

Source: Shelby Steele, *A Dream Deferred: The Second Betrayal of Black Freedom in America* (New York: HarperPerennial, 1998), 58–59, 130–33, 146–51. Copyright 1998 by Shelby Steele. Reprinted by permission of HarperCollins Publishers.

# Immigration: Classical Liberalism Redux

## *The Statue of Liberty and the Promise of America (1986)*

### *Ronald Reagan*

Ronald Reagan (1911–2004) had a classical liberal vision of immigration as central to the American promise of "peace and freedom." Reagan's vision of a society open to immigrants was shared by much of the business press. The *Wall Street Journal* has loudly echoed the classic liberal virtues of immigration and reminded social conservatives that Reagan was on the side of those seeking a freer, more prosperous life in America. In 1986, Reagan signed an important immigration act that legalized millions of aliens and set them on the path to becoming citizens. On the twentieth anniversary of this act, the *Wall Street Journal* editors quoted "the Gipper":

We have consistently supported a legalization program which is both generous to the alien and fair to the countless thousands of people throughout the world who seek legally to come to America. The legalization of this [1986] act will go far to improve the lives of a class of individuals who now must hide in the shadows, without access to many of the benefits of a free and open society. Very soon many of these men and women will be able to step into the sunlight and, ultimately, if they choose, they may become Americans.[26]

The year 1986 also marked the unveiling of the Statue of Liberty, after years of restoration by American and French workers. With French president François Mitterand by his side, Reagan took the opportunity to extol his vision of America as a land of free immigrants.

ℰ℈

President and Madame Mitterand, my fellow Americans: The iron workers from New York and New Jersey who came here to begin restoration work were at first puzzled and a bit put off to see foreign workers, craftsmen from France, arrive. Jean Wiart, the leader of the French workers, said his countrymen understood. After all, he asked, how would Frenchmen feel if Americans showed up to help restore the Eiffel Tower? But as they came to know each other—these Frenchmen and Americans—affections grew; and so, too, did perspectives.

The Americans were reminded that Miss Liberty, like the many millions she's welcomed to these shores, is of foreign birth, the gift of workers, farmers, and shopkeepers and children who donated hundreds of thousands of francs to send her here. They were the ordinary people of France. This statue came from their pockets and from their hearts. The French workers, too, made discoveries. Monsieur Wiart, for example, normally lives in a 150-year-old cottage in a small French town, but for the last year he's been riding the subway through Brooklyn. "A study in contrasts," he said—contrasts indeed. But he has also told the newspapers that he and his countrymen learned something else at Liberty Island. For the first time, they worked in proximity with Americans of Jewish, black, Italian, Irish, Russian, Polish, and Indian backgrounds. "Fascinating," he said, "to see different ethnic and national types work and live so well together." Well, it's how we like to think of America. And it's good to know that Miss Liberty is still giving life to the dream of a new world where old antagonisms could be cast aside and people of every nation could live together as one. . . .

And yet, my fellow Americans, it is not only the friendship of two peoples but the friendship of all peoples that brings us here tonight. We celebrate something more than the restoration of this statue's physical grandeur. Another worker here, Scott Aronsen, a marble restorer, has put it well: "I grew up in Brooklyn and never went to the Statue of Liberty. But when I first walked in there to work, I thought about my grandfathers coming through here." And which of us does not think of other grandfathers and grandmothers, from so many places around the globe, for whom this statue was the first glimpse of America? . . .

Well, the truth is, she's everybody's gal. We sometimes forget that even those who came here first to settle the new land were also strangers. I've spoken before of the tiny Arabella, a ship at anchor just off the Massachusetts coast. A little group of Puritans huddled on the deck. And then John Winthrop, who would later become the first Governor of Massachusetts, reminded his fellow Puritans there on that tiny deck that they must keep faith with their God, that the eyes of all the world were upon them, and that they must not forsake the mission that God had sent them on, and they must be a light unto the nations of all the world—a shining city upon a hill. . . .

Well, that is the common thread that binds us to those [Puritans] on the tiny deck of the Arabella, to the beleaguered farmers and landowners signing the Declaration in Philadelphia in that hot Philadelphia hall, to Lincoln on a train ready to guide his people through the conflagration, to all the millions crowded in the steerage who passed this lady and wept at the sight of her, and those who've worked here in the scaffolding with their hands and with their love—Jean Wiart, Scott Aronsen, Tony Soraci, Robert Kearney, and so many others.

We're bound together because, like them, we too dare to hope—hope that our children will always find here the land of liberty in a land that is free. We dare to hope too that we'll understand our work can never be truly done until every man, woman, and child shares in our gift, in our hope, and stands with us in the light of liberty—the light that, tonight, will shortly cast its glow upon her, as it has upon us for two centuries, keeping faith with a dream of long ago and guiding millions still to a future of peace and freedom.

And now we will unveil that gallant lady. Thank you, and God bless you all.

Source: Ronald Reagan, "Remarks at the Opening Ceremonies of the Statue of Liberty Centennial Celebration in New York, New York, July 3, 1986," http://americanpresidency.org (accessed July 24, 2008).

## "It's Liberty, Stupid": Immigration Makes Us Free and Prosperous (1991, 1999)

### Ben Wattenberg

Ben Wattenberg (1933– ) is a lifelong Democrat disillusioned with the direction his party has taken since the 1960s. His autobiography, *Fighting Words: A Tale of How Liberals Created Neo-Conservatism* (2008), reflects his commitment to bedrock principles. Wattenberg's sunny faith in immigration is one of the principles he shares with classical liberals, a faith that positions him against nativists on the right and labor activists on the left. In *The First Universal Nation* (1991), Wattenberg argued that immigration was central to the American identity and a good thing for the nation (see the first document below). Eight years later, he again advocated immigration by citing statistics—a type of evidence Wattenberg uses to great effect in his books, columns, and television shows. Wattenberg is a senior fellow at the American Enterprise Institute and moderator of the weekly television program *Think Tank with Ben Wattenberg* (www.thinktanktv.org).

☙

### 1991

Adam Smith said that each nation should capitalize on its "comparative advantage." Immigration is the comparative advantage of the first universal nation.

The best arguments for immigration are names. Add these: Toscanini, Kissinger, Javits, I. M. Pei, Robin McNeil, Navratilova, John Kenneth Galbraith, Edward Teller, Oppenheimer, Paul Orrefice (chairman of Dow Chemical), Roberto Goizuta (chairman of Coca-Cola), Adolfo (Cuban), de la Renta (Dominican).

If you believe that America will have problems concerning "competitiveness" in the years to come, if you believe that we are ill-educated and undermotivated, if you believe there will be a labor shortage or a customer shortage in the nineties, if you believe we are short of engineers, physicists, nurses, tile setters, maids, nannies, and busboys—consider the immigration fix.

If you believe we face a problem in funding Social Security liabilities because we are an aging society—consider the immigration fix.

If you believe, as most Americans do somewhat inchoately, that America has some sort of mission (beyond prosperity) in this world, if you believe that global influence has some relationship to population size (Belgium won't be a superpower, no matter what), if you believe that American influence will diminish if it is a slow-growth player in a high-growth world—consider the immigration fix.

Some facts: only immigration provides a society with "instant adults" to deal with labor shortages; increased fertility doesn't provide worker bees until several decades go by. Immigrants are likely to be young workers; they not only relieve a labor shortage, but put a quick dent in any potential "customer shortage" (for example, they need houses). A typical extra young immigrant worker will add about $3,000 per year to the Social Security trust fund; that cuts the deficit now; in the future the now-young immigrant worker will be a middle-aged American, and helping to pay the spiraling pension and health costs of the then-elderly baby-boomers. Immigrants are often educated at another nation's expense; if we are selective in our choosing procedure they are also (typically) ambitious and patriotic. . . .

The economic and environmental arguments against immigration are thin: that immigrants take jobs away from Americans, that America is overpopulated, overpolluted, and running out of resources—and that more immigrants exacerbate these conditions. Less thin are the arguments of those who think, but rarely say, that the racial and ethnic balance is tipping and America will no longer be a country of white European ancestry.

Most serious economists do not believe that immigrants eat up American jobs. Immigrants, of course, do "consume" jobs. But they also "create" jobs. Working immigrants buy food, clothing, and books. That activity yields demand, and demand yields jobs.

Is the world running out of resources? No, but if it were, slower population growth would only mean that we would all hit "empty" a few years earlier. Is America overcrowded? More than a third of its counties are losing population. Is America overpolluted? Pollution is lower than it was two decades ago, even though population, and immigration, have climbed. And, environmentalists, please take note: immigration does not increase global population; it only shifts it around.

The "composition" argument is more troubling. It is true that the proportion of "white-European" immigrants is diminishing and that many Americans are worried that the complexion, and the essence, of the nation will change. (When I give speeches on demographics, to serious and educated audiences, I am frequently asked: " . . . but aren't the wrong people having the babies? Aren't the wrong people immigrating?")

This feeling can be ameliorated (although never eliminated) by some history lessons and by some changes in the immigration code.

Let's remember that immigration has never been popular. One gets the feeling that when the folks on the Mayflower went out to Plymouth Rock to watch the next boats come in, they muttered to one another, "There goes the neighborhood." Americans were once afraid of Irish, Italian, and Jewish immigration. Now the public generally says isn't it wonderful that they came here.

If the immigration code were changed to restore equity to European candidates, that could help counter the "composition" argument.

But there is no going back. A threshold was passed, probably with the passage of the 1965 immigration law. America is becoming the world's first universal nation. That universalizing will not be a painless process, but I believe on balance it is going to be very good for us.

## 1999

The 1999 edition of the "Statistical Abstract of the United States," published by the Census Bureau, is just out, as always one of the great books of the world, this time with a kicker. There are 1,447 tables—a numerical treasure chest of social and economic Americana, worth its weight in gold, an appreciable sum even with gold selling at less than half its 1980 price (Table 1171). The Census folks always make an effort to keep up with the times. . . .

Normally the data in the Abstract go back in time for a decade or two. This year there is a surprise package: Section 34, titled "Century Statistics," containing 36 tables, many of them going back to the year 1900. What's the biggest American story in a century loaded with numbers?

Is it that America became the richest nation in the world, with a $45,000-per-year median family income in 1997? I don't think so; all the advanced nations and most less developed nations have become richer, too.

How about cars? In 1900 there were 8,000 motor vehicles in America, in 1950 there were 49 million, and by 2000 more than 210 million—but there are many more cars everywhere. Relative expenditures for food have dropped sharply here, from 24 percent of disposable income in 1929 to 11 percent now, but the direction—if not the magnitude—of such change has been going on in many other places.

So too with health indicators. Rates of tuberculosis, malaria, typhoid, diphtheria, whooping cough, measles and polio have dropped dramatically, in many cases to the vanishing point. . . . But medical progress is going on all over the world.

These indicators of progress are the fruits of modernism. America was a leader in many aspects of the process, but was by no means a unique player. But there is one way in which America is very, very different from the rest of the world: America is the only nation in modern history that took in nearly unlimited numbers of legal immigrants.

The population of the United States in 1900 was 76 million. In 2000 the count should come in at about 276 million. That's 200 million additional people—and in a country with a birth rate that has sharply decreased.

About 45 million legal immigrants came to America in the 20th century. More than 14 million of those arrived from 1900 to 1920, mostly from Southern and Eastern Europe, which is about the number that will arrive from 1980 to 2000, mostly from Asia and Latin America. But in 1900, about 15 percent of Americans were foreign born. Today, with all the belly-aching about immigration, the rate is about 10 percent.

Much, if not most, of the population gain came from 20th century immigrants and their descendants. The effects are seen and felt everywhere. The population of California was 1.5 million in 1900 and 32.6 million in 1998.

The Florida population was .5 million then and 14.9 million now. New York City was the largest city then, with 3.4 million people, and is the largest city now with 7.3 million. Back in 1900, the number of Americans was about half that of the total of the four most populous countries in Europe: Great Britain, France, Italy and Germany. Today there are more Americans than people in all of those countries combined.

Why did it happen? People wanted to come here, and they were permitted to come. They wanted to come because there was liberty and opportunity. (Ask your next foreign-born cab driver why he's here.) They were allowed to come because the American ethos—admittedly sometimes harshly honored in the breach—was a belief in liberty and opportunity for all.

(In fact, the answer to many of the most important questions about America is elemental: It's liberty, stupid. And that, by the way, is not always good news, only true on balance, a topic for a later column.)

Has such growth been good for America and Americans? I think so. It has changed the nation from what was a remarkably vigorous continental enclave of Northwestern European folk and sub-Saharan slave descendants to an astounding universal nation, with people from everywhere, powerful and emulated beyond belief. Only such a large, polyglot nation, with liberty at its bedrock, could plausibly have gained the 20th century's ultimate prize, summed up by the encomium "the American Century."

Only such an influential nation can aspire to lead the world of the future and have the preemptive gall, and hope, to lay claim to naming rights for the next hundred years: "The Liberty Century." That, of course, will be duly chronicled in the annual edition of the Statistical Abstract, issued at the end of the year 2099.

Sources: Ben J. Wattenberg, *The First Universal Nation: Leading Indicators and Ideas about the Surge of America in the 1990s* (New York: Macmillan, 1991), 72–73, 75; Ben Wattenberg, "Liberty Is Not Abstract," *Jewish World Review*, December 16, 1999, http://www.jewishworldreview.com/cols/wattenberg121699.asp (accessed November 1, 2007). Reprinted by permission of Ben Wattenberg.

## *Out of the Barrio: Assimilation Is Not a Dirty Word* (1991)

### Linda Chavez

A former Democrat and union leader, Linda Chavez (1947– ) became disillusioned with the Democratic Party and labor unions. President Reagan appointed her staff director of the U.S. Commission on Civil Rights. Later, she fought the spread of bilingual education, which she believes makes it more difficult for immigrants to assimilate and succeed in America. Founder of the Center for Equal Opportunity (CEO), Chavez has devoted years to promoting assimilationist policies and color-blind government, just as Louis Marshall and others did in years past.

℘

*Assimilation* has become a dirty word in American politics. It invokes images of people, cultures, and traditions forged into a colorless alloy in an indifferent melting pot. But, in fact, assimilation, as it has taken place in the United States, is a far more gentle process, by which people from outside the community gradually became part of the community itself. . . . Now ethnic leaders demand that their groups remain separate, that their native culture and language be preserved intact, and that whatever accommodation takes place be on the part of the receiving society.

Hispanic leaders have been among the most demanding, insisting that Hispanic children be taught in Spanish; that Hispanic adults be allowed to cast ballots in their native language and that they have the right to vote in districts in which Hispanics make up the majority of voters; that their ethnicity entitle them to a certain percentage of jobs and college admissions; that immigrants from Latin America be granted many of these same benefits, even if they are in the country illegally. But while Hispanic leaders have been pressing these claims, the rank and file have been moving quietly and steadily into the American mainstream. Like the children and grandchildren of millions of ethnic immigrants before them, virtually all native-born Hispanics speak English—many speak only English. The great majority finish high school, and growing numbers attend college. Their earnings and occupational status have been rising along with their education. But evidence of the success of native-born Hispanics is drowned in the flood of new Latin immigrants—more than five million—who have come in the last two decades, hoping to climb the ladder as well. For all of these people, assimilation represents the opportunity to succeed in America. Whatever the sacrifices it entails—and there are some—most believe that the payoff is worth it. Yet the elites who create and influence public policy seem convinced that the process must be stopped or, where this has already occurred, reversed.

From 1820 to 1924 the United States successfully incorporated a population more ethnically diverse and varied than any other in the world. We could not have done so if today's politics of ethnicity had been the prevailing ethos. Once again, we are experiencing record immigration, principally from Latin America and Asia. The millions of Latin immigrants who are joining the already large native-born Hispanic population will severely strain our capacity to absorb them, unless we can revive a consensus for assimilation. . . .

The idea of personal sacrifice is an anomaly in this age of entitlements. The rhetoric is all about rights. And the rights being demanded go far beyond the right to equality under the law. Hispanics have been trained in the politics of affirmative action, believing that jobs, advancement, and even political power should be apportioned on the basis of ethnicity. But the rationale for treating all Hispanics like a permanently disadvantaged group is fast disappearing. What's more, there is no ground for giving preference in jobs or promotions to persons who have endured no history of discrimination in this country—namely, recent immigrants. . . .

Affirmative action politics treats race and ethnicity as if they were synonymous with disadvantage. The son of a Mexican American doctor or lawyer is treated as if he suffered the same disadvantage as the child of a Mexican farm worker; and both are given preference over poor, non-Hispanic whites in admission to most colleges or affirmative action employment programs. Most people think this is unfair, especially white ethnics whose own parents and grandparents also faced discrimination in this society but never became eligible for the entitlements of the civil rights era. It is inherently patronizing to assume that all Hispanics are deprived and grossly unjust to give those who aren't preference on the basis of disadvantages they don't experience. Whether stated or not, the essence of affirmative action is the belief that Hispanics—or any of the other eligible groups—are not capable of measuring up to the standards applied to whites. This is a pernicious idea.

Ultimately, entitlements based on their status as "victims" rob Hispanics of real power. The history of American ethnic groups is one of overcoming disadvantage, of competing with those who were already here and proving themselves as competent as any who came before. Their fight was always to be treated the same as other Americans, never to be treated as special, certainly not to turn the temporary disadvantages they suffered into the basis for permanent entitlement. Anyone who thinks this fight was easier in the early part of this century when it was waged by other ethnic groups does not know history. Hispanics have not always had an easy time of it in the United States. Even though discrimination against Mexican Americans and Puerto Ricans was not as severe as it was against blacks, acceptance has come only with struggle, and some prejudices still exist. Discrimination against Hispanics, or any other group, should be fought, and there are laws and a massive administrative apparatus to do so. But the way to eliminate such discrimination is not to classify all Hispanics as victims and treat them as if they could not succeed by their own efforts. Hispanics can and will prosper in the United States by following the example of the millions before them.

Source: Linda Chavez, *Out of the Barrio: Toward a New Politics of Hispanic Assimilation* (New York: Basic, 1991), 161–63, 169–71. Reprinted by permission of Basic Books, a member of Perseus Books Group. Copyright © 1991 by BasicBooks.

### Free Immigration versus Restriction: Libertarians and Republicans (2004)

Throughout history, classical liberals and conservatives have clashed over the issue of immigration. Most classical liberals believe in free migration, although a few argue that the declining commitment to assimilation and the growing welfare state make open immigration problematic. Even those critics, however, foresee a day when the State withers and open immigration returns.[27] The question comes down to opening the borders before or after eliminating welfare, racial preferences, and multicultural policies that impede assimilation.

The Republican Party includes classical liberals from the business community. Out of self-interest or principle, many business leaders oppose restrictions on the free flow of labor or capital (the *Wall Street Journal* is the most vocal voice for these interests). But the GOP has also attracted nativist conservatives who advocate a physical wall and armed guards to keep "illegal aliens" out. The 2004 Republican Party Platform reflected this point of view.

The Libertarian Party carries the classical liberal tradition of free immigration into the twenty-first century. The following documents pair the Libertarian call for "elimination of all restrictions on immigration" with Republican praise for tough policing of immigrants: "verification of their identity, reconnaissance cameras, border patrol agents, and unmanned aerial flights . . . at the border." There is no starker contrast between the classical liberal and nativist conservative position on immigration, a difference that dates back to the nineteenth century.

の

*Libertarian Party*

### Immigration

The Issue: We welcome all refugees to our country and condemn the efforts of U.S. officials to create a new "Berlin Wall" which would keep them captive. We condemn the U.S. government's policy of barring those refugees from our country and preventing Americans from assisting their passage to help them escape tyranny or improve their economic prospects.

The Principle: We hold that human rights should not be denied or abridged on the basis of nationality. Undocumented non-citizens should not be denied the fundamental freedom to labor and to move about unmolested. Furthermore, immigration must not be restricted for reasons of race, religion, political creed, age or sexual preference. We oppose government welfare and resettlement payments to non-citizens just as we oppose government welfare payments to all other persons.

Solutions: We condemn massive roundups of Hispanic Americans and others by the federal government in its hunt for individuals not possessing required government documents. We strongly oppose all measures that punish employers who hire undocumented workers. Such measures repress free enterprise, harass workers, and systematically discourage employers from hiring Hispanics.

Transitional Action: We call for the elimination of all restrictions on immigration, the abolition of the Immigration and Naturalization Service and the Border Patrol, and a declaration of full amnesty for all people who have entered the country illegally.

*Republican Party*

### Supporting Humane and Legal Immigration

The Republican Party supports reforming the immigration system to ensure that it is legal, safe, orderly and humane. It also supports measures to ensure that the immigration system is structured to address the needs of national security. America is a stronger and better nation because of the hard work and entrepreneurial spirit of immigrants, and the Republican Party honors them. A growing economy requires a growing number of workers, and President Bush has proposed a new temporary worker program that applies when no Americans can be found to fill the jobs. This new program would allow workers who currently hold jobs to come out of the shadows and to participate legally in America's economy. It would allow men and women who enter the program to apply for citizenship in the same manner as those who apply from outside the United States. There must be strong workplace enforcement with tough penalties against employees and employers who violate immigration laws. We oppose amnesty because it would have the effect of encouraging illegal immigration and would give an unfair advantage to those who have broken our laws.

To better ensure that immigrants enter the United States only through legal means that allow for verification of their identity, reconnaissance cameras, border patrol agents, and unmanned aerial flights have all been increased at the border. In addition, Border Patrol agents now have sweeping new powers to deport illegal aliens without having first to go through the cumbersome process of allowing the illegal alien to have a hearing before an immigration judge. We support these efforts to enforce the law while welcoming immigrants who enter America through legal avenues.

Sources: Libertarian Party, "Immigration," *National Platform, 2004*, www.lp.org (accessed October 19, 2007); Republican Party, *National Platform, 2004*, http://americanpresidency.org (accessed October 19, 2007).

## Open Letter on Immigration (2006)

*Alexander Tabarrok, David Theroux, et al.*

In 2006, another wave of anti-immigration hysteria swept America with fears of terrorism and job loss. This is a recurring phenomenon in U.S. history as the native-born seek to preserve "their way of life" from the perceived threat of immigrants. Yet immigration is part of the "American" way of life, however much the American people are troubled by problems that arise from any movement of people. In response, Alexander Tabarrok and David Theroux of the Independent Institute wrote this "Open Letter on Immigration" to President George W. Bush and Congress. Hundreds of economists and social scientists, including several Nobel Prize winners in economics, signed this letter. The signers included both classical liberals and left-liberals. (Disclosure: the editor was one of the signers.)

❧

Dear President George W. Bush and All Members of Congress:

People from around the world are drawn to America for its promise of freedom and opportunity. That promise has been fulfilled for the tens of millions of immigrants who came here in the twentieth century.

Throughout our history as an immigrant nation, those who were already here have worried about the impact of newcomers. Yet, over time, immigrants have become part of a richer America, richer both economically and culturally. The current debate over immigration is a healthy part of a democratic society, but as economists and other social scientists we are concerned that some of the fundamental economics of immigration are too often obscured by misguided commentary.

Overall, immigration has been a net gain for American citizens, though a modest one in proportion to the size of our 13 trillion-dollar economy.

Immigrants do not take American jobs. The American economy can create as many jobs as there are workers willing to work so long as labor markets remain free, flexible and open to all workers on an equal basis.

In recent decades, immigration of low-skilled workers may have lowered the wages of domestic low-skilled workers, but the effect is likely to have been small, with estimates of wage reductions for high-school dropouts ranging from eight percent to as little as zero percent.

While a small percentage of native-born Americans may be harmed by immigration, vastly more Americans benefit from the contributions that immigrants make to our economy, including lower consumer prices. As with trade in goods and services, the gains from immigration outweigh the losses. The effect of all immigration on low-skilled workers is very likely positive as many immigrants bring skills, capital and entrepreneurship to the American economy.

Legitimate concerns about the impact of immigration on the poorest Americans should not be addressed by penalizing even poorer immigrants. Instead, we should promote policies, such as improving our education system, that enable Americans to be more productive with high-wage skills.

We must not forget that the gains to immigrants coming to the United States are immense. Immigration is the greatest anti-poverty program ever devised. The American dream is a reality for many immigrants who not only increase their own living standards but who also send billions of dollars of their money back to their families in their home countries—a form of truly effective foreign aid.

America is a generous and open country and these qualities make America a beacon to the world. We should not let exaggerated fears dim that beacon.

Source: Alexander Tabarrok, David Theroux, et al., "Open Letter on Immigration," June 19, 2006, http://www.independent.org/ (accessed October 23, 2007).

# Toward Color-Blind Law?

## *One Race: American (1995)*

### *Antonin Scalia*

**In a series of court cases, culminating in *Adarand* (1995), the U.S. Supreme Court applied a complex "strict scrutiny" test to the use of race in government contracting. In one of his shortest, most eloquent opinions, Justice Antonin Scalia (1936– ) argued for a forthright statement that the Constitution is color-blind, and that we are "one race here. It is American."**

☙

In my view, government can never have a "compelling interest" in discriminating on the basis of race in order to "make up" for past racial discrimination in the opposite direction. Individuals who have been wronged by unlawful racial discrimination should be made whole; but under our Constitution there can be no such thing as either a creditor or a debtor race. That concept is alien to the Constitution's focus upon the individual, and its rejection of dispositions based on race, or based on blood. To pursue the concept of racial entitlement—even for the most admirable and benign of purposes—is to reinforce and preserve for future mischief the way of thinking that produced race slavery, race privilege and race hatred. In the eyes of government, we are just one race here. It is American.

Source: *Adarand Constructors, Inc. v. Peña*, 515 U.S. 200 (1995). Internal citations have been omitted.

## You Want to Know My Race? "Human" (2000)

### Ben Wattenberg

Racial classification is the key to the government's power to discriminate based on a person's race or national origin. As earlier entries demonstrate, the classical liberal tradition rejects such distinctions in law. Justice is blind to a person's skin color and treats individuals equally "regardless of race." Nothing is worse than a government that requires you to define your race and then limits your choices to predefined "check" boxes. Ben Wattenberg rebels in his witty analysis of how politicians play fast and loose with race, thus pandering to their constituencies— while keeping them "in the box." Wattenberg will have none of it.

℧

Rest assured, future dictionaries will contain the word "Clintonesquely."

I am certain of that as I think about Question 8 on my still un-returned, new and different Census form. It reads: "What is Person 1's race? Mark one or more races to indicate what this person considers himself/herself to be." There are 15 potential boxes to check, including, "White," "Black, African Am., or Negro," "American Indian or Alaska Native," "Asian Indian," "Korean" "Filipino" and "Guamanian or Chamorro." There is a final option: "Some other race."

At last week's meeting of the Population Association of America (PAA) in Los Angeles, I talked to the distinguished demographer Paul Demeny about the new racial classification system. He said: "It's un-American. America fought a war against racism. I know; I'm from Hungary."

It has indeed gotten ridiculous. We're talking ketchup numbers here: The demographers were buzzing that 63 varieties of humanity may now be indicated on the form—for example, a person who marks both "White" and "Guamanian or Chamorro." Actually, if you count Question 7, about Spanish/Hispanic/Latino ethnicity, there are 126 combinations. And you may factor that by four choices within the [rubric]. At the PAA, I heard allusions to Hitler's "Nuremberg Laws" more than once, some comic, some not.

The recent argument about race in the Census began in the real world. As exogamy (inter-marriage) has become more common in America, many of the offspring of the exogames did not want to be labeled as one race or the other. Tiger Woods's mom is Thai, his dad is a black American, and he calls himself Cablinasian. One would assume that, between winning tournaments, Tiger would want to check at least two boxes on his Year 2000 Census form, to express his diverse background.

So, many parents of multi-racial children asked that a new box be added, "multi-racial."

This did not sit well with those involved in what is sometimes called "the race industry." They said that such a new option would diminish or dilute the minority numbers, thereby diminishing political influence of minorities and cutting the amount of public monies flowing to minority communities. But Peter Skerry of Claremont College and the Brookings Institution, author of the newly published "Counting on the Census?" says that minorities are putting far too much emphasis on the actual numbers. Any payoff there may be, he says, comes from the policy that is used to implement whatever the numbers may be.

Still, politics is practiced by politicians, and Bill Clinton is one. Faced with two electoral groups tugging in different directions, he acted in three ways, Clintonesquely. No, his Office of Management and Budget (OMB) ruled, there would be no multi-racial box to check in the 2000 Census. But, yes, the Census form would now list the option of choosing more than one race. And, as a kicker, for purposes of civil-rights monitoring and enforcement, a person who lists white and a minority race would be tabulated wholly as a minority.

Thus, the most racially liberal president America has ever had has codified into law the infamous "one-drop rule." For example, a person who is, say, one-sixteenth black, will be counted wholly as black. Furthermore, as Skerry points out, there has yet to be a determination about how to count the offspring of two minorities. How is Tiger counted when he checks at least the boxes marked "Black" and

"Other Asian"? How will a child who is the issue of Latino and Korean parents be counted? Try consulting the "Allocation Guidance" by OMB, bureaucratic baffle-gab that invites activists to game the system. The directive was issued, Clinton-esquely, on March 10, Friday afternoon, the deadest part of the news cycle.

Is this crazy? I am tempted not to answer Question 8. That would be against the law. But civil disobedience in the cause of conscience is by definition against the law. However, the Census Bureau is one of the great federal agencies, and if anyone has feasted off their harvest of numbers, it's me. Moreover, the academic community is beginning to say there is no such thing as race. Help! I am thinking Clintonesquely.

I will not announce here the beginning of a campaign to eliminate the race question on the 2010 Census. Skerry isn't buying. Race is a legitimate question, he says; it's how we implement it that matters. If we didn't have racial numbers, he says, we'd have race by rumor. He's right about that. For example, most whites think blacks have substantially more children than whites. But black fertility rates have fallen sharply to about the "replacement level" of 2.1 children, just about equal to the national rate. What to do? I pick up my pen. In the space provided for "Some other race" I write "human." So sue me.

Source: Ben Wattenberg, "Why the 'Race Industry' Loves the Census As It Is," *Jewish World Review*, March 30, 2000, http://www.jewishworldreview.com/cols/wattenberg033000.asp (accessed November 1, 2007). Reprinted by permission of Ben Wattenberg.

## Turning Back the Clock to the Civil Rights Act of 1964 (2000)

*Janice Rogers Brown*

In 1996, the people of California passed Proposition 209, Ward Conner-ly's measure to amend the state constitution (see Connerly entry below). The amendment stated:

The state shall not discriminate against, or grant preferential treatment to, any individual or group on the basis of race, sex, color, ethnicity, or national origin in the operation of public employment, public education, or public contracting.

When San Jose reintroduced an affirmative action program, Hi-Voltage Wire Works, Inc. lost a bid because it did not meet the goals set by the city. The company sued and the California Supreme Court struck down the San Jose program. According to the court majority, the amendment returned California to the race neutrality embodied in the Civil Rights Act of 1964.

Justice Janice Rogers Brown (1949– ) wrote the majority opinion in *Hi-Voltage Works*. The daughter of African American sharecroppers, Brown grew up in Alabama and attended segregated schools in her youth; she later went on to a successful legal career in California. After serving on the state courts, Justice Brown—known for her classical liberalism—was appointed to the U.S. Court of Appeals for the District of Columbia Circuit. Commentators mention her as a potential pick for the U.S. Supreme Court. In her *Hi-Voltage* opinion, Brown discusses the rise and demise of "color-blind jurisprudence," beginning with the U.S. Supreme Court's *Weber* decision (1979). The amendment to the state constitution, she ruled, returned California state government to the original meaning of the Civil Rights Act of 1964.

℘

"In the history of this Court and this country, few questions have been more divisive than those arising from governmental action taken on the basis of race (Fullilove v. Klutznick [1980])." In November 1996, the California voters added yet another chapter to the long and tortuous history of this question when they approved Proposition 209, which amended our Constitution to prohibit the state and its political subdivisions from "discriminat[ing] against, or grant[ing] preferential treatment to, any individual or group on the basis of race, sex, color, ethnicity, or national origin in the operation of public employment, public education, or public contracting." (Cal. Const., art. I, § 31.) Subsequent to the approval of Proposition 209, the City of San Jose adopted a program that requires contractors bidding on city projects to utilize a specified percentage of minority and women subcontractors or to document efforts to include minority and women subcontractors in their bids.

The question before the court is whether this program contravenes article I, section 31 of the California Constitution. Although the precise issue is a narrow one, the electorate did not approve Proposition 209 in a vacuum. . . . Viewing the provisions of article I, section 31 from this perspective, it is clear the voters intended to adopt the original construction of the Civil Rights Act and prohibit the kind of preferential treatment accorded by this program. . . .

In 1997, the City solicited bids on a project for which plaintiff Hi-Voltage Wire Works, Inc. (Hi-Voltage), a general contracting firm, was the low bidder. Because it intended to utilize entirely its own work force, it failed to comply with either the MBE/WBE outreach or participation requirement [MBE/WBE: subcontractors who are Minority Business Enterprises or Women Business Enterprises]. The City therefore rejected its bid. Joined by plaintiff Allen Jones, a City taxpayer, Hi-Voltage initiated this litigation challenging the Program as a violation of [the California Constitution] because it required contractors to accord "unlawful preferences" to minority and women subcontractors by giving them "special assistance and information" not provided non-MBE/WBE subcontractors. . . .

We granted the City's petition for review to settle this important question of state constitutional law. To properly measure the relevant analytical context, we trace back almost 150 years before the passage of Proposition 209 and find recurring patterns in the law as to the appropriate role of government concerning questions of race. This extended perspective both illuminates the meaning and purpose of Proposition 209 and guides its application.

The United States was founded on the principle that "all men are created equal, that they are endowed by their Creator with certain unalienable Rights, that among these are life, liberty, and the pursuit of happiness." Yet, our history reflects a continuing struggle to enable every individual to fully realize this "self-evident" article of faith. That struggle demarcates the historical and cultural context within which we decide the issue before us.

While the courts have been instrumental in effecting positive change in the quest for equality, their involvement in articulating a coherent vision of the civil rights guaranteed by our Constitution has not been without its low points. The nadir was perhaps the Dred Scott decision, in which the United States Supreme Court denied citizen status to African-Americans, "whether emancipated or not (Dred Scott v. Sandford [1857])." The true vice of Dred Scott lies not so much in the fact it "treated prohibition of slavery in the Territories as nothing less than a general assault on the concept of property (Washington v. Glucksberg [1997])." Rather, a majority of the United States Supreme Court endorsed the then-prevailing societal view that African-Americans—whether slave or free—were "altogether unfit to associate with the white race, either in social or political relations"; and "had no rights which the white man was bound to respect." (Dred Scott at p. 407; cf. People v. Hall [1854], 4 Cal. 399, 404–405 [holding as a matter of "public policy" under state statute that Chinese, "a race of people whom nature has marked as inferior," were precluded from testifying against White persons]) In legitimating this pernicious concept, the court set the stage not only for the cataclysm of the Civil War but for the contentiousness that continues to this day over government's proper role with respect to race.

Following the Civil War, Congress overturned the Dred Scott decision when it adopted the Fourteenth Amendment expressly defining citizenship and forbidding any state from "deny[ing] to any person within its jurisdiction the equal protection of the laws." Nevertheless, in Plessy v. Ferguson (1896), the Supreme Court validated government-initiated racial restrictions and gave its imprimatur to legally enforced segregation on the theory that "[i]f one race be inferior to the other socially, the Constitution of the United States cannot put them upon the same plane." The court approved "separate but equal" accommodations as a valid exercise of the state's "police power" to prevent racial strife. Although speaking only for himself at the time, Justice Harlan vigorously dissented: "Our Constitution is color-blind, and neither knows nor tolerates classes among citizens." "The destinies of the two races, in this country, are indissolubly linked together, and the interests of both require that the common government of all shall not permit the seeds of race hate to be planted under the sanction of law."

Justice Harlan's view would not prevail for more than half a century. But, in Brown v. Board of Education (1954), a unanimous Supreme Court acknowledged the invidious effect of separating individuals solely because of their race. "The impact is greater when it has the sanction of the law . . ." Repudiating Plessy, the court concluded that "in the field of public education the doctrine of 'separate but equal' has no place. Separate educational facilities are inherently unequal [and] deprive [those affected] of the equal protection of the laws guaranteed by the Fourteenth Amendment."

Brown v. Board of Education concerned state-imposed segregation in education, but the courts did not hesitate to apply its animating principle in other contexts. In summarizing the common thread of these cases, Professor Van Alstyne observed that in the years between 1955 and 1976 following Brown v. Board of Education, "virtually every other race-related decision by the Supreme Court appeared to convey" Justice Harlan's conviction "that the Civil War amendments altogether 'removed the race line from our governmental systems. . . . ' [William Van Alstyne, "Rites of Passage: Race, the Supreme Court, and the Constitution," *University of Chicago Law Review* 46 (1978): 775–810] . . ."

Although the United States Supreme Court had rejected the principle of separate but equal and had directed the admission of students to public schools "on a racially nondiscriminatory basis with all deliberate speed" (Brown v. Board of Education [1954]), many officials charged with implementing the mandate were reluctant if not recalcitrant. Discrimination remained the norm generally, prompting protests and acts of civil disobedience. In response, Congress enacted the Civil Rights Act of 1964 (Civil Rights Act or Act). As the floor debates and committee reports attest, Congress intended that the Act reflect Justice Harlan's understanding of the Constitution and "be 'colorblind' in its application (Bakke II [conc. & dis. opn. of Stevens, J.]). . . ."

The analytical framework of Title VII [equal employment] jurisprudence underwent substantial modification in 1979 when the United States Supreme Court decided Steelworkers v. Weber. In Weber, the employer voluntarily instituted a training program . . . with the proviso that at least half of the trainees chosen be African-Americans "until the percentage of black skilled craftworkers in the . . . plant approximated the percentage of blacks in the local labor force." . . . Because "Congress' primary concern in enacting the prohibition against racial discrimination in Title VII of the Civil Rights Act of 1964 was with 'the plight of the Negro in our economy'" and "private and voluntary affirmative action efforts [were] one method of solving this problem," Congress could not have meant to ban them absolutely [the Court majority concluded]. . . .

Our own decisional law has mirrored this change in focus from protection of equal opportunity for all individuals to entitlement based on group representation. During the period the United States Supreme Court was issuing its great decisions, California was not without its own "judicial harbingers of a prejudice-free society" (DeRonde, 28 Ca1.3d 875, 893 [dis. opn. of Mosk, J.]), opinions in which "this court had consistently maintained that race or similar characteristics are not a qualification or disqualification for the benefits of society. . . ."

Following Weber, however, this court in Price v. Civil Service Com. (1980), declined to reaffirm its categorical hostility toward racial classifications and approved a race-conscious hiring program that required the appointment of minority applicants on a preferential basis until the appointing agency attained a certain percentage of minority employees. Because the program was remedial and intended "to overcome the continuing effects of past discrimination" as well as "bring about the full participation of minority individuals in our society," a majority found it did not violate Title VII or California's Fair Employment Practices Act (FEPA). "[T]he Weber court held that title VII's prohibition against racial discrimination does not mandate a 'color-blind' approach to all employment remedies and does not compel an employer to eschew race-conscious affirmative action programs under all circumstances."

Dissenting, Justice Mosk characterized the majority's reasoning as "doublethink": "[They] . . . purport to eliminate discrimination by means of creating discrimination; they construe equality of all persons regardless of race to mean preference for persons of some races over others; and a hiring program which compels compliance by a reluctant [county agency] is described as voluntary." "It is now clear that undergirding much of the rhetoric supporting racial quotas, and preferential treatment in general, is a view of justice that demands not that the state treat its citizens without reference to their race, but that it rearrange and index them precisely on the basis of their race. The objective is not equal treatment but equal representation."

We move forward a decade to the November 5, 1996 General Election and voter approval of Proposition 209, which added section 31 to article I of the California Constitution. Section 31, subdivision (a), provides: "The state shall not discriminate against, or grant preferential treatment to, any individual or group on the basis of race, sex, color, ethnicity, or national origin in the operation of public employment, public education, or public contracting." The question is: Does the City's Program contravene this injunction?

The argument in favor of Proposition 209 stated in part, "A generation ago, we did it right. We passed civil rights laws to prohibit discrimination. But special interests hijacked the civil rights movement. Instead of equality, governments imposed quotas, preferences, and set-asides. Proposition 209 is called the California Civil Rights Initiative because it restates the historic Civil Rights Act. . . . Real 'affirmative action' originally meant no discrimination and sought to provide opportunity." [Ballot Pamphlet] "Anyone opposed to Proposition 209 is opposed to the 1964 Civil Rights Act. . . ."

. . . Rather than incorporate the judicial gloss of Weber and its progeny, the voters intended to remove it. "Let's . . . return to the fundamentals of our democracy: individual achievement, equal opportunity and zero tolerance for discrimination against—or for—any individual." [Ballot Pamphlet] As originally implemented, "Title VII tolerate[d] no racial discrimination, subtle or otherwise (McDonnell Douglas)." It was applied to "remove barriers that have operated . . . to favor an identifiable group . . . over other employees (Griggs)." With the approval of Proposition 209, the electorate chose to reassert the principle of equality of individual opportunity as a constitutional imperative.

Source: *Hi-Voltage Wire Works, Inc. v. City of San Jose* (2000) 24 Cal. 4th 537. Internal citations have been omitted or abridged.

## The Republican Party Has No Soul (2001)

### Ward Connerly

Ward Connerly (1939– ) was a successful businessman appointed to the University of California Board of Regents in 1993. Awakened to the use of racial preferences in college admissions, he agitated successfully for the end of the practice. In 1996, Connerly persuaded Californians to pass Proposition 209.

Similar measures passed in Washington (1998), Michigan (2006), and Nebraska (2008) despite opposition from both Democrats and Republicans. Connerly's most ambitious measure, Proposition 54, would have banned all racial classifications, but the California referendum failed to pass in 2003. (Ironically, the NAACP, which opposed racial classifications in the 1960s, fought fiercely to preserve them in the twenty-first century.) Author of *Creating Equal* (2000), Connerly is chairman of the American Civil Rights Initiative (www.acri.org) and a self-described libertarian.

Critics of Connerly caricature him as a tool of Republican interests, but GOP leaders have distanced themselves from his classical liberal pursuit of color-blind law. Ever fearful of being tagged "racist," and bound by their commitment to affirmative action, Republican politicians have provided almost no support for Connerly's grassroots successes. Here he blasts the party he joined in 1969 for losing its "soul."

Fellow traveler Clint Bolick echoes Ward Connerly's disappointment with the Republican Party, noting the "Republican abdication" on civil rights. Bolick quotes Shelby Steele, who stated, "Racial quotas came in during the Nixon administration, not because Republicans believed in them, but because they lacked the moral authority to resist them." "Republicans have seemed spineless," Bolick laments.[28] Steele expressed a sliver of optimism: "My hope is that today's conservative will turn out to be a classic liberal."[29]

✧

We learned recently that the Bush administration will defend a government contracting program that is an explicit system of preferences and quotas, based on race. I'm not the least surprised. Why? Because as governor of Texas and as a presidential candidate, George W. Bush avoided taking a position on affirmative action or "triangulated" on the issue in ways that would make Bill Clinton green with envy.

He was essentially silent about the Hopwood case, centering on the University of Texas. He took no position on Measure A in Houston, a ballot initiative patterned after California's Proposition 209 (banning preferences in public institutions). As a presidential candidate, he ducked questions concerning 209: What, after all, did he think about it? In his final debate with Al Gore, he seemed to pray silently that the moderator would step in and call "time" when a question about affirmative action was on the floor. He sought to please everyone and offend no one by expressing support for something named "affirmative access. . . ."

Let's look at some facts, beginning with the 1996 Republican convention.

That year, the most important state ballot initiative was Proposition 209. The cause of getting rid of race preferences was deemed so important that the party included an endorsement of 209 in its platform. That action, sadly, marked the end of the party's clear and unequivocal commitment to true equality and the beginning of its current Jekyll-and-Hyde posture.

Perhaps significantly, even as the party was endorsing Prop. 209, it was denying the requests of then-California governor Pete Wilson and Bill Bennett that I, as chairman of the 209 campaign, address the convention. The reason given was that my appearance might "send the wrong message" to minorities about the GOP's commitment to "diversity." At the convention, I sat as a California delegate while Colin Powell took center stage and voiced his support for affirmative action, opposing the party on a key issue, an issue of principle and conscience. . . .

When we sought the support of Florida governor Jeb Bush and the (Republican-controlled) Florida legislature in placing on the ballot an initiative ending preferences in the state, the governor opposed us by calling us (me, in particular) "divisive." He then tried to preempt our initiative by announcing his "One Florida" plan, a series of baby steps that ended preferences in university admissions while strengthening them through race-conscious "diversity" measures elsewhere.

To think politically for a moment: A full 70 percent of Florida voters indicated that they would vote to end preferences. Yet the chairman of the Florida Republican party said, "Mr. Connerly has a solution looking for a problem which does not exist in Florida. . . ."

In 2000, George W. Bush spoke to the NAACP's convention, and he used the occasion to apologize for his party, saying that it had failed to conduct itself as "the party of Lincoln." I was not alone in wondering, "What is he apologizing for? What have we done to dishonor Lincoln?" Bush should have told the NAACP that Democrats take black Americans for granted, not seeing them and other "minorities" as individuals but as groups. The GOP should dedicate itself to individual rights—which is the ultimate definition of civil rights. . . .

Not only were the likes of me kept from addressing the party convention in 2000 (as before)—our requests to purchase booth space to exhibit the literature of the American Civil Rights Institute were denied by both the national GOP and the Florida GOP. . . .

There is a lot of fuzzy-headed and unsupported punditry making the rounds that the California GOP has fallen on hard times because of three "controversial" ballot initiatives: 187 (illegal immigration), 209 (race preferences), and 227 (bilingual education). Those who subscribe to this view are never able to explain how the GOP is harmed by initiatives that are popular with the voting public. Even blacks, the largest voting bloc in support of preferences, supported 209 at three times the rate of their usual support for GOP candidates. . . .

Well, reality has finally "settled in" for me: I sense that the only chance I will have in my lifetime to discuss race preferences with an American president has already occurred. Strangely, it was Bill Clinton who provided that opportunity. I do not expect as much out of George W. Bush. . . .

Bush's recent decision to defend a morally indefensible government contracting program—the one that resulted in the rejection of the low bid by Randy and Valery Pech of Adarand Constructors, because they are white—speaks volumes about the decline of fundamental values of citizenship in America. Because the victims are white, we look the other way and rationalize our indifference by talk of "providing access to minorities."

When I think of the Pechs, I am also reminded of Xiaolin Li, a student of Vietnamese descent who was a candidate for a "minorities only" scholarship funded by the (tax-exempt) Bill and Melinda Gates Foundation. This program is operated by the United Negro College Fund, and while it excludes whites from eligibility it also sets a higher standard for Asians. Miss Li was in financial need, had a 3.7 grade point average, and boasted an SAT score of 1,380-academic performance that greatly exceeds that of the average black student. But she was rejected because she didn't score high enough in the "non-African-American" pool of candidates. As the young lady said to me in a letter, "It just seems that being Asian has hurt me."

Yet people like her simply don't matter to some of us when we think we are engaged in the noble project of providing "access" to members of anointed minority groups. We don't realize that innocent people are harmed in our preferential schemes. As the critic Shelby Steele often says, "Whenever you give someone a preference, you discriminate against someone else." Why is that so hard to understand?

I became a card-carrying Republican in 1969. No one recruited me (I am a "person of color") in an effort to increase the party's "diversity." In fact, no one much cared whether I became a Republican or not. What inspired me was the bold and decisive leadership of California's governor, Ronald Reagan. He was unequivocal in his views, and those views were right.

Although the "civil rights" establishment sought to portray Reagan as anti-black, millions of Americans like me ignored that portrayal and became Republicans because we respected Reagan and his beliefs. He governed with good humor and made clear that our skin color or ancestry was of no concern to him. We knew that, in his eyes, we were equals. What he wanted from us was that we embrace the pillars of freedom in which he believed. Clarence Thomas and I and numerous others were not "black Republicans"; we were just Republicans. That anonymity and feeling of blending into the political fabric of our nation is what attracted us. We sought no special favors, nor wanted any. . . .

I regret to say that if I had no political affiliation today, I would not be tempted to become a Republican. In its quest for skin-color diversity, the Republican party is subverting its philosophical foundation. The sad fact is, when it comes to principles of individual rights and colorblindness, the Grand Old Party isn't so grand anymore. Principled positions on preferences, bilingual education, and so on are now characterized as "divisive," as "culture war" annoyances, to be avoided at all costs.

The leadership of our party—grossly out of step with ordinary Republicans—doesn't have the stomach to defend the party's principles. But that's not the worst news: The worst news is that the leadership is all too eager to help our opponents on the left when they want to shoot us down for daring to defend, explain, and promote our traditional principles. Truth is, for the last five years, race, gender, and ethnic preferences have been on the ropes—but the knockout blow has been blocked, in part because of the support the Republican grandees give to preferences, either tacitly or explicitly. As long as identity politics and the obsession with skin-color diversity get top billing in the Republican party, there will be no leadership from Republicans, including the Bush administration, to end preferences. They will prefer the slow and agonizing death that preferences will eventually suffer at the hands of court decisions, even as they seek to influence the Supreme Court to delay that richly deserved demise. All the while, people like the Pechs and Xiaolin Li will be expected to seethe in silence, as the nation redefines discrimination against some as "access" for others.

I think of a momentous question posed in the Bible: "[W]hat is a man profited if he shall gain the whole world and lose his own soul?" In this spirit, I ask:

How much skin-color diversity does the Republican party require in exchange for its highest principles?

Source: Ward Connerly, "Losing the Soul of the GOP: Republicans Make a Rotten Peace with Race Preferences," *National Review*, October 1, 2001, 42–44. © 2001 by National Review, Inc., 215 Lexington Avenue, New York, NY 10016. Reprinted by permission.

## Frederick Douglass Still Stands (2003)

### Clarence Thomas

Appointed to the U.S. Supreme Court by President George H. W. Bush, Clarence Thomas (1948– ) came under fierce criticism for his classical liberal views on race. Critics called him a race traitor, an "Uncle Tom," a sellout because he defended nondiscrimination, rather than affirmative discrimination (racial preferences). In a speech before an association of black lawyers, Thomas confronted his critics by defending his right to think, speak, and write as an individual, rather than as a symbol of predetermined "blackness."[30]

Thomas's color-blind view of the Constitution was in keeping with the way he ran the Equal Employment Opportunities Commission (EEOC) in the 1980s, and with the long classical liberal tradition dating back to the Declaration of Independence, which Thomas took as his touchstone. Along with the Declaration, he found inspiration in Frederick Douglass. In his address before the association of black lawyers, Thomas stated:

> Any effort, policy or program that has as a prerequisite the acceptance of the notion that blacks are inferior is a non-starter with me. I do not believe that kneeling is a position of strength. Nor do I believe that begging is an effective tactic. I am confident that the individual approach, not the group approach, is the better, more acceptable, more supportable and less dangerous one. This approach is also consistent with the underlying principles of this country and the guarantees of freedom through government by consent. I, like Frederick Douglass, believe that whites and blacks can live together and be blended into a common nationality.[31]

This document brings us full circle back to the color-blind vision of Frederick Douglass and Justice Harlan, both cited by Thomas. In a college admissions case involving racial preferences, Thomas joined Justice Scalia by stating "the Constitution abhors classifications based on race." Once again, however, the Court muddled its stance on race with a pair of decisions (*Grutter* and *Gratz*) that left open the door to racial discrimination in the name of "diversity."

༄

Frederick Douglass, speaking to a group of abolitionists almost 140 years ago, delivered a message lost on today's majority:

> [I]n regard to the colored people, there is always more that is benevolent, I perceive, than just, manifested towards us. What I ask for the negro is not benevolence, not pity, not sympathy, but simply justice. The American people have always been anxious to know what they shall do with us. . . . I have had but one answer from the beginning. Do nothing with us! Your doing with us has already played the mischief with us. Do nothing with us! If the apples will not remain on the tree of their own strength, if they are worm-eaten at the core, if they are early ripe and disposed to fall, let them fall! . . . And if the negro cannot stand on his own legs, let him fall also. All I ask is, give him a chance to stand on his own legs! Let him alone! . . . [Y]our interference is doing him positive injury. . . .

No one would argue that a university could set up a lower general admission standard and then impose heightened requirements only on black applicants. Similarly, a university may not maintain a high admission standard and grant exemptions to favored races. The Law School, of its own choosing, and for its own purposes, maintains an exclusionary admissions system that it knows produces racially disproportionate results. Racial discrimination is not a permissible solution to the self-inflicted wounds of this elitist admissions policy.

The majority upholds the Law School's racial discrimination not by interpreting the people's Constitution, but by responding to a faddish slogan of the cognoscenti. Nevertheless, I concur in part in the Court's opinion. First, I agree with the Court insofar as its decision, which approves of only one racial classification, confirms that further use of race in admissions remains unlawful. Second,

I agree with the Court's holding that racial discrimination in higher education admissions will be illegal in 25 years. . . . I respectfully dissent from the remainder of the Court's opinion and the judgment, however, because I believe that the Law School's current use of race violates the Equal Protection Clause and that the Constitution means the same thing today as it will in 300 months. . . .

The Constitution abhors classifications based on race, not only because those classifications can harm favored races or are based on illegitimate motives, but also because every time the government places citizens on racial registers and makes race relevant to the provision of burdens or benefits, it demeans us all. "Purchased at the price of immeasurable human suffering, the equal protection principle reflects our Nation's understanding that such classifications ultimately have a destructive impact on the individual and our society." *Adarand Construction* [*sic*], *Inc. v. Peña* (1995) (Thomas, J., concurring). . . .

Justice Powell's opinion in *Bakke* and the Court's decision today rest on the fundamentally flawed proposition that racial discrimination can be contextualized so that a goal, such as classroom aesthetics, can be compelling in one context but not in another. This "we know it when we see it" approach to evaluating state interests is not capable of judicial application. Today, the Court insists on radically expanding the range of permissible uses of race to something as trivial (by comparison) as the assembling of a law school class. I can only presume that the majority's failure to justify its decision by reference to any principle arises from the absence of any such principle. . . .

Finally, even if the Law School's racial tinkering produces tangible educational benefits, a marginal improvement in legal education cannot justify racial discrimination where the Law School has no compelling interest in either its existence or in its current educational and admissions policies. . . .

The Court bases its unprecedented deference to the Law School—a deference antithetical to strict scrutiny—on an idea of "educational autonomy" grounded in the First Amendment. In my view, there is no basis for a right of public universities to do what would otherwise violate the Equal Protection Clause. . . .

The majority grants deference to the Law School's "assessment that diversity will, in fact, yield educational benefits." It follows, therefore, that an HBC's [historically black college's] assessment that racial homogeneity will yield educational benefits would similarly be given deference. An HBC's rejection of white applicants in order to maintain racial homogeneity seems permissible, therefore, under the majority's view of the Equal Protection Clause. . . . Contained within today's majority opinion is the seed of a new constitutional justification for a concept I thought long and rightly rejected—racial segregation. . . .

The silence in this case is deafening to those of us who view higher education's purpose as imparting knowledge and skills to students, rather than a communal, rubber-stamp, credentialing process. The Law School is not looking for those students who, despite a lower LSAT score or undergraduate grade point average, will succeed in the study of law. The Law School seeks only a facade—it is sufficient that the class looks right, even if it does not perform right. . . .

For the immediate future, however, the majority has placed its *imprimatur* on a practice that can only weaken the principle of equality embodied in the Declaration of Independence and the Equal Protection Clause. "Our Constitution is color-blind, and neither knows nor tolerates classes among citizens." Plessy v. Ferguson (1896) (Harlan, J., dissenting). It has been nearly 140 years since Frederick Douglass asked the intellectual ancestors of the Law School to "[d]o nothing with us!" and the Nation adopted the Fourteenth Amendment. Now we must wait another 25 years to see this principle of equality vindicated. I therefore respectfully dissent from the remainder of the Court's opinion and the judgment.

Source: *Grutter v. Bollinger*, 539 U.S. 306 (2003). Case citations and footnotes have been omitted.

## *History Will Be Heard (2007)*

The classical liberal tradition continues to influence, and often decide, today's civil rights debates. For example, in November 2006, Michigan voters passed a constitutional referendum prohibiting the state from granting racial, ethnic, or gender preferences. Then, on June 28, 2007, the U.S. Supreme Court decided *Parents Involved in Community Schools v. Seattle School District* in favor of parents who opposed having their children assigned to schools based on their race. A narrow 5-4 majority agreed that the mechanical use of race in school assignments was unconstitutional. However, Justice Anthony Kennedy wrote a separate opinion emphasizing that race might be considered to promote "diversity." Nevertheless, he concurred with the overall judgment of the majority in these cases: children should not be "racial chits" used to meet predetermined quotas. The remaining four justices vigorously dissented from the majority's interpretation of the Fourteenth Amendment.

Below the reader will find excerpts from the opinions written by Chief Justice John Roberts (1955– ) and Associate Justice Clarence Thomas. Roberts boldly asserts that "the way to stop discrimination on the basis of race is to stop discriminating on the basis of race." Thomas makes the case for a color-blind Constitution set forth by Justice Harlan in his *Plessy* dissent (see chapter 3), and Thurgood Marshall in his *Brown v. Board* brief.

"History will be heard," Roberts writes. Yet the history of the freedom struggle reminds us that "eternal vigilance is the price of liberty." In 1893, Frederick Douglass addressed those who had given up the struggle; he spoke of achieving "one country, one citizenship, one liberty, one law, for all people without regard to race."[32] That is the hope and promise of the classical liberal tradition.

ℰↃ

*John Roberts*

When it comes to using race to assign children to schools, history will be heard. In *Brown v. Board of Education,* we held that segregation deprived black children of equal educational opportunities regardless of whether school facilities and other tangible factors were equal, because government classification and separation on grounds of race themselves denoted inferiority. It was not the inequality of the facilities but the fact of legally separating children on the basis of race on which the Court relied to find a constitutional violation in 1954. The next Term, we accordingly stated that "full compliance" with *Brown I* required school districts "to achieve a system of determining admission to the public schools *on a nonracial basis.*" *Brown II,* 349 U. S., at 300–301 (emphasis added [by Roberts]).

The parties and their *amici* debate which side is more faithful to the heritage of *Brown,* but the position of the plaintiffs in *Brown* was spelled out in their brief and could not have been clearer: "[T]he Fourteenth Amendment prevents states from according differential treatment to American children on the basis of their color or race." What do the racial classifications at issue here do, if not accord differential treatment on the basis of race? . . .

Before *Brown,* schoolchildren were told where they could and could not go to school based on the color of their skin. The school districts in these cases have not carried the heavy burden of demonstrating that we should allow this once again—even for very different reasons. For schools that never segregated on the basis of race, such as Seattle, or that have removed the vestiges of past segregation, such as Jefferson County, the way "to achieve a system of determining admission to the public schools on a nonracial basis," *Brown II,* 349 U.S., at 300–301, is to stop assigning students on a racial basis. The way to stop discrimination on the basis of race is to stop discriminating on the basis of race.

*Clarence Thomas*

Most of the dissent's criticisms of today's result can be traced to its rejection of the color-blind Constitution. The dissent attempts to marginalize the notion of a color-blind Constitution by consigning it to me and Members of today's plurality. But I am quite comfortable in the company I keep. My view of the Constitution is Justice Harlan's view in *Plessy:* "Our Constitution is color-blind, and neither knows nor tolerates classes among citizens." And my view was the rallying cry for the lawyers who litigated *Brown.* ("That the Constitution is color blind is our dedicated belief"); ("The Fourteenth Amendment precludes a state from imposing distinctions or classifications based upon race and color alone"); see also In Memoriam: Honorable Thurgood Marshall, Proceedings of the Bar and Officers of the Supreme Court of the United States, X (1993) (remarks of Judge Motley) ("Marshall had a 'Bible' to which he turned during his most depressed moments. The 'Bible' would be known in the legal community as the first Mr. Justice Harlan's dissent in *Plessy v. Ferguson.* I do not know of any opinion which buoyed Marshall more in his pre-*Brown* days"). . . .

The segregationists in *Brown* embraced the arguments the Court endorsed in *Plessy.* Though *Brown* decisively rejected those arguments, today's dissent replicates them to a distressing extent. Thus, the dissent argues that "[e]ach plan embodies the results of local experience and community consultation." Similarly, the segregationists made repeated appeals to societal practice and expectation. The dissent argues that "weight [must be given] to a local school board's knowledge, expertise, and concerns," and with equal vigor, the segregationists argued for deference to local authorities. The dissent argues that today's decision "threatens to substitute for present calm a disruptive round of race-related litigation," and claims that today's decision "risks serious harm to the law and for the Nation." The segregationists also relied upon the likely practical consequences of ending the state-imposed system of racial separation. And foreshadowing today's dissent, the segregationists most heavily relied upon judicial precedent.

The similarities between the dissent's arguments and the segregationists' arguments do not stop there. Like the dissent, the segregationists repeatedly cautioned the Court to consider practicalities and not to embrace too theoretical a view of the Fourteenth Amendment. And just as the dissent argues that the need for these programs will lessen over time, the segregationists claimed that reliance on segregation was lessening and might eventually end.

What was wrong in 1954 cannot be right today. Whatever else the Court's rejection of the segregationists' arguments in *Brown* might have established, it certainly made clear that state and local governments cannot take from the Constitution a right to make decisions on the basis of race by adverse possession. The fact that state and local governments had been discriminating on the basis of race for a long time was irrelevant to the *Brown* Court. The fact that racial discrimination was preferable to the relevant communities was irrelevant to the *Brown* Court. And the fact that the state and local governments had relied on statements in this Court's opinions was irrelevant to the *Brown* Court. The same principles guide today's decision. . . .

In place of the color-blind Constitution, the dissent would permit measures to keep the races together and proscribe measures to keep the races apart. Although no such distinction is apparent in the Fourteenth Amendment, the dissent would constitutionalize today's faddish social theories that embrace that distinction. The Constitution is not that malleable. Even if current social theories favor classroom racial engineering as necessary to "solve the problems at hand," the Constitution enshrines principles independent of social theories. Indeed, if our history has taught us anything, it has taught us to beware of elites bearing racial theories. See *Dred Scott v. Sandford* (1857) ("[T]hey [members of the "negro African race"] had no rights which the white man was bound to respect"). Can we really be sure that the racial theories that motivated *Dred Scott* and *Plessy* are a relic of the past or that future theories will be nothing but beneficent and progressive? That is a gamble I am unwilling to take, and it is one the Constitution does not allow.

The plans before us base school assignment decisions on students' race. Because "[o]ur Constitution is color-blind, and neither knows nor tolerates classes among citizens," such race-based decisionmaking is unconstitutional. I concur in THE CHIEF JUSTICE's opinion so holding.

Source: *Parents Involved in Community Schools v. Seattle School District No. 1, et al.*, 127 S.Ct. 2738 (2007). Case citations and footnotes have been omitted.

# Notes

1. Steven M. Gillon, *"That's Not What We Meant to Do": Reform and Its Unintended Consequences in Twentieth-Century America* (New York: W.W. Norton, 2000), 129.

2. Ibid., 127.

3. Nathan Glazer, *Affirmative Discrimination: Ethnic Inequality and Public Policy* (New York: Basic, 1975), 44.

4. Clint Bolick, "The Republican Abdication," in *The Affirmative Action Fraud: Can We Restore the American Civil Rights Vision?* (Washington, DC: Cato Institute, 1996); Ward Connerly, "Losing the Soul of the GOP," *National Review*, October 1, 2001, 42–44. For more on Nixon's role in solidifying racial preferences, see Joan Hoff, *Nixon Reconsidered* (New York: Basic, 1994); and Dean J. Kotlowski, *Nixon's Civil Rights: Politics, Principle, and Policy* (Cambridge, MA: Harvard University Press, 2001).

5. Because of this tortured history, classical liberals remain divided: while most favor returning to the original meaning of the Civil Rights Act, a small minority argues for repeal of those sections that invade the private sphere. Legal scholar Richard Epstein argues that those who want to prefer minorities over others could then do so without the long, drawn-out court battles of recent years; likewise, others could associate with whom they please, thus reducing societal conflict and restoring freedom of association. Those favoring a return to the "colorblindness"

of the Civil Rights Act have debated this point with Epstein several times over the years. The debate is an academic one since the Civil Rights Act is clearly here to stay. Richard Allen Epstein, *Forbidden Grounds: The Case against Employment Discrimination Laws* (Cambridge, MA: Harvard University Press, 1992); Roger Clegg et al., "Muddies Waters," *Reason*, May 1999, http://www.reason.com/news/show/31009.html (accessed October 26, 2007); Roger Clegg and Richard Epstein (reply), "Color Schemes," *Reason*, November 2002, http://www.reason.com/news/show/28585.html (accessed October 26, 2007).

6. Milton Friedman and Rose D. Friedman, *Free to Choose: A Personal Statement* (New York: Harcourt Brace Jovanovich, 1980).

7. Stephan Thernstrom and Abigail M. Thernstrom, *America in Black and White: One Nation, Indivisible* (New York: Simon & Schuster, 1997), 101.

8. Robert L. Carter to Mrs. Rhoda Karpatkin, February 3, 1961, in *Papers of the NAACP, Part 22: Legal Department Administration Files, 1956–1965,* ed. John H. Bracey, August Meier, and Randolph Boehm (Bethesda, MD: University Publications of America, 1996), reel 3.

9. "Educator Challenges Use of Word—'Race,'" *Chicago Daily Defender,* November 23, 1965, 9.

10. Thernstrom and Thernstrom, *America in Black and White,* 428.

11. Kevin L. Yuill, *Richard Nixon and the Rise of Affirmative Action: The Pursuit of Racial Equality in an Era of Limits* (Lanham, MD: Rowman & Littlefield, 2006), 143.

12. Jonathan J. Bean, *Big Government and Affirmative Action: The Scandalous History of the Small Business Administration* (Lexington: University Press of Kentucky, 2001), 43.

13. Gillon, *"That's Not What We Meant to Do,"* 146–47; John David Skrentny, *The Ironies of Affirmative Action: Politics, Culture, and Justice in America* (Chicago: University of Chicago Press, 1996).

14. Ed Koch [D-NY], "The Need for Fairness in SBA Loan Policy," *Congressional Record,* June 7, 1973, 18541–42.

15. Nathan Glazer, *We Are All Multiculturalists Now* (Cambridge, MA: Harvard University Press, 1997).

16. Anne Wortham, *The Other Side of Racism: A Philosophical Study of Black Race Consciousness* (Columbus: Ohio State University Press, 1981).

17. Raymond Wolters, *Right Turn: William Bradford Reynolds, the Reagan Administration, and Black Civil Rights* (New Brunswick, NJ: Transaction, 1996).

18. Bean, *Big Government and Affirmative Action.*

19. Nicholas Laham, *The Reagan Presidency and the Politics of Race: In Pursuit of Colorblind Justice and Limited Government* (Westport, CT: Praeger, 1998).

20. Albert Murray, *The Omni-Americans: New Perspectives on Black Experience and American Culture* (New York: E. P. Dutton, 1970).

21. Stephen L. Carter, *Reflections of an Affirmative Action Baby* (New York: Basic, 1991), 102.

22. Carter writes columns on a range of issues, including the role Christianity can play in promoting racial freedom and harmony. See, e.g., "Hope Deferred," *Christianity Today,* July 2004, in which Carter writes, "The sparkling world Brown hoped to build is yet within grasp. But we will have to build it as individuals, with the small decisions of everyday life, rather than through bigger and better government programs. The nation is full of fatherless children to mentor, collapsed families to support, crumbling schools to visit—and human hearts to touch."

23. Shelby Steele, quoted in Sylvester Monroe, "Up from Obscurity," *Time,* August 13 1990, 45.

24. George S. Schuyler, *Racial Intermarriage in the United States: One of the Most Interesting Phenomena in Our National Life* (Girard, KS: Haldeman-Julius, 1929).

25. Frederick Douglass, "Mr. Douglass Interviewed," *Washington Post,* January 26, 1884, 1.

26. "Reagan on Immigration," *Wall Street Journal,* May 16, 2006, A14.

27. Hans-Hermann Hoppe, "Natural Order, the State, and the Immigration Problem," *Journal of Libertarian Studies* 16, no. 1 (2002): 75–97.

28. Bolick, "Republican Abdication," 115.

29. Shelby Steele, quoted in ibid., 119.

30. Clarence Thomas, "Speech to the National Bar Association," Memphis, July 29, 1998, http://www.arthurhu.com/98/06/thomas.txt (accessed July 24, 2008).

31. Ibid.

32. Frederick Douglass, *The Effect of the Accession of the Democratic Party to*

*Power,* press release, January 8, 1893, Frederick Douglass Papers, Manuscript Division, Library of Congress, Washington, DC, http://memory.loc.gov/ammem/doughtml/doughome.html (accessed July 7, 2007).

## Recommended Reading

Bean, Jonathan J. *Big Government and Affirmative Action: The Scandalous History of the Small Business Administration.* Lexington: University Press of Kentucky, 2001.

Carter, Stephen L. *Civility: Manners, Morals, and the Etiquette of Democracy.* New York: Basic, 1998.

———. *The Culture of Disbelief: How American Law and Politics Trivialize Religious Devotion.* New York: Basic, 1993.

———. *The Dissent of the Governed: A Meditation on Law, Religion, and Loyalty.* Cambridge, MA: Harvard University Press, 1998.

———. *Reflections of an Affirmative Action Baby.* New York: Basic, 1991.

Chavez, Linda. *An Unlikely Conservative: The Transformation of an Ex-Liberal; or, How I Became the Most Hated Hispanic in America.* New York: Basic, 2002.

Connerly, Ward. *Creating Equal: My Fight against Race Preferences.* San Francisco: Encounter, 2000.

Conti, Joseph G., and Brad Stetson. *Challenging the Civil Rights Establishment: Profiles of a New Black Vanguard.* Westport, CT: Praeger, 1993.

Crouch, Stanley. *The All-American Skin Game; or, The Decoy of Race: The Long and the Short of It, 1990–1994.* New York: Pantheon, 1995.

Epstein, Richard Allen. *Forbidden Grounds: The Case against Employment Discrimination Laws.* Cambridge, MA: Harvard University Press, 1992.

Gillon, Steven M. *"That's Not What We Meant to Do": Reform and Its Unintended Consequences in Twentieth-Century America.* New York: W.W. Norton, 2000.

Graham, Hugh Davis. *The Civil Rights Era: Origins and Development of National Policy, 1960–1972.* New York: Oxford University Press, 1990.

Kloppenberg, Lisa A. *Playing It Safe: How the Supreme Court Sidesteps Hard Cases and Stunts the Development of Law.* New York: New York University Press, 2001.

Kotlowski, Dean J. *Nixon's Civil Rights: Politics, Principle, and Policy.* Cambridge, MA: Harvard University Press, 2001.

Kull, Andrew. *The Color-Blind Constitution.* Cambridge, MA: Harvard University Press, 1992.

Laham, Nicholas. *The Reagan Presidency and the Politics of Race: In Pursuit of Colorblind Justice and Limited Government.* Westport, CT: Praeger, 1998.

McWhorter, John H. *Losing the Race: Self-Sabotage in Black America.* New York: Free Press, 2000.

Murray, Albert. *The Omni-Americans: Black Experience and American Culture.* 1970. Reprint, New York: Da Capo, 1990.

Newbeck, Phyl. *Virginia Hasn't Always Been for Lovers: Interracial Marriage Bans and the Case of Richard and Mildred Loving.* Carbondale: Southern Illinois University Press, 2004.

Scalia, Antonin, and Kevin A. Ring. *Scalia Dissents: Writings of the Supreme Court's Wittiest, Most Outspoken Justice.* Lanham, MD: Regnery, 2004.

Simon, Julian Lincoln. *The Economic Consequences of Immigration.* 2nd ed. Ann Arbor: University of Michigan Press, 1999.

Sowell, Thomas. *Civil Rights: Rhetoric or Reality?* New York: W. Morrow, 1984.

Steele, Shelby. *A Bound Man: Why We Are Excited about Obama and Why He Can't Win.* New York: Free Press, 2008.

———. *The Content of Our Character: A New Vision of Race in America.* New York: St. Martin's, 1990.

———. *A Dream Deferred: The Second Betrayal of Black Freedom in America.* New York: HarperCollins, 1998.

———. "The Loneliness of the 'Black Conservative.'" *Hoover Digest* 1999, http://www.hoover.org/publications/digest/3506941.html (accessed July 6, 2008).

———. *White Guilt: How Blacks and Whites Together Destroyed the Promise of the Civil Rights Era.* New York: HarperCollins, 2006.

Tabarrok, Alexander. *Economic and Moral Factors in Favor of Open Immigration.* Oakland, CA: Independent Institute, 2000.

Vedder, Richard, Lowell Gallaway, and Stephen Moore. "The Immigration Problem: Then and Now." *Independent Review* 4, no. 3 (1999): 347–64.

Wallenstein, Peter. *Tell the Court I Love My Wife: Race, Marriage, and Law; An American History.* New York: Palgrave Macmillan, 2002.

Wattenberg, Ben J. *Fighting Words: A Tale of How Liberals Created Neo-Conservatism.* New York: Thomas Dunne, 2008.

———. *The First Universal Nation: Leading Indicators and Ideas about the Surge of America in the 1990s.* New York: Free Press, 1991.

Williams, Walter E. *The State against Blacks.* New York: New Press, 1982.

Wolters, Raymond. *Right Turn: William Bradford Reynolds, the Reagan Administration, and Black Civil Rights.* New Brunswick, NJ: Transaction, 1996.

Wortham, Anne. *The Other Side of Racism: A Philosophical Study of Black Race Consciousness.* Columbus: Ohio State University Press, 1981.

Yuill, Kevin L. *Richard Nixon and the Rise of Affirmative Action: The Pursuit of Racial Equality in an Era of Limits.* Lanham, MD: Rowman & Littlefield, 2006.

# Conclusion

*Past, Present, Future*

**WHAT DOES THE TWENTY-FIRST CENTURY** hold for classical liberalism? Classical liberals can no longer rely on the support of either the Democratic or Republican parties. The Democrats remain committed to racial preferences forever, if we take their "diversity" premise at face value: why end something that is good for everyone? Meanwhile, the Republicans are embarrassed by questions of race and wish they would go away. In 2000, candidate George W. Bush fled from issues of race like a vampire escaping dawn's early light. When asked where he stood on affirmative action, the first president of the twenty-first century stated that he opposed quotas but favored "affirmative access," whatever that meant. Yet the Bush administration defended minority contracting quotas before the U.S. Supreme Court (*Adarand,* 2001) and accepted the use of diversity goals to achieve race-proportional results in college admissions (*Grutter* and *Gratz,* 2003). As Bruce Bartlett notes in two provocative books, George W. Bush betrayed the Reagan Revolution and allowed the Democrats to position themselves as the party of civil rights, when the Democrats were "wrong on race" for a very long time.[1] From a classical liberal perspective, both parties are "wrong on race."

U.S. Supreme Court decisions have further muddled the direction of civil rights jurisprudence. In two landmark cases, *Grutter* and *Gratz,* the Court rendered a split decision. The justices ruled that racial discrimination by the government was unconstitutional if it was too numbers-based but acceptable if dressed in "diversity." Furthermore, Justice Sandra Day O'Connor wrote that she *expected* an end to racial preferences within twenty-five years. This is scarcely firm guidance for citizens navigating the contradictory rules set forth by the Court.

State universities can do just about anything in the name of "diversity," while others (for example, government contractors) must be careful not to discriminate too openly. Instead of determining the fate of the civil rights "baby" in Solomon-like fashion, the Court simply cut the baby in half in a pathetic attempt to please both sides. Neither side is satisfied, and so the battle continues. As Senator George Hoar stated long ago: "The question will not down. Nothing is settled that is not right."

The Congress has been equally reluctant to address racial controversies, except for periodic waves of nativist concern over immigration. Cynical opportunism prevails on Capitol Hill. With each legislative session, members of Congress channel pork to their constituents through legalized set-asides for "minority businesses," including the infamous Alaskan Native Corporations (ANCs) sponsored by Senator Ted Stevens (R-AK)—de facto fronts for large corporations such as Halliburton and Battelle.[2]

Although the future looks bleak, classical liberals have survived more difficult times. On the bright side, they have secured constitutional amendments barring racial discrimination in California, Washington, Michigan, and Nebraska. The U.S. Supreme Court, under newly appointed Chief Justice John Roberts, also acted decisively to end "proportional" school assignment. The 2000 census debate over racial categories highlighted the rise of "multiracials"—those people who refuse to adopt only one racial background. The result, as discussed by Ben Wattenberg, was the choice to check more than one box—even if the "minority" box counts for "official" purposes. The debate over the 2010 census will raise the same fundamental issues: What is race? Why should the government define race as it chooses? Why do immigrants get to check boxes that offer them benefits unavailable to other citizens? And the most "dangerous" question that crosses the minds of box checkers: Why is the government in the race business at all?

Race mixing and immigration promise to shake the foundations of the "skin game" played by politicians and government bureaucrats. After all, if Barack Obama's white ancestor owned slaves, does his "white half" owe reparations to his "black" children?[3] The concept is ludicrous but the reality is played out in the lives of millions. They are living proof that race "essence" is unreal. If race is a fiction, then it is a fiction worth disposing with because it has done far more harm than good.

These factors bring us to the election of Barack Obama. A product of racial intermarriage and immigration, Obama stands as a symbol of the "new face of American politics."[4] After initial questions about his "blackness," African American voters rallied around the man who became the first "black" president. White supporters, on the other hand, view Obama as a person transcending race. Obama's multiracial genealogy and inclusive campaign rhetoric make him a different type of candidate. One commentator hopes that Obama might revolutionize affirmative action by basing it on class rather than race.[5]

Despite the chants of "Change!" from the Obama campaign, he has always defended affirmative action "as we know it." True, Obama said that his daughters should not receive an advantage over poorer whites, yet that is a long way from radical change in policies that define us by our racial classification. It is important to remember that Martin Luther King Jr. also advocated compensation to African Americans for past wrongs while extending a form of affirmative action to the "forgotten white poor."[6] Expanding group preferences—race plus class—is not the same as abandoning government-defined racial identity. Call it *Affirmative Action Plus*, but there is little to warm the heart of a classical liberal who believes in individual equality before the law, regardless of race or class.

We are a long way from Frederick Douglass, who was also the product of black and white parents. Despite suffering enslavement and vicious white racism, Douglass refused to define himself by race. After his controversial marriage to a white woman, Douglass stated that "God Almighty made but one race," and he considered himself "a member of the one race which exists." One wonders how Douglass would view today's census and job forms, or how he would deal with the concept of "diversity."

"Diversity liberalism" is the bipartisan consensus of the early twenty-first century. The legal concept emerged from the tortured *Bakke* decision (1978). Justice Lewis Powell stated that quotas were illegal but colleges might consider racial "diversity" as one factor among many. This single decision was the proverbial "camel's nose in the tent" of government-sponsored racial discrimination. Soon, colleges, employers, and others tripped over themselves to promote diversity education, diversity scholarships, diversity hires, and diversity-speak. "Diversity" has become the shibboleth of our age: say "diversity" and you pass through the institutional gates; refuse to speak this word and the gatekeepers identify you as an "enemy" of "multicultural" progress.

Advocates of racial discrimination always profess that they care about the public good. Southern white racists dressed segregation in the language of racial harmony. The races were so different, they argued, that the government needed to regulate the space between them. Woodrow Wilson segregated the federal government because, he insisted, the practice lessened friction between black and white employees. During the 1920s, Franklin Roosevelt defended quotas limiting Jewish admission as a way to preserve Harvard's culture and dampen anti-Semitism. Years later, he interned Japanese Americans for "national defense" purposes. These men took it for granted that there were differences between racial groups and that the "higher good" required unequal treatment, presumably in the interest of all—even those discriminated against!

It is a short leap from this thinking to today's "diversity liberalism." Diversity liberals celebrate racial difference, identity politics, and racialized power. Diversity justifies race preference and discrimination. If "racism" is "prejudice plus power," then the racism they practice serves the positive good, or so they maintain. In *Parents v. Seattle* (2007), Justice Clarence Thomas noted the eerie resemblance between the sociological arguments made by segregationists in *Brown v. Board* and those made by busing advocates in the Seattle case. Thomas was unwilling to let fashionable social theories guide his constitutional thinking:

> Even if current social theories favor classroom racial engineering as necessary to "solve the problems at hand," the Constitution enshrines principles independent of social theories. Indeed, if our history has taught us anything, it has taught us to beware of elites bearing racial theories. See Dred Scott v. Sandford (1857) ("They [members of the "negro African race"] had no rights which the white man was bound to respect"). Can we really be sure that the racial theories that motivated Dred Scott and Plessy are a relic of the past or that future theories will be nothing but beneficent and progressive? That is a gamble I am unwilling to take, and it is one the Constitution does not allow.

There are many problems with group-based diversity policies. By privileging the group, we diminish the individual. Zora Neale Hurston, Anne Wortham, and Stephen Carter spoke eloquently about individual merit. As Hurston put it, "What seems race achievement is the work of individuals. The white race did not go into a laboratory and invent incandescent light. That was Edison. The Jews did not work out Relativity. That was Einstein. The Negroes did not find out the inner secrets of peanuts and sweet potatoes, nor the secret of the development of the egg. That was Carver and Just."

Americans are an "uppity" people who question authority. Yet authority never stands still: power has a tendency to censor, restrict, and suppress speech. When abolitionists questioned the authority of slaveholders, the latter used Congress to impose gag rules on the discussion of slavery. Slaveholders interfered with the distribution of abolitionist mail and firebombed printing presses. Newspaper editor William Leggett warned that the false appropriation of power over a group—African American slaves—emboldened an interest that would defend itself by any means necessary, including suppression of free speech. George Washington Cable discovered a "Silent South" of whites who knew racism was wrong but feared to speak out. Today, on college campuses, we have our own "gag rules" flowing from a defense of race discrimination: speech codes that ban "hate" (see www.speechcodes.org). Diversity administrators label criticism of their policies "hate" and punish it accordingly. The more things change, the more they remain the same.

The questioning will continue. Group-based discrimination cannot last because it fails to satisfy the hunger for an America that transcends race. Race transcendence is what many Obama supporters desire. In his most famous speech, Barack Obama states "how hungry the American people were for this message of unity."[7] Policies based on our inherited identity fail to satisfy the goal originally sought by so many: the rule of law—equality for all and special privileges for none. Old Europe was a society of status; the American promise was a government constitutionally committed to equal protection under the law. Alas, the Constitution often gives way to power. Recall the words of William Graham Sumner: "If you take away the Constitution, what is American liberty and all the rest? Nothing but a lot of phrases."

Although the present situation looks unpromising, classical liberalism has always been an optimistic creed, even as it struggled to overcome slavery, lynching, and anti-immigration hysteria. Despite setbacks, classical liberals remained confident that progress toward equal rights and individual liberty was possible.

Moreover, their religious faith often impelled them to labor onward. Economic forces and changing demographics—namely, waves of immigration—also worked in their favor.

Where will America be in fifty years? Immigration will continue to renew the American promise and challenge old interests. As Ben Wattenberg wrote, "A threshold was passed, probably with the passage of the 1965 immigration law. America is becoming the world's first universal nation." The black-white issues that have dominated racial discourse for three centuries will fade with each passing generation. Racial intermarriage will upset all notions of race as a fixed trait. The greatest Omni-American of all, Frederick Douglass, envisioned what I see in fifty years: "one country, one citizenship, one liberty, one law, for all people without regard to race."[8]

## Notes

1. Bruce R. Bartlett, *Impostor: How George W. Bush Bankrupted America and Betrayed the Reagan Legacy* (New York: Doubleday, 2006); Bruce R. Bartlett, *Wrong on Race: The Democratic Party's Buried Past* (New York: Palgrave Macmillan, 2008).

2. Michael Scherer, "What Ted Stevens, Bolivian Cocaine and Halliburton Have in Common," *Salon,* June 19, 2007, http://www.salon.com/news/feature/2007/06/19/halliburton/ (accessed July 21, 2008).

3. David Nitkin and Harry Merritt, "A New Twist to an Intriguing Family History," *Baltimore Sun,* March 2, 2007, http://baltimoresun.com (accessed May 12, 2008).

4. Martin Dupuis and Keith Boeckelman, *Barack Obama, the New Face of American Politics* (Westport, CT: Praeger, 2008).

5. Richard Kahlenberg, "Barack Obama and Affirmative Action," *Inside Higher Ed,* May 12, 2008, http://insidehighered.com/views/2008/05/12/kahlenberg (accessed May 12, 2008).

6. Martin Luther King Jr., *Why We Can't Wait* (New York: Harper & Row, 1964), 152.

7. Barack Obama, "A More Perfect Union," March 18, 2008, http://www.americanrhetoric.com/speeches/barackobamaperfectunion.htm (accessed May 12, 2008).

8. Frederick Douglass, *The Effect of the Accession of the Democratic Party to Power,* press release, January 8, 1893, Frederick Douglass Papers, Manuscript Division, Library of Congress, Washington, DC, http://memory.loc.gov/ammem/doughtml/doughome.html (accessed July 7, 2007).

# Index

*Note: Page numbers in italics refer to illustrations.*

Santa Ana School Board, 186–87
Scalia, Antonin, 5, 280–81, 295
school choice, 233
Schuyler, George S.
    *Black No More,* 176
    intermarriage of, 261
    on Japanese internment, 176–78
    and Mencken, 172–73
    on private schools, 203
segregation, 77
    *Brown v. Board of Education,* 7, 147,
        185, 286–87, 298–300, 310
    *Buchanan v. Warley,* 7, 126–29
    on campus, 7, 157–60
    in the Census Bureau, 155–56
    *Plessy v. Ferguson,* 111–13, *117,* 126,
        232, 286, 299–301
    rationales for, 310
    school desegregation, 185, 186–87,
        211–12
    "separate but equal" doctrine,
        110–11, 126, 132n11, 286–87
    southern laws on, 110–11
    on streetcars, 6, 113–16, *117*
self-help, 109, 118
self-ownership, 31–34
Sewall, Samuel E., 40
Shaw, Sam, 191
shibboleths, 256–57
silencing dissent, 256–57
Skerry, Peter, 282, 283
slavery
    *Amistad* captives, 6, 28–31
    Christian defense of, 21, 26–28
    *Dred Scott v. Sandford,* 46–47, 48,
        285–86, 300–301
    Kansas-Nebraska Act (1854), 46
    Missouri Compromise (1820), 46
    Northwest Ordinance (1787), 46–47
    *See also* abolitionism; antislavery-era
        writings
Small, Robert, 66, 74n6

Smith, Adam, 269
Smith, Gerritt, 27, 40
Social Gospel of the Left, 3
southern Jim Crow regulations, 9,
    20–21
    *See also* segregation
Sowell, Thomas, 6, 248
Spielberg, Steven: *Amistad,* 28
Spooner, Lysander
    *Address of the Free Constitutionalists,*
        49–53
    American Letter Mail Company
        founded by, 34–35
    on the Constitution, 4
    Frederick Douglass on, 40
    on Lincoln, 45, 48
    on slaves' right to overthrow their
        "masters," 21
    *The Unconstitutionality of Slavery,*
        34–38
state vs. federal power, 8–9
"Statistical Abstract of the United States"
    (Census Bureau), 271–73
Statue of Liberty, 266–69
Steele, Shelby, 233, 261
    *A Bound Man,* 261
    conservative backlash exemplified
        by, 8
    *The Content of Our Character,* 261
    *A Dream Deferred,* 262–66
    on racial quotas, 290, 292
    *White Guilt,* 261
*Steelworkers v. Weber,* 287, 289
sterilization, forced, 4, 153–54
Stevens, John Paul, 244–45
Stevens, Ted, 308
Stewart, Tom, 176
Storey, Moorfield, 10
    Anti-Imperialist League founded by,
        94
    antilynching laws supported by, 141
    *Buchanan v. Warley,* 7, 126–29

# About the Editor

JONATHAN J. BEAN is Research Fellow at the Independent Institute and professor of history at Southern Illinois University. He received his Ph.D. from Ohio State University in 1994. Dr. Bean is a recipient of the Henry Adams Prize for Best Book of the Year from the Society for History in the Federal Government as well as the Herman E. Krooss Prize from the Business History Conference, and he is a member of the Academic Hall of Fame at St. Michael's College. He was named Outstanding Teacher of the Year in 2005 and teaches courses on business history, public policy, the Great Depression, and U.S. history.

His books include *Big Government and Affirmative Action: The Scandalous History of the Small Business Administration* (2001), *Beyond the Broker State: Federal Policies Toward Small Business, 1936–1961* (1996), and *Race and Liberty in America: The Essential Reader* (2009). His scholarly essays have appeared in the *Independent Review*, the *Journal of Policy History*, the *African American National Biography*, *Enterprise and Society*, *Business History Review*, and the *Historian*. His popular articles and interviews have appeared in *U.S. News & World Report*, *National Review*, the *Weekly Standard*, *Fortune Small Business*, *American Banker*, *Business Week*, *Correio Braziliense*, and the *Chronicle of Higher Education*. He has done background research for *Mother Jones*, *Salon*, and *CBS Evening News*. His public appearances have included on-air radio interviews, a C-Span show, and testimony before the United States Senate.

# INDEPENDENT STUDIES IN POLITICAL ECONOMY